Approaches to Gender and Spoken Classroom Discourse

Also by Helen Sauntson

GENDER AND LANGUAGE RESEARCH METHODOLOGIES
(*edited with Kate Harrington, Lia Litosseliti and Jane Sunderland*)

NEW PERSPECTIVES ON LANGUAGE AND SEXUAL IDENTITY
(*with Liz Morrish*)

LANGUAGE, SEXUALITIES AND DESIRES: Cross-cultural Perspectives
(*edited with Sakis Kyratzis*)

Approaches to Gender and Spoken Classroom Discourse

Helen Sauntson
University of Birmingham, UK

First published 2012 by
PALGRAVE MACMILLAN

Palgrave Macmillan in the UK is an imprint of Macmillan Publishers Limited, registered in England, company number 785998, of Houndmills, Basingstoke, Hampshire RG21 6XS.

Palgrave Macmillan in the US is a division of St Martin's Press LLC, 175 Fifth Avenue, New York, NY 10010.

Palgrave Macmillan is the global academic imprint of the above companies and has companies and representatives throughout the world.

Palgrave® and Macmillan® are registered trademarks in the United States, the United Kingdom, Europe and other countries.

ISBN 978–0–230–22994–5

This book is printed on paper suitable for recycling and made from fully managed and sustained forest sources. Logging, pulping and manufacturing processes are expected to conform to the environmental regulations of the country of origin.

A catalogue record for this book is available from the British Library.

Library of Congress Cataloging-in-Publication Data
Sauntson, Helen, 1972–
    Approaches to gender and spoken classroom discourse / Helen Sauntson.
        p.   cm.
    Includes bibliographical references and index.
    ISBN 978–0–230–22994–5 (hardback)
    1. Sex discrimination in education—Great Britain.   2. Interaction analysis in education—Great Britain.   3. Discourse analysis—Great Britain.   I. Title.
    LC212.83.G7S28 2011
    370.81—dc23   2011021390

10   9   8   7   6   5   4   3   2   1
21 20 19 18 17 16 15 14 13 12

Printed and bound in Great Britain by
CPI Antony Rowe, Chippenham and Eastbourne

For Caroline

Contents

Tables and Figures

Tables

Figures

Acknowledgements

I am grateful to the following people for their valuable support and advice during the writing of this book:

Judith Baxter, Adrian Blackledge, Carmen Rosa Caldas-Coulthard, Caroline Heron, Susan Hunston, Liz Morrish, Christine Skelton.

1
Introduction: Language, Gender, Sexuality and Schooling

The main aim of this book is to highlight inequalities around gender which happen in the school environment. We have to understand how and why such inequalities happen before we can start to challenge them. To begin to explain what some of these inequalities are, and the damaging effects of them, I use the voices of some young people in order to highlight some of the problems around gender which are pervasive in UK schools at the time of writing. In the first example, Amy talks about her experiences of expressing gender non-normativity at school. She discusses 'being a tomboy' as a young girl and, in particular, her enjoyment of playing football with boys. At first, she reflects on this as a pleasurable experience. But, over time, she explained how these instances of gender non-normative behaviour led to name-calling and then to more serious verbal and physical bullying. She talks about the devastating effects the bullying had on her self-esteem, social and emotional well-being and academic achievement. Ultimately, the bullying became so bad that Amy refused to go to the school and was home-tutored from the age of 12. Now, at the age of 23, she successfully runs her own business and does voluntary work with a local lesbian, gay, bisexual and trans-gendered/transsexual (LGBT) youth group. Her story is not unique, and others who have been through similar experiences may not have been so resilient and come through their damaging experiences so successfully. Amy's experience highlights the school as an environment in which the boundaries of gender normativity are clearly delineated and enforced. Anyone who transgresses those boundaries is punished – emotionally and, sometimes, physically.

Amy (A = Amy; I = Interviewer)
A: well er I was moving from juniors to senior schools [I: mmm] obviously it's a big leap to begin with em but I never really had any trouble

I'd always made friends very easily [I: yea] em I always er achieved academically [I: yea] em teachers liked me everything was fine er until I was playing football and we I remember being on the pitch and I was playing against all the boys which you know was fairly normal really [I: yea] and er somebody called out 'oy lezza' [I: right] and it tends to be with those kinds of names those kinds of connotations it sticks like superglue [I: yea yea] and it it just escalated from there really to to the gradual name-calling [I: okay] er of course everyone won't sit next to you cuz you're the lezza [I: mmm] and so on and so forth [I: yea]

....

A: and so I decided to go home and lunch times rather than stay in school and [I: yea] sit on my own table and so on so forth so I'd ride my bike back and er and then it escalated to the point where I was going back and forth on my bike and people would start throwing stones kicking the wheels of my bike

er there was a particularly bad incident which is kind of last straw on the camel's back I took a short cut through the park cuz I didn't want to have my bike wheels kicked [I: mmm] or stones thrown at me [I: yea yea] which is er self-preservation that sort of thing [I: yea sure] and er yea I got I got cornered by about five lads and er I came home battered and bruised so it it was at that point I told my mom and dad that I ain't going there again

Two other young people, Tad and Jack, talk about similar experiences of expressing gender non-normativity at school, and the subsequent bullying that arose from this. Tad talks about feeling more comfortable socialising with girls rather than boys, and the discomfort he experienced in PE lessons and, in particular, when he was in the boys' changing rooms. Jack discusses how he received verbal homophobic abuse from other students as a result of his perceived gender non-normativity. Like Tad, Jack talks about the damaging social and emotional effects of this abuse, to the point where he dropped out of school altogether.

Tad (T = Tad; I = Interviewer)
T: luckily I had em in the school which I was being bullied in a teacher who was gay and she worked with physical education and she made it more comfortable for me [I: right] to even be in that environment and in fact she did something really remarkable as I was so uncomfortable with the boys in their changing room and stuff because they taunted me [I: mmm] you know saying things like 'oh he's looking at me' er

and it got a bit bad so I was removed from PE but I wanted to join in with something different

I loved hanging around with girls then because that's when I felt more comfortable [I: mmm] because I couldn't join in with their the girls' activities they opened up a sort of group where it was dance [I: right] and me and the I was the only exception of a boy to be allowed for a dance lesson

I: right

T: yea and that was a good move and I thank that teacher very much

I: yea

T: you know I wish I could see her again I'd thank her very much for sort of opening up that opportunity for me and I wish there was more tutors like her

I: mmm

T: it shouldn't take em a gay or a lesbian teacher to make that movement

Jack (J = Jack; I = Interviewer)

J: all they do right I've experienced bullying and stuff like that in school but it was when because because I wasn't like out or anything like that and em but I still got like 'you poof' and all that crap like that [I: yea] and it makes you feel uncomfortable because you don't wanna say 'yea and what' because then they'd know you don't know where to look so you sort of look on the floor and think 'god where the hell do I look' [I: yea] and most of the time I ended up going into the toilets and just crying like and then that and then it got to the point where I was on home tuition and I had to be taught at home because I refused to go to school [I: right]

In Amy's and Tad's stories in particular, experiences of gender non-normativity are followed by homophobic bullying in varying forms and degrees. Even though none of these young people had come out as lesbian, gay or bisexual at school, their gender non-normative behaviour led to allegations of homosexuality from other students (Amy was called 'lezza', Jack was called 'you poof'). It has been well-documented that gender non-normativity is often equated with homosexuality – in fact, the negative connotations of homosexuality are a key means through which gender normativity is enforced. This crucial relationship between gender and sexuality is one which is too often overlooked in research on gender in schools and it is, therefore, an issue which I wish to stress here in the introductory chapter, and throughout the book. An investigation of this relationship will be returned to explicitly in Chapter 5, but will also be discussed at other relevant points.

These opening examples of reported gender non-normativity in school repeatedly result in feelings of low self-esteem, fear of being in school, gradual disengagement from school and, sometimes, a drop in academic achievement (see, for example, Hunt and Jensen, 2007; Pearson, Muller and Wilkinson, 2007; Wilkinson and Pearson, 2009). What these examples show clearly is that there are still serious problems concerning gender and sexuality inequalities in many schools. Despite decades of research on gender and schooling, school is still experienced as a place where there are strict rules regarding gender normativity, and these rules are constantly enforced through a variety of tacit and more explicit methods. From previous research, we know that language use is one of these methods. The way that language is used within the classroom, in particular, has received much attention over the previous four decades. This work has helped to explain issues concerning gender and achievement, but has also contributed to broader understandings of how gender identities are enacted in school settings. Research on language and gender is important because, in order to change meanings and challenge potentially damaging ideologies about gender, intervention needs to happen at the level of social interaction – and this always entails some sort of linguistic interaction. Changing the patterns of linguistic interaction in a given situation involves re-negotiating social relations and thus challenging the existing social-gender hierarchy, as Swann (1992: 236) states:

> language may be used to subvert routine practice, to challenge expectations, and to contribute towards educational and social change.

Thus, we can never fully understand the processes through which discourses of gender are negotiated and constructed in the classroom until we focus in detail upon the linguistic processes through which those discourses are enacted. This is one of the ultimate goals of the research conducted for this book. Specific questions asked in this book include:

- Are there particular linguistic routines through which gender and sexuality are discursively constructed in classrooms?
- What are those routines and how do we identify and describe them?

- What can the use of multiple methods of discourse analysis reveal about discursive constructions of gender and sexuality that single approaches used in isolation cannot reveal?
- Can the application of multiple methods of discourse analysis serve a socially transformative function in terms of helping us to work towards reducing inequalities around gender and sexuality in our schools?

Through deploying a number of different methods of discourse analysis, the book inevitably explores tensions and contradictions between approaches (and possible ways of resolving these) as well as areas of complementarity. In this way, the book addresses some theoretical and methodological issues in discourse analysis as well as providing a detailed investigation of language, gender and sexuality in classroom settings.

At this point, it is perhaps useful to provide a brief note on the use of terminology. Traditionally, the term 'sex' has been used to refer to the biological state of being male or female whereas 'gender' has referred to a social categorisation system consisting of a polarised set of behaviours classed as 'masculine' and 'feminine'. Sex and gender are ideologically linked so that masculine behaviour is expected of biological males and feminine behaviour is expected of biological females. In reality, though, there is no logical relationship between sex and gender – the relationship is purely ideological. More contemporary understandings of gender tend to move away from viewing it simply in binary terms of 'masculinity' or 'femininity' but conceptualise gender instead as fluid, dynamic and as a potential site of struggle. In relation to language, gender is commonly seen nowadays as *effecting* gender, rather than simply reflecting it. Likewise, contemporary understandings of sexuality tend to see this as something dynamic and active and a site of struggle which is closely linked to, and overlaps with, gender. Gender and sexuality tend to co-emerge in and through discourse, as will be seen in some of the analyses presented throughout this book.

In the remainder of this introductory chapter, I provide some context for the research presented in the rest of the book by outlining previous work on gender and educational attainment. I also discuss related research which has examined the discursive construction of gender identities more broadly in educational settings. I then examine some work which has taken a linguistic approach to the study of classroom discourse. I provide a brief overview of how classroom discourse has been analysed and described, in order to show how linguistic routines function to construct the way learning (both academic and social) takes place. I finally consider research which has focused on classroom discourse in relation to gender, specifically in terms of how the repeated linguistic routines which construe classroom interactions are a mechanism for enforcing the wider social discourses around gender which circulate in the school environment.

Gender, in/equalities and attainment

As the research presented in this book provides a potential contribution to developing understandings of issues to do with gender and attainment, it is worth outlining some of the research conducted over the past twenty or so years which has been concerned with addressing and explaining gender-based inequalities in educational attainment. A predominant concern regarding gender in British education during the 1990s was that of boys' 'underachievement'. This theme has continued and is still being debated today, with a range of possible explanations for boys' underachievement being proposed. Three decades ago, much academic research attempted to challenge gender inequalities in education which disadvantaged girls. Statistics on gender and attainment strongly suggest that, over the past three decades, girls have outperformed boys in most areas of the curriculum (see, for example, http://guardian.co.uk/news/datablog/2010/aug/24/gcse-results-2010-exam-breakdown#data).

However, achievement is not the only issue at stake with regards to gender and education. From a feminist perspective, girls' relatively high levels of attainment should surely be seen as a success. Many studies during the 1990s highlighted what may be seen as a contradiction concerning gender in the context of education and achievement. Even though the evidence suggests that girls are academically at an advantage over boys, other research shows that girls are still *socially* disadvantaged in the education system and in society as a whole (Epstein *et al.*, 1998; Jackson, 1998; Mackinnon *et al.*, 1998; OFSTED, 1996; Skelton and Francis, 2009). At the time of writing, for example, there continues to be concern over unequal pay between women and men, and women's continued failure to occupy the highest professional jobs. The gender pay gap (in 2011) stands at 19.8 per cent. That gap is even greater in the private sector where men's pay is on average 27.5 per cent higher than that of women (the gap in the public sector is 19.2 per cent).[1] And even though there has been increased access into professional occupations for women in Western countries, Bourdieu points out that while some university-educated women have found employment in 'middle-range occupations (middle management, technical staff, medical and social personnel), they still systematically remain excluded from positions of authority and responsibility, particularly in industry, finance and politics' (Bourdieu, 2006: 94). Outside the arenas of education and employment, there is, of course, ongoing concern about the levels of violence committed by men against women. Recent statistics reveal that violence against women is still widespread around the world (http://womankind.org.uk.statistics.html). There has also been a worrying increase in the amount of hate crime committed against both women and men based on transgender and sexuality.[2] This is an issue closely related to gender which I will return to in more detail in Chapter 5. Whilst girls may still be achieving academically in school, then, this does not necessarily mean that unequal gender relations in education (or in any other sphere) no longer need to be addressed. For this reason, the 'boy turn' in research on gender and education has been heavily criticised (see Weaver-Hightower, 2003 for a detailed discussion). Research from as early as the 1980s has examined how girls can be disadvantaged socially at school (Arnot and Weiner, 1987; Stanworth, 1981). And more recent research (Skelton, Francis and Smulyan, 2006; Skelton and Francis, 2009) stresses that in addressing boys' underachievement, issues of girls' ongoing social oppression in schools also still need to be addressed. Reay (2006) also argues that the recent focus on girls' higher attainment levels masks more complex issues concerning gender and education which actually work against gender equity. Thus, there continues to be a need to explain this paradox concerning gender and education – why is it that boys underachieve at school whilst maintaining their relatively high status in various aspects of the wider society? This is one question that this book attempts to address through detailed linguistic analyses of the interactions that routinely take place in the classroom.

It has been pointed out by innumerable researchers that there is actually more overlap than difference in the attainment of boys and girls (Elwood, 2005; Francis and Skelton, 2005; Mendick, 2006) and we should also ask the important question of which boys are 'failing'? Hey *et al.* (1998) point out that the 'underachievement' of boys tends to be a classed and racialised phenomenon. Hey *et al.*'s claim is as relevant today as it was over a decade ago: that is, educational discourses about boys and underachievement have had the effect of silencing demands for increased social justice for girls and women. They state:

> The current discourse of equal opportunity is all about boys needing more help because they are underachieving. This is however, framed by the paradox that boys have in fact always received more resources... (Hey *et al.*, 1998: 128)

Bearing these issues in mind, several arguments have been proposed to explain the apparent reversal of trends in boys' and girls' academic achievement in Britain in recent years. Some have argued that achievement levels have been affected by feminist interventions at all levels in education and in the workplace over the past thirty or so years (Yates, 1997). According to this argument, education policies have worked to girls' advantage but boys' needs have, as a result of this, been ignored and dismissed. However, Swann (2003) points out that specific government interventions around gender and achievement were markedly absent during the 1970s and 1980s, when girls were not achieving at a noticeably higher level than boys. Therefore, it is difficult to equate the introduction of quite general equal opportunities policies with specific issues around gender and achievement in schools.

Another argument is that economic changes in Britain over recent years have resulted in more women working in traditionally 'male' occupations. There has also been a widespread loss of traditional male working-class jobs such as mining and employment in manufacturing industries. Some would argue that this has, in part, resulted in changes in perceptions and expressions of masculinity which, in turn, have affected the way that contemporary masculinities are constructed in the classroom (Epstein *et al*, 1998; Francis and Skelton, 2001; Head, 1999; Kenway and Epstein, 1996; Mac an Ghaill, 1994; Skelton, 1997, 2001). A related argument is that there have been more general shifts in cultural values and attitudes towards gender. These shifts have been instigated and perpetuated through cultural mechanisms such as the mass media. Post-structuralist theories about gender have tended to focus on these issues, emphasising how, in recent years, the concepts of 'masculinity' and 'femininity' have come to mean different things. These arguments are particularly relevant to the kinds of post-structural discourse analysis presented in Chapters 4 and 5 of this book. Connell (2006), for example, suggests that boys' 'underachievement' is often explained through the idea that schools have become increasingly feminised, and that curricula have been remodelled to be more in line with girls' learning needs and so on. Connell argues that this rather crude explanation masks vast differences in educational opportunities and experiences among girls.

Although girls do better academically than boys, then, they are still socially disadvantaged at school, and both of these issues need to be taken into account when examining the relationship between all aspects of gender and education, including gender and classroom interaction. And, as highlighted by the examples cited at the beginning of this chapter, both girls and boys suffer from the restrictive ideologies of gender normativity which pervade the school environment.

Before turning specifically to the role language plays in these processes, I will now briefly consider some proposed explanations for these ongoing issues around gender and achievement.

One early set of arguments proposed to explain gender differences in educational attainment focused upon the idea that, due largely to divergent processes of socialisation, boys and girls typically develop and employ different ways of working and interacting at school. The ways in which male and female students respond to curricula content, as it is mediated through various teaching/learning strategies in the classroom, have been associated with their differing 'learning styles'. Evidence for this was collected throughout the 1980s and 1990s: Gilligan (1982), for example, studied the ways in which males and females address issues in education and concluded that males tend to address issues in a more logical way, looking for patterns of cause and effect and rules of procedure. Males approach tasks in a very rule-bound, legalistic manner, whereas females are more likely to display empathy and place more emphasis on emotions and feelings than on rules and logic. These gender-based differences in approaches to educational tasks have also been found by Kelly (1987), who examined gender-differentiated ways of working in science lessons and discovered that the boys were more likely to choose to work alone or to compete with each other whereas the girls were typically seen as 'helpers' to each other and to the boys. Other work has identified similar gender differences in approaches to tasks in specific subject areas such as Mathematics, Information Technology, English, Science and Technology (see, for example, Murphy and Gipps, 1996).

These differences, then, seem to be characteristic, because they have been found across all age groups and across a variety of different subject areas. Girls' emphasis on verbal interaction and collaboration and boys' emphasis on individuality and competition is a notion which has been addressed and supported by several studies, including those which focus specifically upon gender differences in linguistic interaction in the classroom (Graddol and Swann, 1989; Howe, 1997; Swann, 1992; Thorne,

1993; Tolmie and Howe, 1993). I will outline some key studies on gender and linguistic interaction in the classroom later in this chapter.

Another explanation proposed to explain gender differences in educational attainment has been that curriculum and assessment practices may 'favour' one set of ways of working over others. A body of empirical work exists which has examined relationships between gender, curricula and assessment, with some studies claiming that certain curricula are value-laden and predominantly embody the values, practices and ideologies of men (see, for example, Kessler *et al.*, 1987). Other studies have examined how assessment procedures and practices are related to the curriculum (Gipps and Murphy, 1994; Hildebrand, 1996). Curriculum content determines methods of assessment and, in some ways, assessment practices may be seen to drive lesson content. If the curriculum is ideologically biased and value-laden, the assessment practices which accompany it will be equally as value-laden.

In addition to concerns over boys' academic underachievement and the subsequent development of explanations focusing on factors such as differential ways of working in the classroom, changes in policy, curriculum content and assessment practices, other explanations have focused more upon boys' and girls' own perceptions and expressions of their gender identities in school. These more recent 'post-structuralist' approaches to gender and education have primarily centred around an examination of how 'masculinities' and 'femininities' are performed and constructed through various educational and societal domains. These post-structuralist approaches are closely linked to cultural shifts in values and attitudes towards the meaning of 'gender'. In Britain, for example, there has been a recent shift towards challenging binary constructions of gender and sexuality and allowing for a more diverse plurality of genders and sexualities to be perceived and performed. This will inevitably have an effect upon how the binary concepts of 'masculinity' and 'femininity' are construed through a variety of media, including language, and in a variety of contexts, including education.

Much early post-structurally oriented work tended to centre around girls and how their gendered identities were constructed by and through educational practices, and how these gender constructions worked to place girls in a socially unequal position to boys. Walkerdine (1990) argues that the school, as an institution, embodies powerful ideologies about what the abstract concepts of masculinity and femininity mean and how they should be realised and performed. In this sense, the gender categories of masculine and feminine only appear to exist as facts because they are socially and ideologically constructed as such by dominant forces in society (see also Foucault, 1990). One of the forces which maintain this ideology is education. Education paradoxically enforces dominant ideologies about gender binarism through mechanisms such as curriculum content, teaching strategies and classroom interaction, but also provides a site where students may challenge these ideologies and construct their own gender identities. Walkerdine, like other post-structural theorists researching in the field of education, sees the classroom as a site of struggle – a place where meanings, including meanings about gender and achievement, are negotiated and ultimately produced. Walkerdine (1990: 3) highlights this paradoxical situation by arguing that girls are 'produced as a nexus of subjectivities, in relations of power which are constantly shifting, rendering them at one moment powerful and at another powerless.' Girls are powerful in that they have the autonomy to perform their own gender and sexualities but powerless in that their freedom to perform gender however they want is an illusion and is actually highly constrained by dominant ideologies about gender and sexuality. In addition to the work of Walkerdine, classroom-based performances of dominant (and resistant) forms of femininity have been explored by researchers such as Davies (2005), Francis (1998, 2000), Hey (1997) and Reay (2006).

The exploration of interplays and contradictions has become a central tenet of the post-structuralist approaches to analysing gender and classroom interaction which will be discussed in more detail in Chapter 4. The processes through which genders are produced in the classroom necessarily involve the constructing of 'subjectivities' – individual identities which are constantly shifting in response to the struggle which they are continually involved in over the production of meanings. Moreover, the interplay between ideologies and identities is achieved through discourse. Researchers such as Connell (2006) argue that gender is located in discourse or via cultural representations. The possibility of fluid and unstable subjectivities which are constantly being re-negotiated and re-constructed through discourse is one notion which characterises post-structuralist approaches to gender and education. Post-structuralist thought is centred around the concept of 'difference' which results in identities, relationships and meanings always being in flux and open to re-negotiation by individuals (Baxter, 2003, 2008; Butler, 1990). For this reason, classroom *processes*, in their various forms, are the focus of post-structuralist research in which gender identities are always seen as incomplete and construed through a discursive process of struggle and contestation (for further discussion of post-structuralist approaches to gender and education research, see Skelton and Francis, 2009).

It has been argued that research on gender has, in the past, tended to focus on girls as underprivileged, and little attention, until relatively recently, has been paid to the ways in which boys perform their masculinities in school. Those researching boys and masculinities in education have argued that doing so facilitates a deeper understanding of the processes through which *both* boys and girls construct their gender identities at school and of how relationships *between* boys and girls are perceived, performed and constructed. Francis, Skelton and Read (2010), Kimmel (2009) and Lingard, Martino and Mills (2009) all look at how male students are active performers and producers of their gender/sexuality identities at school whilst at the same time being ideologically driven into performing their gender/sexuality identities in restricted, socially dominant ways. Importantly these studies also address the issue of sexuality identities in relation to gender and explore how gender and sexuality are intricately related to one another – a central principle of the queer theories explored in Chapter 5.

Other post-structuralist researchers argue that effective interventions designed to enhance boys' (and girls') achievement should not be geared towards either boys or girls but should, instead, be concerned with challenging and deconstructing current ideologies about gender and sexuality binarism which pervade schools. For example, Jackson (1998) argues that any interventions in education must move towards allowing for a plurality of different masculinities and femininities to be performed in schools. Such a view also allows for a consideration of the ways in which other social factors, such as social class and race, operate in conjunction with gender to create a further plurality and diversity of different gender performances and identities amongst students. The importance of this argument is highlighted in the examples of gender non-normativity discussed at the beginning of this chapter. The strict policing of gender binaries clearly can have devastating material consequences for those who do not conform. Further examples of gender normativity and non-normativity in schools, the complex relationship with sex and sexuality, are provided and discussed extensively by researchers such as Epstein and Johnson (1998), Renold (2007, 2009) and Youdell (2005). The prevalence of these experiences and examples suggests that, ultimately, we need to challenge the pervasive ideologies of gender normativity which circulate repeatedly in the school environment if we are to seriously confront issues of sexism, homophobia and gender-differentiated attainment in our schools. The research discussed so far is all extremely valuable and we have learnt a lot about the processes which produce gender inequalities, or, at least, gendered experience for students (and teachers) in schools. But what about the role that language plays?

Analysing classroom discourse

The study of classroom discourse begins with an acknowledgement that language and learning are interrelated – it is through the linguistic processes which are enacted in classrooms that learning takes place. Halliday (1985: 96), for example, states that 'most of what we learn, we learn through language'. And Stubbs (1976: 68) argues, 'The classroom dialogue between teachers and students *is* the educational process'. Therefore, we cannot really interrogate the processes through which learning takes place in the classroom unless we pay careful attention to the linguistic routines which characterise classroom interaction. Neither can we fully understand the process of identity formation in the classroom without an explicit examination of how processes of identification (which include gender and sexuality) are enacted and achieved through language. As Swann (2003: 624) argues, 'Insofar as gender is "done" in educational settings it is done, to a large extent, through language.' These are some underlying principles which have driven much research on classroom discourse over the past few decades; before examining studies which specifically focus on gender and classroom interaction, I will outline some key principles, ideas, terms and findings from the study of classroom discourse more broadly.

It is, perhaps, useful to first explain what is meant by the term 'discourse'. 'Discourse' is, of course, a contested term and there has been much debate about what it means. As Cameron (2001) points out, 'discourse analysis' is often used as an umbrella term for many different approaches. But it is generally accepted that there are two broad meanings of the term which, although drawing on different interpretive frames, are nevertheless related to one another. The first 'linguistic' meaning of 'discourse' is that it refers to language above the level of the sentence. In other words, it refers to longer stretches of spoken and written text. This definition also tends to have a 'functional' meaning of referring to language in use and language in context, rather than to notions of language as an abstract decontextualised system. The second meaning of 'discourse' is used in more of a social, rather than a purely linguistic, sense. In this sense, 'discourse' has been defined as a form of social practice (Fairclough, 1992). These social meanings of discourse often draw on the work of Foucault, who defines discourses as socially produced forms of knowledge which organise experience and understandings of the world. They are sets of related statements that produce a particular order of reality. According to Foucault, because there can clearly be different ways or ordering and understanding reality, these 'social' discourses always embody a power dimension and form sites of potential struggle. Moreover, discourses do not simply reflect particular understandings, but actively shape and construct them. Foucault (1972: 49) famously describes discourses as being able to 'systematically form the objects of which they speak'. When using the term 'discourse' in this second sense, researchers often refer to the 'discursive construction' of particular aspects of the social world, and this can include gender and sexuality as well as other forms of social identity. These constructions can be varied and multiple, therefore 'discourse' in its social sense can be plural – different discourses can be constructed within any context. And, as Sunderland (2004: 45) points out, discourses do not exist in isolation but in 'constellations' or, to use Foucault's term, 'orders' of related discourses. In other words, they exist in relation to other discourses, often in hierarchical ways.

Sunderland (2004) similarly makes a distinction between 'descriptive discourses' which operate at a linguistic level, and 'interpretive discourses' which operate at a broader societal, post-structural level. The latter often equate 'discourse' with 'ideology' – as a way of seeing the world. However, Sunderland encourages us to distinguish the terms, whereby ideology is the 'cultural materialist antecedent of the post-structural use of *discourse*' (2004: 6). Within interpretive approaches to discourse, then, discourse is seen as *carrying* a particular ideology or set of ideologies. This point is particularly important when examining gender and sexuality and is a key issue which I explore throughout this book.

These two meanings of 'discourse' are interrelated as social (or interpretive) discourses are realised and enacted through linguistic (or descriptive) discourses, as well as through other semiotic modes of expression. Linguistic analysis can reveal 'traces' (Jaworski and Coupland, 1999) of a particular social discourse as it is enacted through linguistic discourse. In order to identify a social discourse, we need to know what linguistic traces to look for which might be relevant. Stubbs (1976, 1983) was one of the first researchers to discuss in detail how the linguistic routines of the classroom (linguistic discourse) embody many of the wider social discourses circulating outside the classroom, the school and beyond all educational contexts. This book examines both meanings of discourse in relation to classroom settings, with a particular focus on how social discourses of gender and sexuality are enacted through the linguistic discourses of classroom talk between students.

The research presented throughout this book focuses more on the talk that takes place between students in the classroom than on teacher-led interaction. There are several reasons for this. Firstly, teacher-led interaction has received more attention than student group discussion (although there is now also a fairly substantial body of research which examines student–student interaction in classrooms, some of which is discussed below). Secondly, in the classes I observed, student–student interaction constituted substantially more of the talk than teacher–student interaction. Whilst some of the student interaction was set up as a specific task by the teacher – in other words, it was a 'goal-directed activity' (Richards, 2006) – a considerable amount of the interaction that took place between students simply happened whilst they were engaged in other, often more practically oriented, tasks (for example, designing and making products in Design and Technology lessons or engaged in writing tasks in English lessons). This kind of 'unofficial' exchange is rarely noticed in studies of classroom interaction. However, I observed that much of this kind of talk was directed towards whatever task the students were engaged in – they often used this talk to discuss what they were doing, ask each other questions, evaluate their own and each other's work, and so on. As might be expected, not all of the talk was 'on-task' but I did not see this as a reason to discount the on-task talk that occurred in this kind of context. Richards (2006: 57) describes such instances of student talk as 'educationally valuable diversions' and notes that they may provide important learning opportunities for students. He argues that 'interactional legitimacy' in the classroom should not nec-essarily be solely determined by the overall pedagogic purpose of the lesson.

Richards also points out that it is important to consider issues of iden-tity in classroom interaction, as well as issues around pedagogy. A similar point is made by Maybin (2003), who argues that more attention needs to be paid to the social and emotional dimensions of dialogic classroom talk in addition to the cognitive dimensions. In this book, I examine how gender and sexual identities emerge in student–student classroom interaction, as well as considering the potential pedagogic benefits of such interaction.

Gender and classroom discourse

Within the field of classroom discourse analysis, there is a body of research which has paid particular attention to gender. My aim here is not to provide a comprehensive literature review of this research, nor is it to provide a detailed review of theoretical developments in this field of research. For more detailed discussions of the historical and theoretical development of the field, see Cameron (1992), Litosseliti and Sunderland (2002), Talbot (2010) or other introductory textbooks on gender and language. These works provide information on 'older' theoretical approaches of 'deficit', 'dominance' and 'difference'. Because these approaches have been addressed so widely, and because they are not a concern of the work presented in this book, I do not discuss them here. I will, however, provide a brief review of some studies in language and gender which are of more direct relevance to my study.

Gender and classroom interaction has been an ongoing area of study for over three decades. Despite the wealth of empirical studies already conducted, it continues to be a hotly debated area of research today. As stated earlier, a key reason for this continued interest is the fact that girls' increased attainment levels across all areas of the school curriculum do not correspond with the levels of success they achieve later in life. A number of studies on gender-differentiated ways of working in education have focused upon the interactional aspects of these differences. Some of this research specifically addresses linguistic interaction in the classroom. In studies which attempt to explain the social disadvantaging of girls in education, substantive evidence first emerged in the 1980s and early 1990s to show that boys tend to dominate whole-class discussion in the classroom (Clarricoates, 1983; Delamont, 1990; Graddol and Swann, 1989; Spender, 1982; Thorne, 1993). These early findings were often interpreted as being part of a 'hidden curriculum' on gender. Delamont (1990), for example, argues that such differences in behaviour perpetuate existing stereotypes and ideologies about what is acceptable and unacceptable in terms of masculine and feminine genders and help to sustain dominant ideologies which place boys in a superior social position to girls. In this sense, gender differences in classroom interaction help to 'construct' students as gendered beings and place them in unequal power relationships. This is an important point – we cannot dismiss the fact that girls still continue to be subjected to ideologies which place them in a socially subordinate position to males in education and elsewhere. And these ideologies can be damaging in their adherence to narrowly defined conceptualisations of gender normativity, as we have already seen in the examples discussed at the beginning of this chapter.

In an attempt to move away from viewing gender simply in terms of biological 'difference' between boys and girls, researchers such as Sunderland (2004) have adopted more post-structural approaches to examining gender and classroom discourse. In Sunderland's study of gender in foreign language classrooms, she identifies and discusses a number of gendered discourses which emerge simultaneously. Sunderland notes that different discourses can prevail at different times, even within the same class, and there can be a degree of interplay and movement between discourses. Gendered discourses, then, are not necessarily static and fixed, as earlier research might suggest.

In addition to studies which have focused upon gender in whole-class interaction, some research has examined gender and interaction in small group settings in the classroom (Corson, 1997; Davies, 2003; Goodwin, 1998; Swann and Graddol, 1995; Sauntson, 2007). It has long been recognised that group discussion that takes the form of collaborative, 'exploratory' talk is an effective learning strategy employed in the classroom (Barnes, 1976; Lemke, 1985; Mercer, 1995; Mercer *et al.*, 2004; Skidmore, 2000; Wells, 1986). This has continued to be developed following dialogic approaches to exploring the advantages of group interaction in educational settings (Edwards and Westgate, 1994; Maybin, 2003; Wells, 1999). It is important to remember that, whilst the generic benefits of group work have long been established, not all learners will approach group discussion tasks in the same way, and these variations are often linked to social differences such as gender. Given the number of studies which have provided systematic evidence of boys' domination of classrooms, Swann (1998) argues that group work has been one strategy employed in education to increase girls' talk time and reduce boys' interactional dominance of whole-class teaching. In studies that examine girls' and boys' approaches to group work tasks, evidence has been collected to support the notion that boys and girls frequently exhibit different ways of approaching group tasks and interacting in the classroom. Similar to findings of research into adult single-sex conversations (Coates, 1996, 2003; Holmes, 1995), girls' emphasis on collaboration and consensus and boys' emphasis on individuality and competition are notions that have been addressed and supported by several studies (Davies, 2005; Graddol and Swann, 1989; Swann, 1992). These differences seem to be characteristic because they have been found across a range of age groups and subject areas such as Science (Kelly, 1987), Technology (SEAC, 1991), Physics (Tolmie and Howe, 1993) and English (Davies, 2005). Moreover, Davies (2005) found that girls form 'cooperative learning allegiances' in which their use of certain linguistic features, such as the frequent use of minimal responses and inclusive directives, are more conducive to collaborative learning.

In Australia, Reay (1991) produced a landmark study examining gender-based language differences in group work. She noticed in the girls' groups she studied a high dependency on feedback from each other, the teacher and the researcher, an acceptance of suggestions in their initial form and an avoidance of conflict and emphasis on democracy and fairness. The boys' groups used language characterised by less dependency on external validation and more explicit challenging of each other's ideas and suggestions. Similar patterns of girls' collaboration and boys' competitiveness have also been found by Head (1999), Holden (1993) and OFSTED (1993).

It is important to note at this point that much current work in language and gender emphasises that it is impossible to generalise about the behaviour of women/girls and men/boys and criticises work that presents a binary conception of gender. There has, for example, been work indicating that girls can be competitive and boys can be co-operative in some contexts (Cameron, 1997; Hewitt, 1997). In fact, what actually counts as 'collaborative' and 'competitive' has also been problematised (Johnson and Meinhof, 1997). Current gender and language work, therefore, acknowledges the context-bound, multifunctionality of conversational features. Swann (2002) also identifies a concern with research which uncritically equates particular linguistic features or patterns with gender, without considering alternative explanations. In asking the question 'yes, but is it gender?', Swann encourages researchers to pay close attention to what 'warrants' they are drawing on to justify a focus on gender in linguistic analysis. Swann offers seven possible 'warrants' for saying 'yes, it is gender':

1. Quantitative and/or general patterns (derived directly from correlational studies of language use, large, computerised, corpora or other systematic comparison between the language of divergent groups)
2. Indirect reliance on quantitative/general patterns (for example, quantitative data interpreted from earlier studies)
3. 'Participants' orientations' as evident in the text (when participants explicitly evoke gender in their talk – a perspective traditionally associated with conversation analysis)
4. Speakers'/participants' solicited interpretations (for example, in interviews or questionnaires)
5. Analysts' theoretical positions (can be applied to any approach to analysing gender)
6. Analysts' intuitions
7. Speakers/participants are female, male (or whatever).

Throughout this book, different warrants are drawn on in different chapters or parts of the analysis. In Chapter 3, where structural-functional discourse analysis is used as a type of (non-computerised) systematic correlational approach, the quantitative warrant (1) is used. It is also used in parts of the analysis in Chapter 4 which uses critical discourse analysis and feminist post-structural discourse analysis, although other warrants (mainly 3, 4 and 5) are simultaneously drawn on here to account for different aspects of the data. Warrants 3, 4 and 5 are also used in Chapter 5, which utilises aspects of queer theory to explore interrelationships between gender and sexuality in the data (for further discussion of the warrants used to examine gender and language, see Swann, 2002 and Sunderland and Litosseliti, 2008).

Policy context

The research presented in this book responds to a number of recent and current government policies and sets of guidance concerning gender and sexuality in/equalities in UK education. It is hoped that the research may also contribute to developing an understanding of how such policies and strategies may be implemented or, at least, illuminate in greater detail some of the classroom-based issues which need to be considered prior to their implementation.

Introduced under the Children Act in 2004, *Every Child Matters* requires local authorities to make provision for 'every child, whatever their background or circumstances to have the support they need to be healthy, stay safe, enjoy and achieve, make a positive contribution and achieve economic well-being'. It also stipulates that all young people should 'feel safe from bullying and discrimination'. Some of the recent and current research discussed above, and later in this book, suggests that various aspects of the schooling system preclude the possibility of these aims being met for all children, and that there are significant areas of inequality with regard to these aims in terms of gender and other social factors such as race, ethnicity, disability and sexual orientation. Clearly, more work needs to be done to examine the extent to which different groups of students are meeting these aims, and which ones are being prevented from doing so, and how and why this is the case.

In 2007, the *Gender Equality Duty* was introduced as part of the 2006 *Equality Act* in education. This act requires schools to promote gender equality in the same way as race and disability equality. Significantly, the act emphasises the importance of inclusion for children who do not conform to traditional gender norms. Like the examples cited at the beginning of this chapter, the act acknowledges that such children often become subject to homophobic bullying and abuse as a result of their perceived transgression away from culturally sanctioned gender norms, and it consequently makes clear in its guidance that it is impossible for schools to address sexism without simultaneously addressing homophobia.

In 2009, the *Single Equality Bill*, entitled *A Fairer Future*, was introduced. This was a precursor to the introduction of the *Equality Act* designed to tackle discrimination based on race, gender, disability, age, sexual orientation, religion or belief. The act covers discrimination across work, education and other areas, hence a single act to replace a number of other legal provisions. It puts emphasis on gender and sexual orientation as areas of inequality currently needing particular attention in schools. The coalition government established in 2010 has also emphasised sexuality equalities as an area in need of particular attention in schools. In their *Programme for Government* published in 2010, they state their aim to 'help schools tackle bullying in schools, especially homophobic bullying' (http://programmeforgovernment.hmg.gov.uk/schools/).

In addition to this legislation, the previous and current governments have also provided published guidance and support which relates specifically to gender equalities in UK schools. For example, the *Social and Emotional Aspects of Learning* (SEAL) strand of the *Primary National Strategy* specifically highlights gender and sexual orientation as key areas which need to be given more attention in the curriculum. For both primary and secondary schools, the Home Office published guidance on *Transphobic Bullying in Schools* in 2008. This guidance stresses a need for schools to foster an environment in which gender variance is accepted, and a need for all schools to support children who do not adopt traditional gender norms, regardless of whether or not they choose gender re-assignment later in their lives. All of this legislation and guidance is promising in terms of enabling schools to create an environment which is safe and supportive for all students. If implemented effectively, it may ultimately work to prevent the occurrence of experiences such as those related by Amy, Tad and Jack at the beginning of this chapter. But successful implementation requires a thorough understanding of the processes through which gendered experiences, which may or may not be discriminatory, happen in schools – this includes the interactional processes which take place in classrooms. And it is these interactional processes which form the focus for the research presented in the remainder of this book.

Organisation of this book

The organisation of this book moves from the broadly structural to the post-structural (terms which are discussed further in Chapter 2), and from the purely descriptive to the politically transformative (although the boundaries between these orientations are not necessarily clear or straightforward). The final chapter on queer theory is most explicit in advocating an emancipatory and transformative agenda. Although earlier chapters do not enforce this agenda quite so emphatically, it is important to state at the outset that the main purpose of this book is to highlight some of the inequalities and injustices around gender which have been observed in the school environment, as a precursor to understanding how we might continue to eradicate such inequalities. The radical transformational possibilities around gender and sexuality offered by queer theory are, as the name suggests, largely theoretical at present. But a key aim of this book is to investigate how this transformative agenda may be operationalised by joining the theory with more concrete and contextualised methods of classroom discourse analysis. To this end, I explore the combinations of different approaches to discourse analysis in more detail in Chapter 2. I also use this chapter to explain the methods of data collection and other information relevant to the data and methods employed in the research. Chapters 3, 4 and 5 then focus on the analysis of data, with each chapter adopting different discourse-analytic approaches (structural-functional discourse analysis [SFDA] in Chapter 3, critical discourse analysis [CDA] and feminist post-structuralist discourse analysis [FPDA] in Chapter 4, and queer theory/queer linguistics in Chapter 5). Finally, Chapter 6 offers some concluding thoughts, both on the methods of discourse analysis employed throughout the book and on the implications of some of the key findings of the research.

2
Data and Methods

This chapter provides a methodological discussion of how the research was conducted, and how the data were gathered. As the research reported in this book is broadly framed within an ethnographic approach, I firstly discuss some principles of linguistic ethnography which informed the research. I then outline the processes of ethnographic classroom observation, audio-recording, and interviewing participants used to obtain the data. I then introduce the particular methods of discourse analysis used throughout the rest of the book. I discuss how these approaches may be used in complementary ways as well as considering some of the epistemological tensions and contradictions between them, and how these may be addressed.

Linguistic ethnography

UK-based linguistic ethnography is largely influenced by work in linguistic anthropology (Erickson, 2004; Gumperz, 1982; Hymes, 1977; Silverstein, 2003) which advocates the study of language as a social phenomenon and the interlinking of language with its socio-cultural contexts of use. Tusting and Maybin (2007: 578) define linguistic ethnography as:

> ...a cluster of research which studies relationships between the micro-level of language practices and the broader context and social order, drawing on linguistics, social theory, and an ethnographic methodology which places the researcher at the heart of the research.

Thus, linguistic ethnography holds a view that 'language and the social world are mutually shaping' (Rampton *et al.*, 2004: 2) and cannot be separated in the process of conducting and producing research. The main purpose of any ethnographic research is to seek to understand the meanings produced in any particular cultural settings. This can, and does, include classrooms. Ethnographic studies entail the researcher being directly involved in the action and context under study as an 'insider', in order that greater insights can be obtained than would otherwise be possible. In other words, the ethnographer observes *and* participates in the environments they study, and therefore participant-observation is used as a main method of data collection. This is precisely the approach I adopted in the research presented in this book. However, the involvement of the researcher alters the context so that 'the researcher is inevitably part of, and shapes, the research that is being produced' (Tusting and Maybin, 2007: 578). Therefore, the issue of researcher 'reflexivity' is a central concern in linguistic ethnography – the researcher is constantly required to be aware of the impact that their presence may be having upon the research context and the data being produced and analysed in that context. Indeed, there may be issues around the validity of any linguistic data obtained where the researcher is present. However, there are strategies which can be used to counter this potential problem. In my own research, I sometimes asked participants themselves to record their own interactions and removed myself from the room in which those interactions were taking place. This happened particularly when I wanted to collect data from a particular group of students, and my presence would have been more intrusive than at the times when I was sitting in with the whole class. Of course, an advantage of ethnographic research is that the researcher, over time, becomes familiar to the participants and they grow increasingly comfortable with the researcher being involved in the context being studied. I noticed this happening in my research. Any reticent or constrained behaviour noted at the beginning of the research soon disappeared as the participants became used to my presence. After the first few weeks, the participants appeared to be relaxed and seemed to have got used to the presence of myself and the recording equipment during their lessons.

Another tenet of linguistic ethnography is its concern with confronting any differences in interpretation between the analyst and participants of the social practices under scrutiny. Hammersley (2006) argues that the dynamic relationship between analysts' and participants' understandings is at the heart of ethnographic research. Tusting and Maybin (2007: 579–80) note that: this presents particular challenges for linguistic ethnography, arguing that:

linguistic ethnographers need to take on the epistemic authority to make truth claims which may differ from those of their research participants. However, this may sit uneasily with an ethnographic commitment to representing participants' perspectives, and may raise particular ethical issues where these claims challenge, or even directly contradict, participants' understandings.

Some methods of discourse analysis, for example, require the structured analysis of language using pre-coded categories which emphasise the analysts' interpretations and understandings, rather than those of the participants. However, such frameworks are necessary to identify patterns of language use which may not be identified by the participants themselves, and those linguistic patterns may be very significant to the context in question (see, for example, Eckert, 2000).

Linguistic ethnography often starts from a neutral or apolitical position, unlike approaches such as critical discourse analysis (CDA). This may be seen as an advantage as it reduces researcher bias, which is a criticism that has been levelled at CDA. However, this may also be a weakness as 'the political commitments of many linguistic ethnographers...entail a belief in, and a critique of, the pre-existing social structures and power relations which shape and constrain actions and interactions' (Tusting and Maybin, 2007: 581). However, I argue that, if CDA is used as an analytical tool or framework *within* a broadly ethnographic approach, this tension may be reconciled, at least temporarily. In Chapter 4, for example, I use CDA as a means of identifying dominant discourses and ideologies around gender which circulate in the classroom contexts studied (I also do this, to a certain extent, in Chapter 3 through the use of structural-functional discourse analysis), but I also use feminist post-structuralist discourse analysis as a means of considering discourses which may emerge as marginalised or resistant. Thus, the use of particular analytical frameworks within linguistic ethnography may be used strategically to resolve some of the inevitable tensions and challenges which arise from this kind of research. In fact, these arguments around 'interdisciplinarity' have appeared in recent discussions of linguistic ethnographic research in the UK. Rampton *et al.* (2004), for example, discuss how linguistic ethnography draws on a number of different traditions, despite being largely influenced by linguistic anthropology. They argue that the boundaries between different traditions are themselves 'permeable, with a lot of cross-fertilisation, synthesis and for the most part, not much policing' (Rampton *et al.*, 2004: 11). They also note that ethnography is more pronounced in some approaches than it is in others. Furthermore, Creese argues that it is 'the interdisciplinary nature of linguistic ethnography that allows us to look closely and look locally, while tying observations to broader relations of power and ideology' (2010: 140–1) and she notes a recent emphasis on combining analytical approaches, rather than relying on one single approach, within ethnographic studies of interaction (see, for example, Holmes *et al.*, 1999; Rampton *et al.*, 2002; Stubbe *et al.*, 2003; Zuengler and Mori, 2002). Creese provides examples of how the different discourse-analytic approaches of SFDA and conversation analysis (CA) might be used in complementary ways within an ethnographic study to analyse classroom interaction. She claims that 'a linguistic ethnographic approach might analyse a piece of classroom data using a range of discursive traditions, while keeping the ethnographic context central to its interpretation' (2010: 141). This is precisely what I attempt to do in the research presented throughout this book. Even SFDA, arguably the most decontextualised discourse-analytic framework used in this book, still incorporates the use of observational field notes to enhance the interpretations of the data. Thus, the combination of an ethnographic approach with different types of discourse analysis should allow for a more nuanced account of what is happening in terms of gender in the classroom interactions being studied.

Tusting and Maybin (2007) discuss in more detail how linguistic ethnography can be usefully combined with detailed linguistic analysis 'in order to probe the interrelationship between language and social life in more depth' (2007: 576). Drawing on the work of Rampton *et al.* (2004), they argue that 'combining linguistics with ethnography brings a formal, abstract discipline and tried-and-tested, finely-tuned methods for analysing text together with the more open, reflexive social orientation of ethnographic methods, which offer analytic purchase on the related social practices and structures' (2007: 576). This is what the research presented throughout this book aims to do. Data were collected using a broadly ethnographic approach. But the detailed data analysis draws on a number of discourse-analytical approaches taken from the discipline of Linguistics. This approach arguably also addresses the two key criticisms of ethnography, as discussed by Rampton *et al.* (2004). The first is that it fails to enable generalisations to be made beyond the limited number of situations that the researcher has observed and been involved in. The use of SFDA (or similar approaches), as an approach which is well-suited to yielding quantitative data whilst still enabling that data to be gathered using ethnographic methods of participant observation, could at least enable the identification of linguistic patterns which may reveal particular trends. A second criticism of linguistic ethnography is that in focusing on micro-interactional analyses it neglects broader socio-cultural and socio-historical processes and systems (Hammersley, 1992). The incorporation of an analytic method such as CDA alongside ethnography may function as a means of addressing this criticism. In addressing both criticisms, the data collection would still rely largely on ethnographic methods of participant observation, participant interviews and so on. But the detailed analyses of the data collected could draw on any number of discourse-analytic frameworks in order to offer a more comprehensive account which considers both the micro- and macro- systems operating in the context under scrutiny. This is what I attempt to do in the research presented throughout this book. In the following section, I explain how I used an ethnographic approach to collect the data for the research. I then consider the specific approaches which were used in the analysis of that data, the tensions which exist between them, especially in relation to gender and language, and how some of these tensions may be resolved.

Methods of data collection

Within the broadly linguistic ethnographic approach, a variety of methods were employed, the main ones being the audio-recording of group discussions in the classroom and interviews with teachers and young people. I also used field notes as a means of gaining contextual information to support the data gained from the audio-recordings.

The classroom-based research took place in a British co-educational urban comprehensive school in the city of Birmingham over a period of three years. Some of the interviews also took place during this period but further interviews were conducted over a longer period of time and included participants from schools other than the one where the classroom-based research took place. These additional interviews were conducted in order to explore more fully some aspects of the interrelationship between gender and sexuality in schools, a point I will return to later. Most of the students in the classroom-based research came from working-class or lower middle-class backgrounds. The majority of the students in the school are white, with 17.2 per cent coming from ethnic minority backgrounds. At the time that the fieldwork was conducted, the school had 135 bilingual students. I chose a school with which I was very familiar for the research. A high level of familiarity provided me with an in-depth knowledge and understanding of all aspects of the school's activities, thus facilitating the ethnographic approach. The majority of the staff were already familiar with my research. The teachers and students at the school were all used to having observers, in the form of parents, inspectors and researchers, and the school as a whole had a positive attitude towards educational research being carried out. This meant that neither the teachers nor the students felt inhibited or uncomfortable about having a researcher present during their lessons.

As gender issues are high on the agenda in the school, the staff were keen for my research to be carried out in the school on the premise that, when completed, it could be put to some practical use within the school. Gender differences in attainment nationally are particularly marked within the subjects of English and Design and Technology, with girls consistently outperforming boys in these subjects. The 2010 GCSE results reveal quite a large difference between girls' and boys' achievement in the A* to C grades in these subject areas and this has been the case for some years now.[1] It is for these reasons that I was encouraged by the senior staff in the school to focus my investigation in these particular subject areas. The school does, however, see gender issues, and the contribution this research makes to understanding gender issues, as a cross-curricular issue. For example, whilst conducting the research, many of the staff were keen to comment upon the boys' low literacy skills relative to those of the girls and the effect that this had on all subjects across the curriculum, including Design and Technology.

I observed three main classes at regular intervals over a three-year research period. Classes were mainly observed during each of their Design and Technology lessons during the times in which fieldwork was taking place in the school. A smaller number of observations of the same classes in English lessons also took place (about one class per month). This was done partly because I wanted to see whether the class produced the same kinds of interactions in different subject areas. There were no noticeable differences in their interaction across these two subject areas. Although, as a former English teacher, I continued to be interested in focusing my research on English classes, I also wanted to collect data from students in different subject lessons. Many existing studies of classroom discourse do focus on the interactions that take place in English lessons (including a large body of work on EFL classrooms). In these lessons, language is both the subject matter of the lesson and the medium of instruction – which makes it more difficult to focus only on what is happening structurally in the lesson in relation to the subject content (see Willis, 1992 for further discussion of this issue). In my own research, I am less interested in the actual content of what is discussed and more interested in the structural and social aspects of the discourse. In classroom discourse analysis, the focus is more on *how* things are said and what that can reveal about the interactional and ideological processes at work in the context under scrutiny. A further reason for shifting the subject focus of the research away from English towards another quite different discipline was simply because there is still a lack of research on classroom discourse which focuses on subjects other than English. Design and Technology is one such subject. Within the school's Technology department, the curriculum is organised so that all students in Key Stage 3 (11–14 age range) study a variety of different disciplines within the broad subject area of Design and Technology. These disciplines are Resistant Materials, Systems and Control and at least one of the Food and Textiles product areas.[2] Throughout the course of the research, students were observed in all of these disciplines.

Although there is a fairly even mix of male and female teachers in the Design and Technology department, the female teachers tend to teach those disciplines which are traditionally perceived as being 'feminine' domains (Food and Textiles) and the male teachers teach disciplines traditionally viewed as 'masculine' domains (Resistant Materials, and Systems and Control). However, the teachers reported no explicit gender stereotyping in the students' attitudes towards the subject and this was reflected in my own observations of the classes. The boys displayed no explicit objection or reluctance to participate in Food Technology or Textiles lessons and the girls displayed no obvious objections to studying Resistant Materials and Systems and Control. The girls also consistently outperformed the boys in all disciplines, not only in those traditionally associated with feminine activities.

I started observing the key classes when they were in Year 7 (age 11) and continued to observe them at regular intervals across most of Key Stage 3. The classes had Technology lessons three times per fortnight. I observed each lesson, and recorded group discussions occurring in them, for a total of 55 weeks. In addition, I observed and recorded about one English class per month for the duration of the research period. A total of approximately 50 hours of classroom data were recorded and transcribed. When whole lessons were recorded, only the group work components were transcribed, in most cases. The group discussions which were the most audible, and which lasted for more than five minutes, were transcribed. Throughout the research period, recordings of single-sex male and female and mixed-sex group interactions were made so that, after the conversations had been transcribed and analysed, comparative analysis across the groups could then be conducted if necessary (the SFDA required this kind of comparative analysis).

In all classes, the students were told that I was a researcher investigating the use of group discussion as a means of enhancing learning in the classroom. They were not told that I was investigating gender in relation to linguistic interaction in the context of group work as this might have affected the linguistic behaviour of the groups. All student participants were fully de-briefed about the project during the student interviews which took place at the end of Year 9 (age 14). The students gave their consent for me to use the audio-recordings of their discussions and interviews for the purposes of this research. Consent was gained from the students' parents, via their teacher, to use the recordings in this research. The students quickly got used to me being present during their lessons. In lessons, I attempted to interact as little as possible with the students but built up a rapport with them by talking to them at the beginnings and ends of lessons. The students quickly adapted to this way of working and accepted that they should not engage in conversation with me during lessons. The names of all participants involved in the research have been changed or removed in all transcriptions as a means of anonymising them.

Recordings of student–student group discussion

Any group discussion that took place during lessons was audio-recorded using digital voice recorders placed on the tables where the students were working. Two recorders were used simultaneously, which enabled two groups to be recorded at any one time. I was responsible for switching the recorders on and off, although I tended to move away from the groups while they were being recorded. The use of video-recording in the Technology classrooms could not be permitted, due to safety regulations, therefore I decided to use only audio-recordings for all of the lessons observed. The use of group work was a strategy frequently employed by all of the teachers in the study. Group work was employed for approximately 60 per cent of the total lesson time observed throughout the period of research. In many cases, the whole lesson was recorded but only the elements of group discussion were transcribed. This enabled me to analyse and comment upon the group discussion data in the context of the overall aims and structure of the whole lesson. When recording group discussions, the audio-recorder was positioned at the side of the room with an external microphone fixed to the desk where the students were working. The students generally talked in groups of two to four.

Observational field notes

For each lesson observed and recorded, I compiled a set of field notes to accompany the transcripts obtained from the recordings of the student group discussions. Field notes are used primarily as a means of providing contextual information for each transcript and are a method which is commonly used in ethnographic research. They provide information about the overall aims and objectives of each lesson, the nature, requirements and goals of any group work employed, the times allocated to each activity within the lesson, the overall structure and progression of the lesson, the relationship between the lesson being observed and previous lessons, and general notes on the behaviour and activities of the students and teacher during the lesson. Any contextual information considered relevant to the data recordings, but which could not be captured by the recording itself, was recorded in the field notes.

Interviews

Some of the students in the key class being observed for the three years were interviewed at the end of the research period when they were in Year 9, although not all students were available to be interviewed at this time. The main objective in interviewing the students was to try to obtain information from them about their own perceptions of gender and linguistic interaction with their peers in the classroom. The students were interviewed in single-sex pairs or groups of three and, where possible, in friendship groups. By the time the students were interviewed, they were used to me being present in their lessons and seemed relaxed and keen to talk openly about their experiences. The students were taken out of the classroom to be interviewed. The interviews took place in the English and Design and Technology departmental offices which were quieter and more comfortable than the classrooms. These relaxed and informal surroundings also encouraged the students to talk freely.

I also conducted later interviews with teachers and young people in other schools about the issues raised by the research. A key finding which emerged from the classroom-based research was that sexuality was integral to gender and vice versa. I subsequently used interviews with teachers and young LGB-identified (i.e. lesbian, gay or bisexual) people in schools to investigate this issue further (see Sauntson and Simpson, 2011) and these data were also helpful for providing further insights into the ways in which gender and sexuality emerge simultaneously through classroom interaction. These data are used primarily in

Chapter 5 which uses elements of queer theory to focus explicitly upon the interrelationship between language, gender and sexuality in schools.

Methods of data analysis: discourse-analytic frameworks

As discussed above, a body of recent research on linguistic interaction, both in schools and other contexts, emphasises the advantages of combining analytical approaches rather than relying only on one approach or framework. Hammersley (2003) asserts that there is much to be gained from an eclectic and inclusive research environment in linguistics. And Rampton *et al.* (2002: 387) argue that a range of approaches to analysing classroom interaction 'offer more to the analysis of classroom discourse in combination than they do alone'. Stubbe *et al.* (2003) also consider the benefits of utilising different discourse-analytic approaches to interpret professional talk. They note that different discourse-analytic approaches may not necessarily conflict with each other, but may, in fact, be used in complementary ways. Stubbe *et al.* use five different discourse-analytic approaches (conversation analysis, interactional sociolinguistics, politeness theory, critical discourse analysis and discursive psychology) to study different facets of one spoken workplace interaction. They note that the key differences between these approaches lie in their varying treatments of context, the level of detail with which linguistic features are analysed, and the degree to which an interaction is seen and/or analysed as a joint construction between speakers, rather than a simple 'transmission' of information or intent. I would also add, drawing particularly on insights from the field of gender and discourse analysis, that the differences between approaches lie in how linguistic and social categories are conceptualised (for example, as pre-discursive or as emergent). Stubbe *et al.* conclude:

> Each approach...provides a slightly different lens with which to examine the same interaction, highlighting different aspects or dimensions of its key features. These are not necessarily in conflict with one another...rather, they are complementary in many ways, with each approach capable of generating its own useful insights into what is going on in the interaction (2003: 380).

This same principle is adopted in the analysis of classroom interaction presented throughout this book. However, I use different discourse-analytic approaches from Stubbe *et al.*, which are detailed below. In Stubbe *et al.*'s paper, different authors also conduct different types of analyses on the same piece of data, whereas I conduct the different analyses myself, thus providing a degree of consistency in terms of what the researcher is bringing to each analysis.

As discussed earlier, the use of a range of discourse-analytic frameworks sits well within a broad linguistic ethnographic approach. A characteristic of linguistic ethnography is its openness to including other traditions of linguistic analysis to enhance the ethnographic analysis. Combining an ethnographic approach with a multi-strand discourse analysis should allow us to build a more nuanced and detailed account of what is happening in the classroom interaction under scrutiny. However, it is important to acknowledge and address the issue that the different epistemological assumptions underlying each analytic approach are not necessary mutual and do not always sit comfortably together. But this should not be a deterrent to conducting such analysis. Discussions in the field of discourse analysis will not move on unless researchers rise to the challenge of testing out combining different methods. Indeed, the discussions presented in this book contribute to wider debates across the social sciences about interdisciplinarity and the use of multiple analytic frameworks. Rampton *et al.* point out that applied linguistics often involves a lot of 'hybrid interdisciplinarity' (2002: 373) and they illustrate this concept by looking specifically at how combinations of different discourse-analytic approaches can be used in the analysis of classroom discourse. They consider ethnography of communication (EC), conversation analysis (CA) and systemic functional linguistics (SFL) as frameworks for the analysis of classroom interaction. They explain how approaches such as CA and SFL lend themselves well to quantitative and statistical validation, whereas EC is more suited to yielding detailed and qualitative insights (the appropriateness of CA to gender and language study has also been debated extensively in various issues of *Discourse and Society* – see, for example, Stokoe; 1998; Stokoe and Smithson, 2001; Wetherell, 1998). These distinctions similarly apply to the approaches of CDA, FPDA and queer theory in contrast to SFDA used in this book. I will explore some of the tensions between these approaches, along with some possible resolutions, as each one is dealt with throughout Chapters 3, 4 and 5. Combining multiple approaches will hopefully bring a new dimension to developments in linguistic ethnography and discourse analysis.

There are many different strands of discourse analysis, even within the disciplinary field of linguistics. It is obviously not possible to consider a large number of different strands or approaches within one book, so the types of analysis adopted here are necessarily selective. Other possible approaches not drawn on in this book include, amongst others: discursive psychology, conversation analysis, corpus linguistics. This wider range of discourse-analytic approaches, specifically in relation to the study of gender, is examined in greater detail in two useful edited collections on gender and language methodologies – *Gender Communication: Theories and Analyses* (Krolokke and Sorensen, 2006) and *Gender and Language Research Methodologies* (Harrington *et al.*, 2008).

In this book, I am particularly interested in providing examples of discourse analysis which can yield quantitative information and contrasting that with approaches which are generally seen as being more qualitative. The selection of approaches is also partly based on my own experience and expertise in using different methods of analysis. I am also interested in contrasting methods which are traditionally viewed as falling within a broadly 'structuralist' paradigm with those which are more 'post-structural' in their orientation. In other words, I want to address the challenge of seeing if and how it is possible to combine approaches to analysis which are seen to embody particular theoretical and methodological tensions and contradictions. In the remainder of this chapter, and throughout the rest of the book, I consider whether there are ways of resolving some of the underlying epistemological tensions between approaches to see if they can be used in complementary ways, even if this is just in a temporary and localised way. Cameron (2001: 57) argues that:

> Insider-observers have to put some distance between themselves and the phenomena they are observing; they have to notice what normally passes unnoticed... it may help them to do this if they come to the task with a systematic framework for making observations.

Combining qualitative approaches such as CDA, FPDA and queer theory with a quantitative, systematic framework such as SFDA, all within an overarching ethnographic framework, enables us to do precisely that.

It has been argued that approaches to discourse analysis more broadly have moved in recent years towards more contextualised and localised studies within what is commonly referred to as a 'discursive turn' in the humanities and social sciences. Swann (2002: 43) notes that there has, likewise, been a general shift in language and gender research characterised as 'running from relative fixity to relative fluidity in terms of how "language" and "gender" are conceived and how the two are seen to interrelate'. In other words, there has been a move away from quantitative variationist approaches to language and gender research, which treat gender as a pre-discursive category, towards more post-structural approaches, which see gender as emergent and discursively constructed through contextualised practices. Whilst acknowledging the value of such developments, Swann questions whether post-structural approaches actually do (or whether they can) dispense with gender as an *a priori* category. And Hultgren (2008: 33) more vehemently argues that:

> ...the theoretical steering away from 'essentialism' to social constructionism is not consistently reflected in practice and it has certainly not led us to discard the old binary categories of 'men' and 'women'...

However, neither Swann nor Hultgren necessarily see this as problematic, as long as researchers are explicit about why and how it is useful, or perhaps even necessary, to draw on these pre-discursive categories in ways which are appropriate to the research in question. As a self-reflexive analyst, I do not see how gender can emerge from the data collected for this research in ways which are not influenced in any way by my own preconceptions and experiences of gendered and gendering practices. And part of these preconceptions is seeing and experiencing gender in a binary way which is ideologically premised on the biological categories of sex. However, this does not prevent me from critically analysing these discursive constructions of binary gender and, sometimes, how those binary constructions may be challenged. Indeed, approaches such as queer theory are a particularly effective means of exploring what happens when the binary categories of gender are discursively contested, as I will show and discuss in Chapter 5.

Swann also suggests that many localised studies are actually framed by earlier research which has already established patterns of gender difference in language use. Localised studies may be driven by this research to test the validity of the sometimes overstated and over-generalised claims of this earlier research, or they may be of use and interest because 'they are able to qualify, or complexify, or introduce counter-examples' (2002: 60). Holmes (1996) also argues that quantitative studies of language and gender can provide a background for more detailed qualitative research. In view of such discussions, Swann (2002) advocates using what she terms 'pragmatic eclecticism' in combining different approaches and methodologies in the study of language and gender. Swann does acknowledge, however, that there may be fundamental incompatibilities between generalised/quantitative and localised/qualitative approaches, particularly in terms of how they conceptualise 'language' and 'gender' and in what kind of role the researcher is seen to play in the research process. This does not necessarily mean that approaches cannot be combined, but that the researcher needs to carefully consider which approaches can be used, and the specificities of how they may be combined in a particular research project. In discussing similar issues, Sunderland and Litosseliti (2008: 13) have asked:

> ...can Approach A always go with Approach B, in a pick-and-mix sort of way? Might some approaches be particularly compatible and others incompatible? Must some always serve and supplement others? And can a researcher achieve accountability to more than one method?

These are all questions which it has been necessary to consider in the process of selecting the approaches used within this book and they are, perhaps, questions which have, to a certain extent, been overlooked in discussions about the use of multiple approaches in discourse analysis more broadly. In both Rampton *et al.*'s theoretical paper on the use of different methods in the analysis of classroom discourse, and Stubbe *et al.*'s data-oriented paper on the use of different approaches to analysing workplace interaction, the rationale for the selection of approaches is not particularly clear. Stubbe *et al.* select their methods based on the experience and expertise of each of the authors/researchers. Whilst this is a valid reason for selecting those methods, it could be asked whether such an 'opportunistic' approach has its limitations, and whether more objective criteria for the selection of specific methods and approaches could be used instead? Rampton *et al.*, on the other hand, seem to focus on methods which are selected because they provide a clear contrast with one another in terms of their epistemological and methodological assumptions. This seems appropriate given that their paper is primarily concerned with theoretical explorations rather than with actual data analysis. However, if those particular frameworks were to be applied to some data, would the selection of that combination necessarily be the most effective or appropriate one?

In selecting the approaches to be used in the analysis of data throughout this book, I have attempted to base my choice on a careful and critical consideration of what each approach may offer, how appropriate each one is to the context and type of data in question, and how much scope there is for exploring and possibly resolving some of the underlying epistemological differences between them. This is in addition to the levels of experience and expertise I consider myself to have in applying each method of analysis. No researcher will ever have a comprehensive knowledge of all available frameworks of discourse analysis, and some discourse-analytical approaches had to be dismissed simply because I do not have the necessary knowledge or experience in using them. But I wanted to ensure that the methods used would yield both quantitative and qualitative data, and would enable the identification of structural patterns as well as be able to account for discursive constructions of ideologies, both dominant and marginalised, and the contextualised details of how such ideologies are brought into being, reinforced and perhaps contested through the interaction under scrutiny.

Within the broadly ethnographic approach used to collect data, four specific approaches to the discourse analysis were used to analyse the classroom interaction and interview data. I explain each approach in more detail throughout the chapters which follow, but I will provide a brief introduction to each approach below, along with some consideration of the tensions and areas of complementarity between them.

Structural-functional discourse analysis (SFDA)

SFDA is arguably the most quantitative approach used in this book. This approach is similar to, and was partly developed from, systemic functional linguistics (SFL). Whereas SFL focuses on grammatical description and analysis, SFDA moves beyond grammar to the level of discourse – rather than describing sentences and clauses, and their constituent structures, SFDA describes the utterances which occur in spoken interaction and the relationships between them. What it draws from SFL is a classification system which focuses on the functions of linguistic elements (in the case of SFDA, these are utterances) rather than on their form. And the functions ascribed to each particular utterance are identifiable only through examining the utterance in relation to those that occur around it. SFDA is also partly influenced by conversation analysis in that it sets out to identify and describe the routines used in naturally occurring spoken interaction. However, SFDA is less interested in classifying all of the conversational features which routinely occur in everyday conversation (pauses, overlapping speech, and so on) and is more interested in categorising the functions that utterances are performing in relation to each other, and in identifying any notable patterns which emerge from this functional analysis of utterances.

Some of these patterns may emerge around gender. In this sense, SFDA is well-suited to revealing comparative patterns in the interaction produced by boys and girls in the classroom. However, this approach has been criticised. One common critique centres around the lack of detailed, contextually informed analysis of extracts of data. Another criticism is that, like 'variationist' approaches to language and gender, SFDA treats gender in binary terms and does not account for any differences which may occur within those binary categories. Sunderland and Litosseliti (2002) note that early variationist studies of gender differences were often criticised for downplaying the importance of context and 'intragroup' variation and overlaps, for treating gender as a binary opposition, and for rendering 'gender' the equivalent of biological 'sex'. The same criticisms could potentially be applied to SFDA. Sunderland and Litosseliti contrast studies of gender difference with more recent 'discourse approaches' to gender and language which incorporate a consideration of the agency of the subject and of gender identities as potentially fluid, multiple and contextualised. However, despite the criticisms of variationist and comparative approaches, and the general shift in recent years towards more discourse-based approaches, some researchers continue to emphasise the value of approaches which take more of a quantitative approach and are informed by more 'structuralist' methods of analysis. And, as discussed above, some researchers claim that a combination of different approaches can be beneficial (Hultgren, 2008; Swann, 2002; Swann and Maybin, 2008). In support of these arguments, I use SFDA alongside the more 'post-structural' approaches of critical discourse analysis, feminist post-structuralist discourse analysis and queer theory.

Critical discourse analysis (CDA)

CDA sets out to examine the ways in which ideologies and power are achieved, reinforced and also contested through language. CDA examines how 'social' discourses are enacted and realised through the 'linguistic' discourses which operate at a more micro level in different forms of speech and writing. In conducting CDA, the analyst can focus on various aspects of language, including lexis, grammar and larger textual structures (see Fairclough, 2001: 92–3). But the analysis then focuses on how these linguistic features function to construe particular ideologies and/or social identities. This can include gender, and a growing body of research has emerged in the field of feminist CDA which specifically examines the ways in which gender is discursively constructed and negotiated in texts. I will discuss this research more in Chapter 4. CDA is also helpful because of the particular attention it pays to the relationship between language and social and institutional structures which are infused with power. CDA tends to focus quite explicitly upon the ways in which power and dominance are produced in social practice through routine linguistic interaction.

At a first glance, an approach such as CDA does not sit comfortably with more structurally oriented approaches such as SFDA. However, CDA and SFDA arguably do share similarities, and those similarities can help to reconcile some of the tensions between approaches. Rampton *et al.* (2004) explore the combined used of CDA with another 'structural' approach – conversation analysis (CA). Like SFDA, conversation analysis uses a pre-coded system of analysis to uncover the interactional routines and practices that govern everyday talk. Rampton *et al.* discuss how, despite the differences between approaches such as CDA and CA, they do, in fact, share similarities in terms of enabling the researcher to uncover or deconstruct the commonsense or taken-for-granted assumptions that may pervade a particular interactional context:

> ... both critical discourse analysis and conversation analysis provide ways of stepping back from the taken-for-granted in order to uncover the ideological (CDA) or interactional (CA) processes that constitute commonsense and everyday practice (Rampton *et al.*, 2004: 7)

Although CA is not used in this book, SFDA similarly uses a pre-coded analytic framework to describe the structures and patterns in spoken interaction. Therefore, I argue that just as CDA and CA can work alongside each other in complementary ways, so can SFDA and CDA. The combination of these approaches is particularly effective in uncovering both the ideological and interactional processes that constitute gendered practices in the classroom, as I will show in Chapter 4.

Feminist post-structuralist discourse analysis (FPDA)

FPDA is, in many ways, similar to CDA. Judith Baxter, who devised FPDA, describes it as a 'supplementary' approach which can be used effectively with other approaches, including CDA. FPDA and CDA share a focus on how identities emerge through discourse, rather than viewing identities (including gender) as pre-discursive. Both approaches also tend to focus on localised and contextualised instances of language use. Both approaches also explicitly acknowledge the subjectivity of the analyst and, as a result, encourage the analyst to be self-reflexive when conducting research. This subjectivity and self-reflexivity is seen as a strength in both CDA and FPDA, as it means that the analyst can draw on a more in-depth 'insider' knowledge and experience of the particular context under scrutiny, which can help to validate the analysis.

However, FPDA does also differ from CDA in some key ways. Firstly, although both approaches see identities as emergent – as emerging in and through discourse – CDA places more emphasis on how those emergent identities may actually be constrained by prevailing social and institutional structures and ideologies. FPDA places more emphasis on how identities are flexible and can be multiple, and not necessarily linked to ideological power structures in any given situation. Secondly, in terms of their theoretical orientations, CDA has traditionally been informed more by Marxist ideas, whereas FPDA draws more explicitly on feminist theories (although feminist CDA does try to pull these two theoretical orientations together). Thus, FPDA is specifically designed to focus on the discursive construction of gender, whereas CDA is more broad-ranging in that it focuses on discursive constructions of different kinds of social identities in relation to power and ideology. A final key difference between CDA and FPDA is that CDA has more of an explicitly emancipatory agenda. Because of its overriding concern with power and power relations, CDA ultimately has a socially transformative agenda. FPDA, on the other hand, does not necessarily seek to transform that which it sets out to investigate, although transformation may be a by-product of such analysis. Due to these differences, FPDA tends to focus more on the multiplicity of gendered subjectivities which may emerge from the data under scrutiny. It also focuses on how gendered identities may shift and change, even across the same text or stretch of interaction. FPDA offers more scope for focusing on what Baxter terms 'marginalised' or 'silenced' voices in interaction, whereas CDA tends to focus more on identifying loci of power (and relative lack of power) in discourse.

Queer theory

In terms of its underlying principles, queer theory shares similar characteristics with both CDA and FPDA. Applications of queer theory to linguistic analysis (queer linguistics) typically focus on describing localised and contextualised texts and interactions, rather than trying to identify patterns, trends and routines across larger, decontextualised data-sets. In this sense, it shares a broad 'post-structural' approach with CDA and FPDA. Queer theory also sees identities as emerging from discourse. However, recent work in queer theory, particularly by Judith Butler, has focused more explicitly upon the tensions between structure and agency in relation to discourse and identity. Whilst Butler (2004) maintains that gender (as a form of social identity) is something which the subject has agency to 'perform', speakers are still to a certain extent constrained by hegemonic discourses of gender which operate in any given context. Butler claims that, although we are basically 'free' to perform gender however we want, we also know that different gendered discourses are 'hierarchised under constraint'. In other words, some emerge as hegemonic and valid, whereas others are more marginalised.

Queer theory is also different from CDA and FPDA in that there is an explicit focus on the interrelationship between gender and sexuality. Whereas CDA and FPDA are well-suited to researching language in relation to either gender or sexuality, there is no real critical interrogation of the relationship between these forms of social identity. Queer theorists argue that there is a special 'definitional' relationship between gender and sexuality in that one cannot fully be described or even conceptualised without reference to the other. I will return to this point in Chapter 5.

Like CDA, queer theory is socially transformative, or at least it has the potential to be. Queer theory takes 'normality' as its starting point and sets out to critically interrogate discursive constructions of 'normal' and 'queer' in relation to a range of contexts. In particular, queer theory is interested in examining how heterosexuality, and the related hegemonic discourses of gender that are associated with heterosexuality, are normalised and naturalised through discourse, and how other forms of identity are 'queered'. It is also important to note that queer theory is more of a social theory rather than a specific analytical framework which is rooted in linguistics and discourse analysis. However, I argue and attempt to illustrate in Chapter 5, that elements of queer theory can be incorporated into other linguistic analyses in order to offer new perspectives and insights on the data, especially in relation to examining the interrelationship between gender and sexuality.

In order to summarise and highlight the key areas of similarity and difference between the four approaches to the analysis of classroom interaction used throughout this book, Table 2.1 lists the key underlying principles of each approach.

It is clear, then, that there are particular differences between the four approaches which may create tensions when conducting data analysis. But these tensions, I argue, are not irreconcilable – in fact, they can actually be very productive.

Table 2.1 Summary of approaches

SFDA	CDA	FPDA	Queer theory
Non-transformative starting point	Transformative starting point	Non-transformative starting point	Transformative starting point
Analyst is objective	Acknowledgement of subjectivity of analyst	Acknowledgement of subjectivity of analyst	Acknowledgement of subjectivity of analyst
Describes systematic patterns and routines	Describes localised and contextualised instances but can link these to larger patterns and routines, depending on which linguistic frameworks are being applied at the level of 'description'	Describes localised and contextualised instances, rather than patterns and routines	Describes localised and contextualised instances, rather than patterns and routines
Uses pre-discursive social categories	Social identity categories are emergent but constrained	Social identity categories are emergent	Social identity categories are emergent but constrained

Unlike the other three approaches, SFDA is the only one which uses binary sex as a starting point for comparative analysis. The other approaches see social gender as emerging *through* discourse, rather than having any *a priori* existence. A criticism of SFDA is that the researcher imposes a binary system onto the data and assumes in advance that the binary will be played out somehow in the analysis of that data. However, Hultgren (2008) makes the same criticism of post-structural approaches, claiming that many studies which adopt these approaches still tend to treat the analysis of data in binary terms according to gender (for example, by focusing on how binary discourses of 'masculinity' and 'femininity' emerge in the data). So the tension between structural and post-structural approaches to gender and language is perhaps not as great as it first seems. Like Hultgren, I argue that taking binary sex as a starting point for analysis, as in SFDA, does not mean that the binary cannot then be critiqued through a more critical linguistic analysis. And it also does not mean that the emergent discursive categories of gender cannot be seen as multiple, dynamic and context-dependent. Sunderland and Litosseliti (2008) also note that a further problem with post-structural 'gender in discourse' approaches is that they often fail to resonate with most people outside academia (especially the post-structural view that there is no pre-discursive gendered reality). Combining an approach such as SFDA, then, with more post-structural approaches may help to facilitate understanding of issues around gender and discourse outside academia. The combination of approaches may provide a bridge between seeing gender in binary terms and simultaneously challenging and questioning this view.

In practical terms, what worked best in terms of effectively combining the different approaches, was to use SFDA as a descriptive framework which could be applied *within* CDA. SFDA was used to describe the formal properties of the interactional data at the level of description within the larger CDA framework. FPDA was then used as a supplementary approach in order to account more fully for the fluidity and multiplicity of gendered discourses emerging from the data. FPDA was also useful for re-conceptualising 'power' as something more dynamic and fluid, rather than viewing power and a lack of power as a rather static binary. Queer theory was then seen more as a critical, interpretive framework which could offer alternative perspectives on the data within the interpretation and explanation levels of the broader CDA framework. Whilst CDA does offer a clear framework for deconstructing taken-for-granted and commonsense assumptions around gender, queer theory explicitly focuses its critique of 'normality' around the ideological interrelationship between gender and sexuality. This adds a further dimension to the understandings of gender and discourse which can be gained from combining SFDA, CDA and FPDA. Whilst queer theory does not conflate gender and sexuality, it does acknowledge that there is a definitional and ideological relationship between them which means that understandings of gender are never fully complete without a consideration of sexuality and vice versa.

Another key tension is between approaches which are transformative and those which are not. Unlike the other differences and tensions, this is arguably one which cannot be resolved. Ultimately, the arguments made throughout this book cannot be both politically motivated and apolitical, or both transformative and non-transformative. As an activist as well as an academic, my work is driven by a socially transformative agenda which is more consistent with the epistemological principles of CDA and queer theory. Ultimately, I would like the research presented in this book to contribute towards the attainment of greater social equality in terms of gender and sexuality.

How, then, can the non-transformative frameworks of SFDA and FPDA be accommodated into this overarching emancipatory agenda? As explained above, in treating SFDA as a specific descriptive framework (rather than a critical, interpretive framework) which operates within CDA at the level of description, the apparent objectivity of SFDA actually gets supplanted by CDA's transformative agenda. Thus, SFDA becomes a means of identifying and describing the interactional patterns and routines which systematically embody and reinforce (and sometimes challenge) wider social ideologies of gender and sexuality in the classroom context. In this sense, the findings revealed through the application of SFDA provide quantitative support to the transformative arguments made through a more critical analysis of the data. However, because FPDA works *alongside* CDA rather than *within* it, this same principle cannot be applied to the combination of CDA and FPDA. But as FPDA is a supplementary approach perhaps the tension between transformative and non-transformative agendas does not actually need to be resolved. In fact, it may not be necessary to resolve any of the tensions but to simply accept that the different approaches provide alternative interpretations of the data. And the reader can then decide which interpretation they find the most valuable and which sits the most comfortably with their own gendered experiences and understandings.

In sum, the four approaches selected for use in this book each bring something different to the analysis of data. And the collective combination of these approaches, arguably, works to produce a more comprehensive understanding of how gender works than would the use of a single approach. SFDA is able to identify interactional patterns and routines which can provide quantitative support to the claims made using the other approaches. SFDA can show that the ways in which gender and sexuality emerge and are discursively constructed and constituted through classroom interaction happen routinely. In other words, the gendered (and sexualised) discourses which emerge can be shown to be systematic, rather than isolated instances. However, this does not preclude other non-dominant discourses from emerging, as it simply shows which discursive patterns are more and less frequent. Both CDA and FPDA are then able to focus more explicitly upon the emergence of gendered discourses (in a social sense) through the discursive patterns previously identified at the level of description through the SFDA. But CDA and FPDA have slightly different emphases in terms of how they interpret the emergence of gendered discourses. CDA focuses more upon how the dominant interactional patterns reflect and maintain hegemonic ideologies and structures of social power. FPDA focuses less on power and more on the fluidity and dynamism of gender. FPDA can say more about the possible multiplicity of gendered discourses which emerge and the interplay between gendered subject positions in the classroom. A further incorporation of a queer theory perspective can highlight how sexuality is inevitably tied up with gender in classroom interaction, just as it is in any kind of interaction and context. Queer theory adds another dimension to the other approaches in that it explicitly acknowledges that any analysis of gender is never fully complete unless the analyst has considered the inevitable interrelationship between gender and sexuality.

The four approaches, then, can be used in complementary ways to offer a more detailed account of gender and classroom talk than would be available using a single approach (although any analysis, even using different approaches, can never be fully comprehensive). The following three chapters develop and exemplify this argument by applying each of the approaches to the data.

3

From Form to Function: Structural-Functional Discourse Analysis

As discussed in the preceding chapter, much recent work on language and gender in education has tended to rely upon more qualitative and/or post-structuralist approaches to discourse analysis. However, the importance of more quantitative perspectives is acknowledged and, in this research, the two approaches are seen as complementary and equally necessary. This chapter focuses on the use of structural-functional discourse analysis (SFDA), as an example of a more quantitative approach to analysing classroom discourse. SFDA uses descriptive labels to classify utterances according to their discursive function, rather than their form, in relation to other utterances. Such approaches utilise a 'rank scale' system, whereby each unit of analysis is realised by the units below it. The approach was developed in the 1970s with the specific purpose of providing a linguistic framework which could account for the highly ritualised patterns of language typically found in classroom-based teacher–student interaction. In the first part of this chapter, I will explain why such approaches are useful and, indeed, necessary if we seek to thoroughly investigate gender and classroom interaction. I will discuss examples of how such approaches could usefully add another dimension of analysis and interpretation to previous studies which have taken different approaches. I then go on to provide an explanation of the particular analytical framework used within this chapter, before applying it to the data. The discussion of the findings will highlight what SFDA is able to reveal about gender and classroom discourse that other approaches are not designed to account for, as well as considering the limitations of the approach.

Filling a gap in existing research on gender and language

As discussed in Chapter 1, research on gender and linguistic inter-action constitutes a rich and diverse field of study. There are many studies which have investigated gender and interaction in educational settings, but also more broadly and in a range of other contexts. But research on gender which utilises SFDA has been limited, especially in recent years, when the emphasis in gender and language research has shifted towards more post-structural approaches. These recent and current trends in gender and language research arise largely from a recognised need to be cautious about the idea of a straightforward binary divide between female and male speakers. Swann (1992: 59) notes: 'On the whole... there does seem to have been a shift towards more localised studies... [there is] far less reliance placed on quantifiable and/or general patterns.' This point is also emphasised by McElhinny (2003) who argues that certain theoretical assumptions about gender have led to a focus on more localised studies on language and gender to the neglect of other kinds of studies and approaches. Whilst such studies are valuable in enhancing our understanding of the relation-ship between language and gender, and in moving the field forward in methodological terms, I argue in this chapter that the claims that can be made from such research are limited. And approaches such as SFDA can help to substantiate and develop many of these claims.

Furthermore, SFDA is not inconsistent with these approaches, but rather provides a valuable contribution to such research in facilitating analysis of classroom conversation in both structural and functional terms simultaneously. It enables the analyst to observe structural pat-terns in discourse, but the analytical categories themselves are based on the contextualised functions of each part of the discourse, rather than adopting a decontextualised focus on form. Because this kind of dis-course analysis allows the analyst to quantify the frequencies of certain components of conversation, there has been a tendency to dismiss its value on the grounds that it does not link structural patterns to the details of the social context that surround the discourse. This is a huge misconception. Baker (2005), in discussing quantitative approaches to the study of gender, sexuality and discourse, importantly questions the split between quantitative and qualitative approaches and argues that both forms of research can complement each other and may in fact be part of the same process. Quantitative research is helpful for revealing general patterns in discourse, whilst a qualitative examination of data can reveal how the specific features identified in quantitative comparisons are actually used, and can thus help us to understand quantitative patterns. Therefore, there is no legitimate reason why the quantitative empirical data gained from a structural analysis of discourse cannot be interpreted and explained qualitatively in terms of exploring how speakers deploy the linguistic resources available to them as a means of discursively constructing their gender in any given context. Despite the apparent wealth of international research that points to important gender-based differences in student group discussion, relatively little work has systematically explored features of group discussion from a functional discourse-analytical perspective. There are still fewer studies that examine in detail gender differences in the use of specific structural features of discourse that occur in either single-sex or mixed-sex student group discussions.

Out of all the approaches used and illustrated in this book, SFDA probably has the longest and most established tradition in terms of analysing classroom discourse. Sinclair and Coulthard's (1975) seminal work was one of the first to identify structural patterns in classroom discourse. Building on earlier work by Bellack *et al.* (1966), they propose a systematic linguistic model designed to capture the interactional details of spoken discourse. Although classroom data were originally used simply as a convenient example to illustrate the systematic analysis of spoken discourse using their new model, what the analysis reveals about classroom discourse has since gained so much importance that Sinclair and Coulthard's framework is now considered an extremely valuable means of capturing the patterns which characterise classroom interaction. Their model has subsequently been modified, developed and applied to a wider range of interactional contexts than that of the 'traditional' teacher-led classroom dialogue in which it was first devised. Subsequent frameworks (for example, Francis and Hunston, 1992; Mercer, 1995; Mercer *et al.*, 2004; Stubbs, 1983) have thus accounted for a wider range of discursive situations than Sinclair and Coulthard's single teacher-many students model. Work by Cullen (2002), Maybin (2006), Mercer (1995), Mercer *et al.* (2004) and Richards (2006) has also been important in terms of relating patterns of discourse structures to the construction of knowledge and identity in the classroom and in wider school settings. SFDA is still an obligatory component in most undergraduate and taught postgraduate modules in discourse analysis, thus highlighting its continued importance in the field.

A significant advantage of this type of analysis is that it enables the identification of patterns of use across large amounts of data. SFDA can yield quantitative information about patterns of interaction which can be very important for examining aspects of social identity such as gender. If the data show that girls are using particular discursive features substantially more than the boys in the same contexts, or vice versa, this provides a strong 'warrant' (Swann, 2002) for investigating that part of the interaction in relation to gender. In this case, the warrant is not based on a researcher's subjective interpretation of a particular part of the data as being interesting in terms of gender, but rather on the relative frequencies of a particular feature being used by the boys and girls. A close analysis of how gender is constructed in particular extracts of interaction is, of course, very valuable, but this approach raises the question: 'what if it only happens occasionally in the data, and the researcher has chosen to focus their analysis only on that small handful of extracts?' How reliable is the analysis in this case? But if we can show that particular patterns of interaction, which seem to be marked in some way in terms of gender, happen repeatedly and systematically across fairly long stretches of data, then this could ultimately support and enhance the interpretations and analyses gained from more qualitative and localised approaches. As discussed in Chapter 2, this point is made by several researchers in the field of gender and language, including Hultgren (2008), who emphasises the benefits of combining quantitative 'correlational' approaches (defined broadly as approaches which seek to identify general patterns of language use and rely on quantifications to support these) with qualitative ethnographic ones.

Hultgren presents a convincing case for the argument that 'numbers count', especially in research that pursues a feminist political agenda. Hultgren directly addresses the key criticisms which are commonly levelled against correlational sociolinguistics and its applicability to studying gender, and it is worth outlining these criticisms and the counter-arguments presented by Hultgren (and others), as this will function to support and justify the use of SFDA in this chapter. The first criticism of correlational sociolinguistics that Hultgren addresses is that the category of 'sex' should not be taken as a starting point, because it presupposes that gender emerges from the binary categories of biological sex and does not, therefore, allow for possibilities of fluid and contested gender identities emerging in and through discourse. Hultgren points out that the suggestion not to take biological sex as a starting point for analysis in linguistics has, in reality, proven difficult to achieve, and in fact, many studies of gender and language which purport to be 'post-structural' and to treat gender as something emergent rather than pre-discursive, actually still do take sex as their starting point but simply fail to acknowledge it. She argues:

> ...adherents of 'gender in discourse' approaches might object that the behaviour they are studying is not so much linked to the categories 'female' and 'male' as to the gendered expectations that these categories produce, but, even so, studying the way gendered expectations affect women does not solely, as is purported, locate gender in discourse but also in a material and binary reality...the theoretical steering away from 'essentialism' to social constructionism is not consistently reflected in practice and it has certainly not led us to discard the old binary categories 'men' and 'women' – and may even have led us to conceal them under a smokescreen of postmodern rhetoric. (Hultgren, 2008: 32–3)

Hultgren argues that sex should be seen as a legitimate starting point for analysis precisely because it does have a material reality. And taking sex as a starting point does not necessarily preclude possibilities of critiquing it through linguistic analysis. Baker (2008) similarly notes this criticism and how it has resulted in such approaches being regarded as 'essentialist' in the way they allegedly reduce gender to biological binary sex presented as a pre-discursive category. But, like Hultgren, he argues that using sex as a starting point is viable because of its material reality and this does not mean that quantitative approaches cannot be used to critique dominant ideological notions of both sex and gender. Baker uses the largely quantitative approach of corpus linguistics to demonstrate how frequent patterns of particular words can contribute to discursive constructions of gender.

A second criticism of correlational approaches contested by Hultgren is that an interest in treating women and men (and girls and boys) as separate groups does not allow for an analysis of variation within those groups, or of the similarities between them. Hultgren maintains that accounting for complexity within and across groups is not unattainable in correlational sociolinguistics. Indeed, I will show later how SFDA (as a broadly correlational approach) is used effectively in this study to reveal the similarities between some of the discourse features used by the girls and the boys, as well as the differences. It can also show differentiation within groups, albeit in a limited way.

A third criticism, related to the second one, is that quantitative correlational approaches to gender and language always run the risk of reifying (often negative) stereotypes. But Hultgren asks whether more localised, qualitative, smaller-scale studies necessarily solve this problem. She notes that there is always a danger that the analyst may read into data an interpretation of what they expect to find in terms of gendered behaviour. Correlational approaches, on the other hand, strive to reduce researcher interference in the data analysis through their use of pre-determined linguistic categories. The fact that these approaches start out from the categories 'woman/girl' and 'man/boy' is not to say that they set out to find differences. Swann and Maybin (2008) similarly advocate the use of quantitative approaches to gender and discourse analysis, especially when they are combined with more qualitative approaches. They cite studies (albeit a limited number) in the field of gender and language which are seen to have successfully combined approaches in this way (for example, Eckert, 1989, 2000). In fact, Swann and Maybin question the assumption that there is necessarily a tension between the ways in which 'gender' is conceptualised within quantitative and qualitative approaches, claiming that gender may be seen both as a pre-discursive category *and* as a contextualised and performative practice within the same research:

> ... gender is clearly not done afresh in each interaction. Speakers necessarily bring with them a 'gendered potential' – the sedimentation of accrued prior experience, of prior genderings – and this may be drawn on (performed, renegotiated, contested, subverted or of course ignored) in response to particular interactional contingencies. In this sense, gender may legitimately be seen as both a prior category (something that one has) *and* a contextualised practice (something one does, that bolsters, subverts, etc. the category). (Swann and Maybin, 2008: 26)

They also argue that to interpret an action in terms of gender, researchers themselves must have some prior conception of what 'gender' is. And this conceptualisation must somehow be recognisable to the readers of their research. Swann and Maybin also point out that focusing upon the details of localised interactions could mean that researchers actually miss connections with other contexts, and those connections and points of similarity could be important (as could any areas of difference). Such connections and continuities are more easily recognisable through the use of quantitative approaches.

Baker, in his discussion of the use of corpus linguistics in gender and language research, also argues that 'numbers count' in the sense that the frequencies with which speakers use particular linguistic features can be used to uncover the 'cumulative effects of language' (2008: 77). He argues:

> A single word or phrase might just suggest the existence of a discourse. But other than relying on our intuition...it can sometimes be difficult to ascertain whether such a discourse is hegemonic, mainstream, resistant or marginal. It is only by collecting numerous supporting examples of similar linguistic phenomena, that we can start to witness the cumulative contribution of specific linguistic items to a given discourse (2008: 76)

SFDA is well-suited to being able to make such claims about frequencies, albeit across smaller amounts of discourse than may be analysed using corpus linguistics. But SFDA can certainly be used to identify quantitative patterns and the cumulative effects of those patterns in terms of gender, as this chapter will show.

In order to make quantitative claims about gender and language, the system of discourse analysis itself has to be systematic and reasonably self-contained and objective. Prior to analysing the whole data-set of classroom interaction, the system of analysis was tested out on a small section of the data by myself and another researcher (who did not have an interest in gender per se). We applied the system independently and then compared our results. There was about 90 per cent similarity in the application of the system, which seems adequate for ensuring the reliability of the system.

Structural-functional discourse analysis – explaining the system of analysis

The analysis of sequences of classroom dialogue presented in this chapter utilises Francis and Hunston's model (1992), which accounts for discourse where there is a peer relationship, as well as interaction where there is a hierarchical power relationship, between speakers. This is important as the data cited in this chapter involve student–student discussion in the classroom, rather than teacher-led sequences of talk. The chapter focuses upon analysis of interactional components such as specific types of exchanges, moves and acts, and sequences of particular types of exchange to see if their varying functions play any kind of role in the discursive construction of gender in the students' classroom conversations. SFDA provides an overall systematic framework for analysing the patterns of interaction and their potential relevance to discursive constructions of gender. However, it has been criticised for being rather 'uncritical' and for being limited in terms of accounting for the social meanings of the discourse. Hence, other ways of analysing spoken classroom discourse may be needed to account for the social and political implications of the discourse patterns identified, including possible implications for gender and achievement. Thus, this chapter ends by bridging to other approaches considered in conjunction with SFDA in subsequent chapters. The chapter also includes an explanation of the coding schemes used in this part of the data analysis.

Classroom discourse has been studied within linguistics since the 1960s. Early studies focused on producing structural-functional descriptions of teacher–student interaction, while later and current work is more diverse and draws on a variety of approaches and analytic frameworks. One of the earliest and still most influential studies on teacher–student interaction was by Sinclair and Coulthard (1975). Their work was informed by discourse analysis in which the descriptive labels used to classify utterances focus on the function each utterance performs within the context of other utterances, rather than on its form. In the following example, the pupil interprets the teacher's interrogative 'What are you laughing at?' as a command to stop laughing rather than as a question:

> T: What kind of person do you think he is? Do you – what are
>   you laughing at?
> P: Nothing
>
> (Sinclair and Coulthard, 1992: 10)

The system of analysis would, therefore, label the teacher's interrogative as a *directive* rather than a question. Discourse analysis arranges its descriptors into hierarchical units of analysis such as those found in structural-functional models of grammar. Sinclair and Coulthard's model consists of the following units: Interaction, Transaction, Exchange, Move, Act. Each unit of analysis is realised by the units below it. So transactions are realised by exchanges which, in turn, are realised by moves, and so on.

A key contribution of Sinclair and Coulthard's model is the identification of the three-part exchange which, they argue, is a key characteristic of classroom discourse. Drawing on Bellack *et al.*'s (1966) previous identification of a three-part 'teaching cycle' in classroom interaction, Sinclair and Coulthard characterise traditional, teacher-led exchanges as typically consisting of three structurally linked moves: Teacher Initiation (I), Student/Pupil Response (R) and a Teacher Follow-up or Feedback move (F) An example of an IRF exchange is shown below:

T: what sort of poems are they   (I)
   Paul
P: they're shape poems sir   (R)
T: shape poems   (F)

Although the (F) move is optional, it does occur frequently in classroom discourse, as teachers constantly evaluate students' responses to their questions. The dominance of this IRF exchange structure in classroom discourse is a key means through which teachers control the interaction. Since the publication of Sinclair and Coulthard's work, subsequent studies have developed the model to account for more diverse and complex types of classroom discourse, and to extend it to other interactional contexts (Coulthard and Montgomery, 1981; Francis and Hunston, 1992; Hoey, 1993; Sinclair and Brazil, 1982; Stubbs, 1976). The basic IRF structure identified by Sinclair and Coulthard is still seen as pervasive in most kinds of teaching environments.

In the kind of teacher-initiated exchanges addressed to the whole class studied by Sinclair and Coulthard during the development of their original framework, all three elements tend to be present. However, in other types of discourse, such as more informal group discussion, only the 'I' (Initiation) element is obligatory, with the subsequent 'R' and 'F' moves being optional. This is a modification to Sinclair and Coulthard's original model. The main types of exchanges found occurring in the data collected in my own research are Elicit, Inform, Direct, Boundary and Structure.[1] Definitions and examples are provided as follows. In each case, the definition refers to the first move in the exchange. The element of exchange structure (I, R or F) that each utterance realises is indicated in brackets.

(a) *Elicit* – functions to elicit information, decision or agreement.
    G1: (I) which one are you doing
    G2: (R) I've gotta draw the design

(b) *Inform* – functions to offer information.
    G1: (I) mine's at the side you know where you see it through
    I'm doing mine at the top
    G2: (R) cool

(c) *Direct* – functions to request action.
   B1: (I) give me my pencil back

(d) *Boundary* – functions to mark boundaries in the conversation.
   G2: (I) right

(e) *Structure* – functions to structure the conversation, either prospectively or retrospectively.
   G3: (I) to do
   think about designing a small cake for one of the following occasions
   G1: (R) okay

(Definitions adapted from Francis and Hunston, 1992)

Exchange structure in the system is expressed in terms of moves. The main move types are opening, answering, eliciting, informing, acknowledging, directing and behaving. Definitions and examples are provided as follows:

(a) *Framing* – functions to mark boundaries in the conversation. Occurs at I in a Boundary exchange.
   G3: (I) okay
   when you beat the fat and sugar together (reading from text)

(b) *Opening* – functions to initiate or impose structure on the conversation in some way. Occurs at I in a Structure exchange.
   G2: (I) we're we're talking about what you're meant to eat
   G2: (R) all right all right all right

(c) *Answering* – functions to indicate willingness (or not) to participate in the conversation.
   G2: (I) we're we're talking about what you're meant to eat
   G2: (R) all right all right all right

(d) *Eliciting* – functions to elicit information, agreement, clarification or repetition, depending on which act realises it.
   B3: (I) are they the ones what you put disks in
   B4: (R) yeah and you can get playstation ones to put your playstation in
   B2: (F) yeah

(e) *Informing* – functions to offer information.
   B3: (I) are they the ones what you put disks in

B4: (R) yeah and you can get
playstation ones to put your playstation in
B2: (F) yeah

(f) *Acknowledging* – functions to provide positive or negative
follow-up.
B3: (I) are they the ones what you put disks in
B4: (R) yeah and you can get playstation ones to put your
playstation in
B2: (F) yeah

(g) *Directing* – functions to request action.
G2: (I) in brackets put girl and boy
G3: (R) okay girl and boy

(h) *Behaving* – functions to supply an action or to state that the
required action will not be provided.
G2: (I) in brackets put girl and boy
G3: (R) okay girl and boy

(Definitions adapted from Francis and Hunston, 1992)

A complete list of the acts used in the system of analysis is provided in
the Appendix as it is too lengthy to include here. This list also shows
the abbreviations for the acts which have been used in the data extracts
included in this chapter. All of the acts in Francis and Hunston's system have been used except *prompt*, *observation* and *terminate*. These acts
were not found to occur in any of the data analysed and so have been
removed from the system. The acts of *greeting*, *reply-greeting*, *reformulate*,
endorse and *engage* were found to occur rarely in the data examined,
perhaps, again, due to the nature and context of the interaction in
question. They have, however, been retained in the system of analysis
because of the few occasions where they do occur in the data. Whilst
some acts have been removed from the model, three new acts have
been added to account for utterances found in the data which could
not adequately be assigned any act which exists in the Francis and
Hunston model. Acts are the smallest and most 'delicate' level of analysis in any SFDA framework. For this reason, it is not unusual for the
specific acts which appear in the system to alter slightly, depending on
the specific context of interaction under scrutiny. The acts which have
been added are called *suggestion*, *dictate* and *repeat* and I will provide a
brief explanation of each of these.

Suggestion

The act of *suggestion* realises the head (the central or most important component) of an eliciting move at I or R/I and is realised by questions which seek a 'yes' or 'no' answer. In terms of its discourse function, a *suggestion* is similar to the other acts which occur in eliciting moves and which also select polarity – *marked proposal* and *neutral proposal* – but there are functional differences between these acts which are significant in examining this kind of interaction. Since both *suggestions* and *marked proposals* function to elicit the agreement (or, if rejected, the disagreement) of the other speaker/s, the informing move which a *suggestion* or *marked proposal* predicts can only be realised by the acts of *concur*, *confirm* (agreement), *reject* (disagreement) or *qualify* (tentative response). This is different from a *neutral proposal* which functions to elicit information rather than agreement and is, therefore, typically followed by *informative* at the head of the informing move which follows it.

But *suggestion* and *marked proposal* also differ from each other in that a *suggestion* does not explicitly indicate the polarity of the expected answer. The lexico-grammar of *marked proposals* usually contains some explicit strategy for marking the polarity of the expected answer. The most common of these strategies is the use of a tag question. For those *marked proposals* that do not employ a declarative utterance with a tag question, one could be inserted without changing its function, as the following examples illustrate:

G1: and you just put it in a folder?		m.pr.	eliciting
G2: no		rej	informing
B1: and you just put it in a folder <u>did you</u>?		m.pr.	eliciting
G2: no		rej	informing

If a tag question cannot be inserted into an utterance it is likely to be a *suggestion* rather than a *marked proposal*. *Suggestions* may also be recognised through their modality, as in these examples from the data where the modality is predominantly epistemic rather than deontic (modal verbs are <u>underlined</u>).

B1:   well it's colour innit
       you <u>could</u> do some red

G2:   it's a child you <u>can</u> have it it's a girl well
       <u>shall</u> we do a girl so we can do pink icing around

Dictate and repeat

The acts of *dictate* and *repeat* occur only within sections of interaction in which the speakers are engaged in producing a written text based on their group discussion. This is fairly characteristic of classroom group discussion but not of the casual telephone conversations analysed by Francis and Hunston when they were developing the system of analysis, and this is why they do not appear in the original model. *Dictate* and *repeat* usually co-occur as the head of an informing move and an acknowledging move respectively in Elicit and Inform exchanges. *Dictate* is realised by a statement, command or moodless item and functions to supply information concerning the construction of a written text that the speakers are in the process of producing. *Repeat* is realised by a statement or moodless item and functions to indicate positive endorsement of a preceding *dictate*. An example is included in Extract 3.1, in which the speakers are engaged in the production of a written text. To see transcription conventions and an explanation of how the analysis is presented using Francis and Hunston's model of SFDA, please refer to the Appendix.

Extract 3.1

Dialogue	Act	E.S.	Move	E.S.	Exchange	Exch. No.
G1: a hundred grammes of margarine	dict	h	informing	I	Inform	114
G3: of magazine	rep	h	acknowledging	R		
G1: and two eggs	dict	h	informing	I	Inform	115
G3: two eggs	rep	h	acknowledging	R		
G1: and twelve em paper cups	dict	h	informing	I	Inform	116
G3: twelve paper cups	rep	h	acknowledging	R		

In the study, I applied the system of analysis to all of the interactional data collected (about 50 hours). I then counted the number of instances that each component of the model (types of each exchange, move and act) occurred in the interaction of the single-sex girls' groups, single-sex boys' groups and mixed-groups. This enabled easy comparison across the different groups to see where the most notable similarities and differences occurred, and which patterns stood out the most. In the analysis presented here, I focus on the levels of exchange, move and act as they are the most revealing in terms of the details of the interactions that take place when the students are working in groups. The levels of lesson and transaction are simply too large to be able to reveal anything significant or details about the interaction that takes place between students in the lessons. Focusing on exchanges, moves and acts is adequate for accounting for the discursive similarities and differences between the different gender-based groups in the study. In discussing the findings, I first focus on exchanges, then moves and finally, acts. I will present the quantitative findings for exchanges, moves and acts first, and then move on in the latter part of the chapter to considering possible interpretations and implications of these findings.

Exchanges

This section will present and describe the distribution of exchange types across all of the data for the three types of groups (single-sex girls, single-sex boys and mixed-sex). Most of the tables contain two sets of figures – one set shows the number of items found within the data and the other set shows this number as a percentage of the total items found in the data. Table 3.1 shows the percentage of the total interaction occupied by each exchange type across all of the data collected for the three types of groups.

The most notable differences are the percentages of Elicit, Inform, Direct and Structure exchanges occupying the total interaction. Elicit exchanges are proportionately more frequent in the discourse of the girls and mixed-sex groups than in the discourse of the boys (48.3 per cent, 48.7 per cent and 37.2 per cent respectively). Inform exchanges occur more frequently in the boys' discourse than in the girls'. The mixed-sex groups also use Inform exchanges more frequently than the girls. The boys also employ proportionately more Direct exchanges than the girls and mixed-sex groups. The number of organisational exchanges (Boundary, Structure, Greet and Summon) employed in the boys' and mixed-sex interaction is very low – 3.6 per cent and 1.9 per cent respectively. Organisational exchanges (Boundary, Structure, Greet and Summon) in the girls' interaction, on the other hand, take up 8.2 per cent of the total number of exchanges in all of their data.

Table 3.1 Exchange type distribution for girls', boys' and mixed-sex groups

Exchange type	% of total exchanges					
	Girls		Boys		Mixed	
	No. of exchanges	% of total exchanges	No. of exchanges	% of total exchanges	No. of exchanges	% of total exchanges
Elicit	322	48.3	500	37.2	327	48.7
Inform	211	31.6	574	42.7	249	37.1
Direct	59	8.8	192	14.3	53	8
Clarify	13	2	19	1.4	13	1.9
Repeat	7	1.1	11	0.8	16	2.4
Structure	47	7.1	20	1.5	9	1.4
Boundary	7	1.1	2	0.2	2	0.3
Greet	0	0	0	0	1	0.1
Summon	0	0	25	1.9	1	0.1
TOTAL	**667**	**100**	**1343[2]**	**100**	**671**	**100**

It is also interesting to note that in the mixed-sex groups it is the girls who initiate the vast majority of the Boundary and Structure exchanges which occur in the interaction. The examples in Extract 3.2 illustrate this point (Boundary and Structure exchanges are highlighted using a **bold font**).

Extract 3.2

Dialogue	Act	E.S.	Move	E.S.	EXCH.
B2: what's the time G2: five past	inq inf	h h	eliciting informing	I R	Elicit
come on then	**fr**	**h**	**framing**	**I**	**Boundary**
- - - - - - - - - - - - -					
B1: can I borrow your ruler ⇑ B2: course you can I've got another one	n.pr. inf com	h h post-h	eliciting informing	I R	Elicit

G1: right now we have to find first design ideas	fr ms	pre-h h	opening	I	Structure
- - - - - - - - - - - - - -					
G1: I think he knows his own name B1: shut up	inf prot	h h	informing acknowledging	I R	Inform
G1: weren't we supposed to be discussing something B2: yes food eat	ms acq	h h	opening answering	I R	Structure

Even in the mixed-sex interaction, then, it is the girls who are predominantly producing the organisational exchanges, with the boys' use of these types of exchanges being relatively low. In fact, they are hardly produced at all by the boys. The possible meanings and implications of these findings in terms of gender will be discussed later in the chapter. I will first examine the quantitative SFDA findings for the move and act levels of analysis.

Moves

Table 3.2 presents the move type distribution across the interaction of the three types of groups.

Table 3.2 shows, firstly, that the girls employ higher percentages of opening and answering moves in their interaction than the other two groups, as would be expected if the girls are employing higher percentages of Structure exchanges than the other two groups. The mixed groups employ the highest proportion of eliciting moves out of all of the groups, and the boys' and mixed groups employ higher percentages of informing moves than the girls' groups. There is a considerable difference in the relative percentages of acknowledging moves used by the groups, with the girls' acknowledging moves occupying 13.3 per cent of their total moves, the boys' acknowledging moves occupying a lower 9.7 per cent and the mixed groups' corresponding moves taking up only 8.6 per cent of the total number of moves in their interaction. The act distribution within acknowledging moves across the three groups also varies considerably. Figures 3.1–3.3 illustrate more clearly the overall move type distribution across the interaction of the three groups.

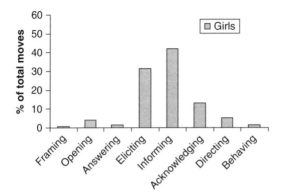

Figure 3.1 Move type distribution – girls' interaction

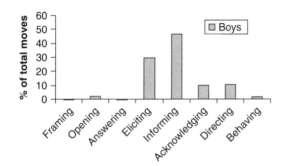

Figure 3.2 Move type distribution – boys' interaction

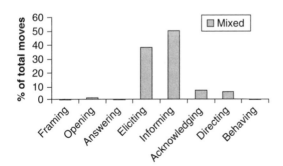

Figure 3.3 Move type distribution – mixed-sex interaction

Table 3.2   Move type distribution for girls', boys' and mixed-sex interaction

Move type	% of total moves					
	Girls		Boys		Mixed	
	No. of moves	% of total moves	No. of moves	% of total moves	No. of moves	% of total moves
framing	7	0.6	2	0.1	2	0.2
opening	47	4.2	45	2.4	11	1.1
answering	17	1.5	7	0.4	2	0.2
eliciting	358	31.6	556	29.5	370	37.1
informing	476	42.1	870	46.1	487	49
acknowledging	151	13.3	182	9.7	66	6.6
directing	60	5.3	193	10.2	53	5.3
behaving	16	1.4	31	1.6	5	0.5
TOTAL	1132	100	1886	100	996	100

Acts

It is at this level of acts that most variation seems to occur in the data collected for this research. Table 3.3 presents information about the distribution of each of the acts across the discourse of the three types of groups. The acts in **bold** in Table 3.3 are those which are, on the whole, used the most frequently in the interaction of all three of the groups, as the percentage figures in the table indicate. Although the percentage figures for *starter* and *comment* are also relatively high for all of the groups, they have not been bolded because these acts only occur at the pre-head or post-head of a move and are, therefore, not considered to be major acts.

Eliciting acts – *inquire, suggestion, neutral proposal* and *marked proposal*

The first major difference which can be identified in these figures relates to the acts which realise the head of eliciting moves in Elicit exchanges – *inquire, suggestion, neutral proposal and marked proposal*. For both the boys

Table 3.3 Act type distribution

Act type	% of total acts		
	Girls	Boys	Mixed
	(Total acts = 1367)	(Total acts = 2305)	(Total acts = 1119)
Organisational acts			
framer	1.7	0.7	0.5
starter	8.6	8.1	5.8
metastatement	2.2	0.5	0.8
conclusion	1.2	0.4	0
acquiesce	1	0.1	0.1
greeting	0	0	0.1
reply-greeting	0	0	0
summons	0	1.1	0.1
reply-summons	0	0.1	0
Eliciting acts			
inquire	8	10.7	13.3
suggestion	7.3	4.5	2.3
neutral proposal	3.4	2.6	5.2
marked proposal	5.9	5	9.2
return	1	0.9	1.2
loop	0.5	0.5	1.4
Informing acts			
informative	20.6	32.4	35.7
concur	4.6	0.9	1.4
confirm	2.5	2	3.5
qualify	1	0.4	0.5
reject	3.2	3	2.9

Table 3.3   (Continued)

Act type	% of total acts		
	Girls	Boys	Mixed
	(Total acts = 1367)	(Total acts = 2305)	(Total acts = 1119)
dictate	3.6	0.5	0.2
Acknowledging acts			
receive	3.3	1.5	1.5
react	3.4	2.4	1.2
reformulate	0.1	[0.04]	0
endorse	0.1	0	0
protest	1.3	3.9	2.7
repeat	3	0.3	0.2
Other acts			
directive	4.4	8.3	4.7
behave	0.8	0.3	0.2
comment	7.2	8.9	5.3
engage	0.1	0	0
TOTAL	100	100	100

and the mixed-sex groups, *inquire* occupies the highest percentage of the total acts out of these four eliciting acts. The boys' *inquire* acts occupy 10.7 per cent of their total acts and the mixed groups' *inquire* acts occupy a higher 13.3 per cent of their total acts. The girls' use of *inquire* is lower – 8 per cent of their total number of acts comprise *inquire* acts. The girls' employment of *suggestions*, however, is considerably higher than the other two groups: 7.3 per cent of the girls' total acts comprise *suggestion* compared to only 4.5 per cent of the boys' acts and an even lower 2.3 per cent of the mixed groups' acts. The mixed groups employ a slightly higher percentage of *neutral proposals* but the difference between the use of *marked proposals* is even greater. Whilst there is little difference between the girls' and the boys' use of *marked*

Table 3.4 Relative distribution of eliciting acts

Eliciting act	% of total eliciting acts		
	Girls	Boys	Mixed
inquire	32.5	47	44.3
suggestion	29.7	19.7	7.7
neutral proposal	13.8	11.4	17.3
marked proposal	24	21.9	30.7
TOTAL	100	100	100

proposals – with the girls employing 5.9 per cent and the boys employing 5 per cent – the mixed groups' *marked proposals* occupy a much greater 9.2 per cent of the total acts in their discourse. Table 3.4 shows the distribution of eliciting acts relative to the total number of eliciting acts found in the interaction of the three types of groups.

Table 3.4 shows that *inquire* is the eliciting act which occurs with the highest frequency for all of the groups, although the boys' and the mixed groups' proportional use of *inquire* is higher than that of the girls. Relative to the total eliciting acts in the interaction, the boys' use of *inquire* is the highest (47 per cent) and the girls' the lowest (32.5 per cent). There is a marked difference in the second most frequently occurring eliciting act between the three groups. For the girls, *suggestion* is used with the second highest frequency, with their *suggestions* comprising 7.3 per cent of their total acts and 29.7 per cent of their total eliciting acts. The boys use *marked proposals* slightly more than *suggestions*. In the mixed interaction, however, both *marked proposals* and *neutral proposals* are used much more frequently than *suggestions*. *Marked proposals* and *neutral proposals* comprise 30.7 per cent and 17.3 per cent respectively of the total eliciting acts occurring in the mixed-sex interaction whilst *suggestions* only comprise 7.7 per cent.

Informing acts – *informative, concur, confirm, qualify, reject* and *dictate*

Within the acts which realise the head of informing moves, Table 3.5 shows that the boys' and mixed groups' use of *informatives* is considerably higher than that of the girls. The girls' use of *concur* and *confirm* is also considerably greater than that of the boys and mixed groups. The girls' use of *concur* and *confirm* comes to a total of 7.1 per cent of the total number of acts in their interaction. The boys' *concur* and *confirm* acts combined comprise a much smaller 2.9 per cent of the total acts in their interaction and the mixed groups' corresponding acts come to 4.9 per cent of the total acts in their interaction. Table 3.5 shows the distribution of the different informing acts relative to the total number of informing acts found in the interaction of the three groups.

Table 3.5 shows that *informative* occurs with the highest frequency for all of the groups. This is to be expected, as *informative* is the only informing act which can occur at both the I and R positions in an exchange. The other acts can only occur at R. However, the boys' and mixed groups' use of *informative* is considerably higher than that of the girls. For the girls, the second most frequently occurring inform-ing act is *concur/confirm* (20 per cent) followed by *dictate* (10.2 per cent). The informing act which is used the least is *qualify* (2.8 per cent). For the boys, the second most frequently occurring informing act is *reject* (7.7 per cent) with *confirm/concur* comprising only 7.4 per cent of the boys' total informing acts – a much lower figure than the girls. The boys' use of *dictate* is noticeably lower than that of the girls. The boys' use of *dictate* comprises only 1.2 per cent of their total informing acts compared to the girls' 10.2 per cent. In the mixed-sex interaction, *con-firm* and *concur* are the second most frequently occurring informing acts, although they occur less frequently than those of the girls. The mixed groups use *dictate* even less than the boys. *Dictate* comprises only 0.4 per cent of the total informing acts in the mixed-sex interaction and only 0.2 per cent of their total acts.

Table 3.5   Relative distribution of informing acts

Informing act	% of total informing acts		
	Girls	Boys	Mixed
informative	58	82.7	80.8
concur/confirm	20	7.4	11.1
qualify	2.8	1	1.1
reject	9	7.7	6.6
dictate	10.2	1.2	0.4
TOTAL	100	100	100

Acknowledging acts – *receive, react, reformulate, endorse* and *protest*

Within the set of acts which realise the head of acknowledging moves at R or F, the most noticeable differences, illustrated in Table 3.6, are between the girls', boys' and mixed groups' use of *receive*, *react* and *protest*. The girls' use of *receive* and *react* is considerably greater than that of the boys and mixed groups. The girls' combined employment of *receive* and *react* comprises 6.7 per cent of the total acts in their interaction. The boys' *receive* and *react* acts occupy a smaller 3.9 per cent of their total interaction and the mixed groups' corresponding acts occupy 2.7 per cent of the total number of their acts. The boys' and mixed groups' use of *protest* is, however, higher than that of the girls. The difference between the boys' and the girls' use of *protest* is particularly marked, with the boys' *protests* occupying 3.9 per cent of their total interaction and the girls' *protests* occupying only 1.3 per cent of their total interaction. Tables 3.6–3.8 highlight the differences in the use of acknowledging acts between the girls and boys' single-sex and mixed-sex interaction respectively by showing the distributions of the different types of acknowledging acts relative to the total number of acknowledging acts in the interactions of each group. Table 3.6 shows the percentage distributions of the different types of acknowledging acts in the girls' single-sex interaction.

Table 3.6 shows that *receive* and *react* comprise the highest percentages of the total acknowledging acts employed by the girls in their single-sex interaction. *Repeat* also comprises a high percentage – 25.8 per cent of the girls' total acknowledging acts are *repeat*. The girls' use of *protest* is

Table 3.6 Act type distribution across acknowledging moves – girls' interaction

Act realising head of acknowledging move at R or F	% of girls' total acknowledging acts
receive	28.4
react	29.1
reformulate	1.3
endorse	1.4
protest	12
repeat	25.8
TOTAL	100

Table 3.7 Act type distribution across acknowledging moves – boys' interaction

Act realising head of acknowledging move at R or F	% of boys' total acknowledging acts
receive	18.1
react	29.7
reformulate	0
endorse	0
protest	48.9
repeat	3.3
TOTAL	**100**

low (12 per cent) relative to the other acknowledging acts. Their use of *reformulate* and *endorse* is minimal. These percentage figures mean that the majority of the girls' acknowledging acts indicate some kind of consensus or positive endorsement of preceding utterances within the exchanges in which they occur. This is a notable finding, which I will discuss in more detail later. Table 3.7 shows the relative distribution of acknowledging acts in the boys' interaction.

In the boys' single-sex interaction, *protest* comprises the highest percentage of their total acknowledging acts. At 48.9 per cent of the total acknowledging acts, the boys' use of *protest* is over four times that of the girls (12 per cent). The boys' use of *receive* and *react* is lower than that of the girls. The boys' *receive* and *react* comprise a total of 47.8 per cent of their total acknowledging acts, whereas the girls' *receive* and *react* comprise a higher total of 57.5 per cent of their total acknowledging acts. The boys' use of *repeat* is very low – only 3.3 per cent of the boys' total acknowledging acts are comprised of *repeat*. Consensus and positive endorsement feature proportionately less in the boys' interaction than in the girls' as a result of the distribution of acknowledging acts. The high use of *protest* means that explicit disagreement proliferates in the boys' acknowledging acts. Again, I will discuss the finding later as it is a key area of difference that emerges from this part of the data analysis. Finally, Table 3.8 shows the relative distribution of acknowledging acts in the mixed-sex interaction.

Like the boys, the mixed groups' use of *protest* is also the highest out of all of the acknowledging acts. *Protest* comprises 43.9 per cent of the

Table 3.8 Act type distribution across acknowledging moves – mixed-sex interaction

Act realising head of acknowledging move at R or F	% of mixed-sex total acknowledging acts
receive	25.8
react	27.2
reformulate	0
endorse	0
protest	43.9
repeat	3
TOTAL	100

mixed groups' total acknowledging acts, which is only slightly lower than the boys' and still much higher than the girls' use of *protest*. The mixed groups' use of *receive* and *react* is higher than the boys' but lower than the girls' use of the same acknowledging acts. As in the boys' single-sex interaction, in the mixed-sex interaction *repeat* is used infrequently compared to the girls' single-sex interaction. In the mixed-sex groups, *repeat* comprises only 3 per cent of the total acknowledging acts.

The act analysis, then (like the exchange and move analysis), reveals a number of notable differences in relative frequencies of usage across the three types of groups. Again, I will start to consider possible interpretations and explanations for this variation in the final sections of this chapter. Before doing so, however, it is also worth commenting on one more notable finding in terms of gender which is revealed through the application of the SFDA, but which does not appear as a distinct 'rank' in the system of analysis. This is the feature of 'exchange clusters'.

Exchange clusters

In all of the discourse observed and analysed, particular types of exchange were seen to occur frequently in clusters rather than in isolation. This happened with Direct exchanges in particular. However, this phenomenon is particularly marked in the boys' interaction. Even though the Direct exchanges may not necessarily follow on directly from one another, they do tend to occur close to each other (within one or two exchanges) in the interaction. Extract 3.3 illustrates this feature.

Extract 3.3

Dialogue	Act	E.S.	Move	E.S.	EXCH.
B4: shut up Bugs {laughter}	dir	h	directing	I	Direct
B1: hey don't call me Bugsy man	dir	h	directing	I	Direct
look at his teeth compared to mine	com	post-h			
you're like this man {laughter}					
B2: look how big your teeth are man	dir	h	directing	I	Direct
B4: mind my coat	dir	h	directing	I	Direct

Many Boundary and Structure exchanges also tend to occur in clusters in the interactional data analysed. This phenomenon is particularly marked in the girls' interaction, although these exchanges are also used (mainly by the girls) in the mixed-sex interaction too. Extract 3.4 illustrates this feature.

Extract 3.4

Dialogue	Act	E.S.	Move	E.S.	EXCH.
G2: there you go	con	h	opening	I	Structure
right	fr	pre-h			
and then question D	ms	h	opening	I	Structure
G3: hang on	s	pre-h			
G2: your reasons why do you think it's a good idea	ms	h	opening	I	Structure

The phenomenon of exchange clustering tends to occur most notably around Direct exchanges in the boys' interaction and Structure and

Boundary exchanges in the girls' and mixed-sex interactions. Possible explanations for this will be considered in the following discussion sections. Before moving on to discuss the findings revealed through the application of SFDA, it is perhaps useful to provide a summary of the key discursive features of the girls', boys' and mixed-sex interaction, in order to highlight where the key areas of difference lie. Table 3.9 summarises these results. The table shows each type of group's use of each discourse feature relative to the use of that discourse feature by the other two groups. For example, the mixed groups' use of Inform exchanges have been labelled as 'mid' meaning that they are high relative to the girls' use of Inform exchanges but low relative to that of the boys. Thus, Table 3.9 shows clearly where the main similarities and differences lie in the discourse structures systematically produced by the three groups.

Summary of results

In Table 3.9, 'mid' indicates key areas of similarity between the different types of group and 'low' and 'high' indicate key areas of difference. Table 3.9 shows that there are more 'lows' and 'highs' than 'mids' in the dataset as a whole. This means that the differences between the groups are more prevalent than the similarities. This, then, provides a warrant for focusing more on the differences than the similarities which emerge across the different types of group in the study.

The key areas of similarity, especially between the boys' and girls' single-sex groups, tend to occur in relation to those discourse features which are not used frequently by any of the groups. This includes the use of Greet and Summon exchanges, the use of framing and behaving moves, and the use of *framer, starter, greeting, reply-greeting, summons, reply-summons, return, loop, reformulate, endorse, comment, engage* and *qualify* at the level of acts. As these are all features which are used relatively infrequently by all of the groups, this means that much more of the data are characterised by difference than by similarity. As stated earlier, this provides a statistical warrant for focusing more on differences than similarities using this approach. However, we should still be cautious about making generalisations based on this data-set, a point which I will return to in subsequent chapters.

What we have seen so far in this chapter, then, is that SFDA is very useful for highlighting patterns across the single-sex and mixed-sex group interaction in the classrooms observed. It provides an effective means of enabling us to see where the main areas of similarity and difference lie

Table 3.9   Summary of results

Discourse feature	Relative frequency of occurrence		
	Girls	Boys	Mixed
Elicit exchanges	High	Low	High
Inform exchanges	Low	High	Mid
Direct exchanges	Low	High	Low
Boundary and Structure exchanges	High	Low	Low
Eliciting moves	Mid	Low	High
Informing moves	Low	Mid	High
Opening, answering and framing moves	High	Low	Low
Acknowledging moves at R and F	High	Low	Low
Suggestion	High	Low	Low
Inquire	Low	Mid	High
Marked proposal	Low	Low	High
Concur/confirm	High	Low	Mid
Receive/react	High	Low	Low
Protest	Low	High	Mid
Directive	Low	High	Low
Dictate and *repeat*	High	Low	Low

in terms of the potentially gendered use of particular discursive features. But what do these patterns and areas of similarity and difference actually mean? And what effects do they actually have in terms of shaping the overall interaction of the groups? In order to answer such questions, we need to look more closely at the ways in which particular discursive features are being used by the girls and boys in the study. This interpretive level of the analysis is necessarily selective, given the length of the lists and the amount of statistical information provided so far. Because differences, especially between the single-sex groups, seem to outweigh the similarities, this provides us with a warrant for focusing on the discursive differences produced by the girls and boys in their single-sex classroom interactions. Therefore, in the following sections, I will focus on what some of the key areas of difference mean and what effects they seem to have in terms of constructing gendered discourses in the classroom contexts studied.

From the key findings presented above, the main areas of difference seem to fall into a number of key areas in terms of the functional groupings of the discourse features included in the system of analysis. Main differences emerge around: discourse features which function to express individuality and competitiveness; features which contribute to collaboration within the group and the co-production of outcomes; features which express agreement and consensus; features which express disagreement and conflict; features which function to indicate interactional engagement and attention to face needs; and features which contribute to the creation of interactional coherence. I will discuss and exemplify each of these areas of difference in the sections which follow.

Features which express individuality and competitiveness

The features in the framework which function most effectively to express individuality and competitiveness and found to frequently occur in the data are: Direct exchanges and the corresponding directing moves which occur within them at I, and informing moves at I which are not followed by an R move within an Inform exchange. Both of these features were found to occur more in the interaction of the single-sex boys and mixed-sex groups. When they occurred in the mixed-sex interaction, these features were used more noticeably by the boys in those groups. Therefore, the statistical results of the SFDA strongly suggest that the use of these features is gendered.

Directing moves

Within the boys' single-sex interaction, they make more frequent use of Direct exchanges, and the directing moves which occur within them. Direct exchanges function to give a command or request an action. In a classroom context, they are typically used by the teacher and are associated with asserting authority and controlling the actions and behaviour of others. This is, of course, seen as entirely appropriate, given the hierarchical relationship between teacher and students. However, the use of Direct exchanges in non-hierarchical peer group interactions may be seen as less appropriate. So when they are used, this may be seen as potentially threatening by other members of the group. In the boys' interaction, the Direct exchanges tend to occur in sequences together, as in Extract 3.5.

Extract 3.5

Dialogue	Act	E.S.	Move	E.S.	EXCH.	EX.
B2: draw it	dir	h	directing	I	Direct	97
draw the spatula	com	post-h				
B1: yeah you do	rej	h	behaving	R		
B3: draw the spatula	dir	h	directing	I	Direct	98
B2: I can't see it all the way over there	rej	h	behaving	R		
B3: look	s	pre-h				
it's got a hole in it	inf	h	informing	I	Inform	99
{laughter}						
B3: boys boys Alex look	s	pre-h				
it's got one there	inf	h	informing	I	Inform	100
B1: Alistair get on with it	dir	h	directing	I	Direct	101
B2: I can't draw	ref	h	behaving	R		
B3: Alex stop being rude	dir	h	directing	I	Direct	102

When Direct exchanges occur together in the way illustrated by Extract 3.5, each tends to be initiated by different speakers in the group. This seems to be one way in which the boys vie for power within their group. If one speaker initiates a Direct exchange, this puts the initiator in a position of power and the other interactants in relatively powerless positions, at least temporarily. This poses a potential threat to the social status of the other speakers. One way of combating this is to initiate another Direct exchange which has the effect of shifting the power relationships between the interactants. Another way is to reject the *directive* produced by the speaker who initiates the Direct exchange and, thus, fail to perform the behaviour which is predicted by the preceding *directive* at I in the exchange. Both of these discourse features occur in Extract 3.5. Sequences of Direct exchanges occurring in the interaction could, then, be interpreted as a struggle for power and status amongst the group members based on this kind of systematic usage. This is a point I explore in more detail in Chapter 4.

Another feature of the boys' Direct exchanges is that they tend to be followed by a sequence of off-task talk, even when the propositional content of the Direct exchanges initially refers directly to the task in hand. This is also exemplified by Extract 3.5. When the boys begin to produce Direct exchanges in their interaction, they compete for social power within the group and attempt to exercise control over the actions of others. Direct exchanges seem to be particularly threatening to the boys in terms of each individual's autonomy and control over their own behaviour. Direct exchanges threaten the positive social relationships between the interactants in a group – they signal that the social hierarchy within the group is open to contestation and debate. As soon as these concerns over social status become a particularly salient feature of the interaction through the use of a sequence of Direct exchanges, they seem to lose focus, and the task that they are working on seems to become less important. It is as though the boys' vying for social status suddenly becomes more important than the necessity of working on the task that they have been set by the class teacher. These sorts of sequences of Direct exchanges never occurred in any of the girls' single-sex interaction, and when they occurred in the mixed-sex interaction it was the boy members of the group who most frequently participated in them. The boys' more frequent use of Direct exchanges and directing moves (and *directive* acts within the moves) thus supports the more post-structuralist work of researchers such as Reay (1991) who have found that boys use more explicit, imperative commands than girls in the classroom. The SFDA provides much-needed quantitative support for these other studies.

High use of informing moves accompanied by relatively low use of acknowledging moves within and across exchanges

The boys also employ a much greater use of informing moves within Inform exchanges than the girls in the study. This applies particularly to informing moves which are not followed by an accompanying acknowledging move at R within the exchange. These are referred to as 'single-move exchanges'. In Sinclair and Coulthard's original model, single-move exchanges do not occur, although their model does allow for them to take place. As Sinclair and Coulthard only considered teacher-led exchanges in the development of their model, it may be that single-move exchanges are simply less likely to occur in teacher–student interaction than they are in peer group interaction, which is structurally and functionally different. A typical example of the boys' use of sequences of these single-move Inform exchanges is included in Extract 3.6.

Extract 3.6

Dialogue	Act	E.S.	Move	E.S.	EXCH.	EX.
B3: what	s	pre-h				
I'm doing the equipment list before I do the star profile ⇓	inf	h	informing	I	Inform	13
B4: I'm doing Bakewells ⇑	inf	h	informing	I	Inform	14
B2: I am ⇓	inf	h	informing	I	Inform	15
B3: I'm doing pizza again I am ⇑	inf	h	informing	I	Inform	16
B1: I'm doing mini pizza	inf	h	informing	I	Inform	17
B3: oh I made eleven right my mom had six	inf	h	informing	I	Inform	18
B1: I made em I made twelve I made twelve I had about six and my nephew had two and I don't know where the rest went	inf	h	informing	I	Inform	19

The boys' interaction in Extract 3.6, with this characteristic proliferation of single-move Inform exchanges, seems to embody a collation of each speaker's individual contributions, assertions and opinions, whereas the girls' single-sex interaction, with its characteristic two- and three-move exchanges (particularly Elicit exchanges), seems more genuinely 'collaborative' in that individuals within the group seem engaged in the co-creation of new knowledge and meanings. The boys' reluctance to produce an R move following an *informative* at I could be one way of construing competition amongst the interactants. Through a series of single-move Inform exchanges, the boys may be seen to be competing for who holds the most knowledge, opinions and so on. It also suggests that the boys are confident about asserting their own individual knowledge within the group and about valuing it as a learning resource which can be used by others. At the same time, through systematically not producing acknowledging moves in response to each other's informing moves, their interaction contains relatively little evaluation of each other's contributions. It is difficult to see how meanings and knowledge are being 'co-created' by the group in this sense. The notion of the boys using single-move Inform exchanges as a means of competing for the floor is also salient, as their informing moves often take the form of short personal narratives. This is illustrated in the final two exchanges in Extract 3.6. The boys here seem keen to share their personal knowledge and experiences within the group through the use of Inform exchanges. Producing an acknowledging move which indicates positive endorsement of a preceding informing move would add value to the informing move. This places the speaker of the informing move in a powerful position, at least temporarily, at this point during the interaction. A possible effect of this is that it contributes to a sense of the boys being continually engaged in struggles over who holds the most power and status within the group. If we pursue this interpretation, we start to analyse the example critically. The SFDA itself does not provide us with this interpretation – it simply provides us with a pattern. In interpreting this pattern, we begin to move into more critical forms of discourse analysis – a point which will be developed further in the next chapter.

The boys' single-move Inform exchanges, such as those in Extract 3.7, often function to provide a kind of commentary on what each individual interactant is doing whilst the group discussion is taking place. In this way, the boys' actions and achievements are continually being put on display to the rest of the group. The frequent use of the pronoun 'I' within these exchanges highlights the boys' concern with their individual achievements rather than with the group's collaborative achievements. The boys seem more confident to display their knowledge even when acknowledging moves occur relatively rarely in the discourse, as in Extract 3.8.

Extract 3.7

Dialogue	Act	E.S.	Move	E.S.	EXCH.	EX.
B: I've got eighteen now eighteen I've got eighteen	inf	h	informing	I	Inform	77
B1: you got eighteen	s	pre-h				
fourteen I've got	inf	h	informing	I	Inform	78
B1: what you copying me for	inq	h	eliciting	I	Elicit	79
B2: I don't need to copy	inf	h	informing	R		
look how many I've got	com	post-h				
I've got eighteen						
- - - - - - - - - -						
B2: I've got twenty-three anyway	inf	h	informing	I	Inform	88

Extract 3.8

Dialogue	Act	E.S.	Move	E.S.	EXCH.	EX.
B1: mine's forty-four	inf	h	informing	I	Inform	33
B5: my bed's about that big	inf	h	informing	I	Inform	34

B2: I'm doing mine fifty centimetres	inf	h	informing	I	Inform	35
- - - - - - - - - - - -						
B4: you can make that out of wood	inf	h	informing	I	Inform	45
B2: you can make it out of fabric as well	inf	h	informing	I	Inform	46
not not one of those shelves like a carry case just like a case where you can carry them around	com	post-h				

In the boys' discourse, R moves are more likely to be absent but this does not prevent the boys from continuing to share their personal knowledge and experience with each other. The interpretation of girls as less confident at displaying their knowledge is supported by interviews with the students who were observed. In the interviews, the girls tended to focus upon on how group work can be useful when they do not have enough individual knowledge to complete the task which has been set for them by the class teacher:

> just in case someone gets stuck er other people are there to help 'em...I think like if you're stuck on a question you can just ask someone and they'll help you

This suggests the girls may have less confidence in their individual academic abilities than the boys. Whilst the girls seem happy to ask each other for help, and to share work and ideas with each other in their classes, the greater reluctance on the part of the boys is further seen in particular sequences of data in which they become protective of their own work. During the classes observed, it was not uncommon to see instances of the boys accusing each other of 'copying', even when the teacher had set up the group work as a collaborative exercise in which the group was asked to produce a single collaboratively produced written outcome.

Issues around 'copying' in the boys' interaction

The boys were often observed to copy each other's written work and, in the mixed-sex groups, the boys often copied the girls' written work whilst being reluctant to engage in co-constructing any required written outcomes, as Extracts 3.9 and 3.10 illustrate.

Extract 3.9

Dialogue	Act	E.S.	Move	E.S.	EXCH.	EX.
B2: he's copying you	inf	h	informing	I	Inform	152
B1: I'm not	prot	h	acknowledging	R		
does that look like hers	com	post-h				

Extract 3.10

Dialogue	Act	E.S.	Move	E.S.	EXCH.	EX.
B1: now what you doing	inq	h	eliciting	I	Elicit	5
B2: I'm just copying them like that	inf	h	informing	R		
B1: not with my work you're not	prot	h	acknowledging	F		
B1: give me my work back	dir	h	directing	I	Direct	6
B2: shit man {aside}						
B1: Sir	s	pre-h			Inform	7
he's trying to copy me	inf	h	informing	I		

In both of these extracts (mixed-sex in Extract 3.9 and single-sex in Extract 3.10), the boys seem very protective of their own individual written work. In the student interviews, the girls also reported a feeling of frustration that when working in mixed-sex groups the girls did the majority of the work whilst the boys took credit for it:

> yeah they'd I think they'd just let us do all the work and then in the end just like go along with it and then get all the credit for it like

This further contributes to the emphasis on individuality and competitiveness that seems to be more highly valued by the boys in the study but less so by the girls. Therefore, we can begin to see how the SFDA results reveal how gendered discourse emerges, at least partly, as a cumulative effect of the systematic repetition (or marked absence) of particular discourse features within the three types of groups.

The features and examples discussed above support previous studies on gender and conversational interaction which have also concluded that men/boys often display a greater orientation towards competitiveness in their interactions (Coates, 2003; Davies, 2005; Goodwin, 1990; Head, 1999; Reay, 1991; Swann, 1992). However, as discussed earlier, these studies have been criticised for making such claims based on relatively small amounts of selected data, and for presenting arguments which could actually be seen to perpetuate negative stereotypes and help to maintain binary constructions of gender. I argue here that SFDA helps to counter these criticisms by providing quantitative support for the claims. But this quantitative support is not just provided in the form of numerical tables, charts and so on. It is also possible to look at detailed examples in the data of where and how particular features are used. And contextual information can be added to these examples, if necessary, because, in taking a broadly ethnographic approach, the researcher was present in the classes when the recordings took place. Despite criticisms levelled at work which presents gendered discourse in a binary way, it is difficult to dispute the fact that the SFDA in this study reveals more differences than similarities, especially across the boys' and girls' single-sex groups. And those features which function to construe a sense of competition (as well as other characteristics discussed below) are unarguably, at least according to the SFDA, more frequently used by the boys than the girls in the study.

Features which contribute to collaboration and co-production of outcomes

Likewise, the SFDA also supports previous studies which have found greater levels of collaboration amongst female speakers, particularly in single-sex friendship groups (Coates, 1996; Davies, 2005; Goodwin, 1998; Reay, 1991; Swann, 1992). Again, SFDA is able to provide both the details of exactly which types of utterances produce this discursive effect, and quantitative information which illustrates the frequency of use. The components of the framework occurring most frequently in the data which functioned to realise greater degrees of collaboration and co-production of outcomes for the groups were the use of Inform exchanges realised by the acts of *dictate* at I and *repeat* at R, and the use of multi-move exchanges (exchanges which consisted of an I and R, or I, R and F moves).

Dictate-repeat Inform exchanges

The occurrence of Inform exchanges which consist of a *dictate* (I)-*repeat* (R) structure, such as those appearing in Extract 3.11 below, are largely characteristic of the girls' single-sex interaction and rarely occur in the interaction of the boys or the mixed-sex groups.

Extract 3.11

Dialogue	Act	E.S.	Move	E.S.	EXCH.	EX.
G2: the bin behind the door	dict	h	informing	I	Inform	20
G3: bin the bin	rep	h	acknowledging	R		
G2: the bin ⇑	[rep	h	acknowledging	R]		
G1: by a fridge	dict	h	informing	I	Inform	21
G2: bin bin should should have em the top on	dict	h	informing	I	Inform	22

G1: should have the	rep	h	acknowledging	R		
G1/3: top on ⇑	[rep	h	acknowledging	R]		
G2: em and the rule is always?	inq	h	eliciting	I	Elicit	23
G3: always keep the top on always	dict	h	informing	R		
G1: keep	dict	h	informing	I	Inform	24
G3: keep	rep	h	acknowledging	R		
G1: the	dict	h	informing	I	Inform	25
G3: the	rep	h	acknowledgng	R		
G1: top on	dict	h	informing	I	Inform	26
G3: top on	rep	h	acknowledging	R		
G2: on yeah ⇑	[rep	h	acknowledging	R]		

The main functions of these types of exchanges is to enable the speakers to collaboratively construct a written text. *Dictate* and *repeat* exchanges ensure that the written outcomes produced at the end of the group discussion are the same for each speaker in the group if they are required to produce one each for assessment purposes, as was often the case. Sequences of *dictate* and *repeat* acts also function as a checking mechanism for technical aspects of the textual outcome. As no one participant is continually providing utterances in the informing moves at I, the result is that the group collectively constructs each sentence.

For the majority of the time, when the girls produce these kinds of sequences of exchange, they have already collaboratively decided the content and, sometimes, the overall structure of the textual outcome. The ensuing section of interaction is, therefore, concerned strictly with the technical aspects of writing, such as sentence structure, lexical choice, spelling and punctuation. The following extract shows such an example of the girls making a decision about what to write in a part of their text, and then engaging in a sequence of negotiations regarding the technical aspects of producing it.

Extract 3.12

Dialogue	Act	E.S.	Move	E.S.	EXCH.	EX.
G3: right	s	pre-h				
what's the hygiene I mean the safety rule	inq	h	eliciting	I	Elicit	3
G1: what's the safety rule em	sugg	h	eliciting	R/I		
carry the pot with two hands?						
G2: okay	conc	h	informing	R		
G1: carry	dict	h	informing	I	Inform	4
G2/3: carry	rep	h	acknowledging	R		
G1: the pot	dict	h	informing	I	Inform	5
G2: the pot	rep	h	acknowledging	R		
G1: with	dict	h	informing	I	Inform	6
G3: with	rep	h	acknowledging	R		
G1: two hands	dict	h	informing	I	Inform	7

Again, it is the repeated and systematic use of these types of exchanges in the girls' interaction which has the cumulative effect of contributing to a gendered discourse whereby the girls emerge as more collaborative and collegial in their groups than the boys or the mixed-sex groups.

Multi-move exchanges

In contrast with the boys' high use of single-move exchanges (especially single-move Inform exchanges), the girls' exchanges (of all types) were typically longer and more frequently consisted of more than one move. As moves have a direct link in terms of their function and propositional content to other moves within an exchange, this creates a sense of collaboration and coherence within exchanges. It shows that the girls are characteristically providing direct verbal responses to each other's utterances as the interaction progresses. Extract 3.13 illustrates this feature.

Extract 3.13

Dialogue	Act	E.S.	Move	E.S.	EXCH.	EX.
G1: oh well	s	pre-h			Inform	51
so it's a small child {laughter}	inf	h	informing	I		
G3: a small child	rec	h	acknowledging	R		
G2: it's a child you can have it it's a girl well	s	pre-h			Elicit	52
shall we do a girl	sugg	h	eliciting	I		
so we can do pink icing around ⇓						
G3: hang on ⇑	s	pre-h			Elicit	53
how about how about both a girl and a boy you know like teletubbies	sugg	h	eliciting	I		
G2: yeah	conc	h	informing	R		
G1: yeah	end	h	acknowledging	F		
that's a good idea						
G1: em a small child {aside} G2: a small child {aside}						
G2: in brackets put girl and boy	dir	h	directing	I	Direct	54
G3: okay	beh	pre-h	behaving	R		
girl and boy						
G3: I still say we should do a cake for both a girl and a boy	sugg	h	eliciting	I	Elicit	55
G2: yeah ⇓	[conc	h	informing	R]		
G1: yeah we have	conf	h	informing	R		
G1: em design your ≠						

G3: hang on	s	pre-h					
we could have a picture of a teletubby on the cake with pink icing for a girl	sugg	h	eliciting	I	Elicit	56	
G1: yeah	conc	h	informing	R			

*see page 100 for the distinction between conf and conc.

In this typical example, we can immediately see, simply from the way the data analysis is presented, that these exchanges are longer than those characteristically produced by the boys and mixed-sex groups.

Features which express disagreement and conflict

Components of the SFDA framework which function most explicitly to express disagreement and conflict are the production of sequences of Direct exchanges and the relatively frequent use of the acts of *protest* and *reject*.

Direct exchange sequences

As discussed earlier, the boys in the study displayed a higher use of sequences of Direct exchanges than the girls or the mixed-sex groups. As well as functioning to express a sense of competitiveness, these types of exchanges can also function to express disagreement and conflict, or they can at least create conflict as a result of their use. This was seen repeatedly in the boys' single-sex interaction. At a point in the interaction when Direct exchanges started to be used, this often initiated a dispute amongst the group members. This is illustrated in Extracts 3.14 and 3.15. In Extract 3.14, the boys' dialogue also noticeably increased in volume between exchanges 37 and 41 to the point where they were shouting aggressively at each other. The sequence culminates in the teacher becoming involved with the group and reprimanding them.

Extract 3.14

Dialogue	Act	E.S.	Move	E.S.	EXCH.	EX.
B1: give me my ruler back	dir	h	directing	I	Direct	37
B2: just hold on B1: okay yeah okay	dir beh	h pre-h	directing behaving	I R	Direct	38

B1: give me give me	dir	h	directing	I	Direct	39
B2: okay	beh	pre-h	behaving	R		
B2: let me just write	dir	h	directing	I	Direct	40
B1: please please please	s	pre-h				
Mario has got my ruler Sir	inf	h	informing	I	Inform	41
Teacher: hand it back	dir	h	directing	I	Direct	42
B2: this is mine this is	rej	h	behaving	R		

A similar instance occurs in Extract 3.15. Again, the boys raise their voices as the short sequence of Direct exchanges progresses and is accompanied by an aggressive tone of voice and some physical posturing.

Extract 3.15

Dialogue	Act	E.S.	Move	E.S.	EXCH.	EX.
B2: put the bin there	dir	h	directing	I	Direct	87
B1: Nick come here	dir	h	directing	I	Direct	88
B2: Woody	s	pre-h				
Miss said she don't like wasting paper	dir	h	directing	I	Direct	89
B3: you're in the scrapyard you are Alex	inf	h	informing	I	Inform	90
B1: Michael stop blazing me	dir	h	directing	I	Direct	91
B4: I ain't blazed you once	rej	h	behaving	R		

It seems that Direct exchanges are perceived as potentially threatening because they constitute an attempt by one group member to try to exert authority or control over the rest of the group by telling them to do something. In student group interaction, where the peer relationship is not supposed to be hierarchical, this action is perhaps interpreted as inappropriate which could be a reason why the use of Direct exchanges is often followed by a challenge or dispute.

Protest

Disagreement and conflict are also realised through the relatively frequent and systematic use of particular kinds of act. For example, the boys' higher employment of *protest* suggests that they are more ready to challenge rather than support each other's utterances, as Extract 3.16 illustrates.

Extract 3.16

Dialogue	Act	E.S.	Move	E.S.	EXCH.	EX.
B2: you shake it ≠						
that's for em putting the collies in	inf	h	informing	I	Inform	257
B3: no it's not	prot	h	acknowledging	R		
that's a drainer	com	post-h				
B3: does that look like a drainer to you	m.pr.	h	eliciting	I	Elicit	258
B3: drainers are metal not plastic cos ≠						
B2: it's a big circle thing with a end on the end	inf	h	informing	I	Inform	259
it's a drainer there's all the little holes look and you	com	post-h				
B3: no it's not	prot	h	acknowledging	R		
you stick your you stick sugar in it	com	post-h				

In some ways, it could perhaps be argued that this can have a positive effect upon the students' learning because the occurrence of *protest* allows for further possibilities and ideas to be explored. In Extract 3.16, the boys' *protests* are followed by *comments* at the post-head of the move which provide explanations and justifications for the preceding *protest*. The *protests* are often quite direct and are realised grammatically through a declarative form, as in B3's *protests* in exchanges 257 and 259. Mercer *et al.*'s (2004) study on the use of group exploratory talk in school Science lessons similarly found such challenges being used in the students' discussions. The authors claimed that these challenges had a positive function in that they led to an exchange of reasoning between the group members and a better understanding of someone else's position. However, because Mercer *et al.* do not set out to examine gender in their research, they do not explore whether the boys and girls in their study are using challenges in the same way. Mercer *et al.* unequivocally state that 'Challenges are constructive and all members of the group are involved in working towards a joint decision' (2004: 369). But in my research, it is often difficult to see how the production of verbal challenges (realised through the use of *protest* in particular) result in an exchange of reasoning and a better understanding. This is largely because the *protest* acts which realise the challenges are not usually followed by alternative suggestions or opinions. In my own study, although the boys' *protests* may be followed by an explanation or justification in the form of a *comment* at the post-head of the move, they are not usually followed by further suggestions or proposed solutions. Mercer *et al.* note that children tend to produce longer utterances when they explain and justify their views. In SFDA terms, this is because these utterances would typically consist of more than one act – one which provides a positive or negative response to the preceding utterances and then a *comment* which expands on or explains the positive or negative response. In Extract 3.16, the boys fail to reach a compromise in the end. They disagree with each other's utterances and explain why they disagree, but they fail to come up with an alternative which the whole group agrees with. There can be no compromise between the two individual assertions being made. In fact, the boys then give up trying to negotiate agreement between themselves and resort to asking the teacher for the correct answer. It is difficult to specify the conditions under which systematic disagreement with preceding utterances may be productive, as in Mercer *et al.*'s study, and when it may be counter-productive and simply result in an argument and subsequent breakdown in the conversation, as happened fairly frequently in the boys' interaction in my own research. A range of factors, such as the particular individuals involved, the nature of the task in hand, the class teacher, and other contextual factors may all play a part in influencing whether the use of disagreement in group discussion can have a positive or a negative outcome in terms of facilitating effective learning or completion of the group task. There is clearly potential for both outcomes and, rather than trying to decipher the complexities of why it sometimes has positive or a negative effect, perhaps this is something that class teachers simply need to be aware of when monitoring the use of group discussions.

Reject

The boys in the study also used the act of *reject* as an expression of disagreement more frequently than did the girls. Again, as Mercer *et al.* (2004) suggest, the use of this act, as a means of expressing disagreement, could potentially serve a positive function in facilitating the exploration of a greater number of possibilities by the group, rather than all group members simply agreeing with the first speaker's suggestion. But in order for this to happen successfully, the *reject* really needs to be accompanied by a *comment* at the post-head of the move, which functions to explain or justify the *reject*. It is also expected that alternative suggestions would subsequently be forthcoming following a *reject* in the acknowledging moves. This does not happen particularly frequently in the boys' interaction. In the boys' interaction, the *reject* is sometimes followed by a *comment* justifying the *reject*, but is less frequently followed by a further *suggestion* which produces an alternative solution. This highlights the notion that the boys rely heavily on each other's individual knowledge when they are engaged in group discussion. If nobody has the relevant or required knowledge, the boys are reluctant to co-construct new knowledge through their interaction as a solution to this problem. In the following two examples, a *reject* at R follows a preceding *marked proposal* at I. In the first extract, a *comment* is provided to briefly explain the *reject* at the post-head of the R move, but alternative answers or suggestions are not offered in the following extract (as was found be more typical in the girls' single-sex interaction):

Extract 3.17

Dialogue	Act	E.S.	Move	E.S.	EXCH.	EX.
B1: gas mark six?	m.pr.	h	eliciting	I	Elicit	115
B4: no	rej	h	informing	R		

you don't need to do it for those just for pizza	com	post-h					
B1: you got six on yours	inf	h	informing	I	Inform	116
B2: write it out	dir	h	directing	I	Direct	117

In Extract 3.18, the *reject* is not accompanied by a *comment*, nor is it followed by an alternative suggestion. B3 simply initiates the next exchange with a directing move.

Extract 3.18

Dialogue	Act	E.S.	Move	E.S.	EXCH.	EX.
B1: why don't you do this one	sugg	h	eliciting	I	Elicit	9
B2: I can't do that one	rej	h	informing	R		
B3: what you doing	s	pre-h				
you're meant to write the writing like a blue sign ⇓	dir	h	directing	I	Direct	10
B2: yeah ⇑	beh	pre-h	behaving	R		

It seems reasonable, then, to question the real value of the use of *reject* (and *protest*) as expressions of disagreement in terms of enabling the group to explore a greater range of ideas and possibilities in relation to the task in question. It seems that disagreement and conflict are only valuable if they are accompanied by alternative suggestions which lead on directly from the expressions of disagreement, and this simply does not happen with any noticeable frequency in the boys' interaction.

Features which express agreement and consensus

Within the analytical framework, as with the components which most clearly function to express disagreement and conflict, the components which most explicitly function as expressions of agreement and consensus occur most clearly at the level of acts. These acts are *confirm, concur, receive, react* and *repeat* (there are others but these are the ones which occur most frequently in the data). What emerges from the quantitative SFDA is that all of these acts are used notably more frequently in the girls' interaction than in the interaction of the boys' or mixed-sex groups. This supports previous work by Davies (2005) who found that girls, in their group talk in classrooms, exhibited a strong disposition towards seeking agreement.

Confirm and *concur*

The acts of *confirm* and *concur*, by their definition, function to express agreement with a preceding move in an exchange. Whereas *concur* functions to give agreement to a preceding utterance, *confirm* functions to give or assert agreement more strongly than *concur*. This is often determined by the tone and pitch of the voice (how audibly and forcefully the assertion is made) rather than simply by the content of what is said. Both acts are used more by the girls than the boys in the study and the girls' frequent use of these acts thus contributes to a more general orientation towards agreement and consensus in their single-sex interactions. An example is included in Extract 3.19.

Extract 3.19

Dialogue	Act	E.S.	Move	E.S.	EXCH.	EX.
G1: rolly jam G2: okay Cadbury's rolly jam	sugg conc com	h h post-h	eliciting informing	I R	Elicit	111
G1: jam rolly G2: jam rolly that's a good one	sugg s conf	h pre-h h	eliciting informing	I R	Elicit	112
G1: jam roly poly	sugg	h	eliciting	I	Elicit	113

shall I have that G2: jam roly poly yeah	conf	h	informing	R		
G3: jam roly poly	sugg	h	eliciting	I	Elicit	114
jammy roly poly G1: yeah I'm gonna have that	conf	h	informing	R		
good one Nicky						

Receive and *react*

Like *confirm* and *concur*, the acts of *receive* and *react* also function to express a positive evaluation or endorsement of a preceding move within an exchange. The difference is that *receive* and *react* realise acknowledging moves, while *confirm* and *concur* realise informing moves – so the difference is primarily a structural one in that it refers to which position the acts can occur in within an exchange. Again, the girls' use of *receive* and *react* was much higher than that of the boys or the mixed-sex groups, thus adding to the cumulative emergence of a gendered discourse whereby the girls showed a much stronger orientation towards collaboration and consensus than the boys or the mixed-sex groups. Two examples of the girls using *receive* and *react* (only the act of *receive* is used in the first of these two examples) in their single-sex interactions are included in Extracts 3.20 and 3.21.

Extract 3.20

Dialogue	Act	E.S.	Move	E.S.	EXCH.	EX.
G1: ingredients em the ingredients	s	pre-h				
you'll need a hundred grams of caster sugar	inf	h	informing	I	Inform	107
G2: hundred grams	rec	h	acknowledging	R		
G3: I've got the ingredients	inf	h	informing	I	Inform	108

G1: hundred grams of sugar	ret	h	eliciting	Ib	Elicit	109
G2: it's self-raising flour	inf	h	informing	R/I		
G1: self-raising flour	rec	h	acknowledging	R		

Extract 3.21

Dialogue	Act	E.S.	Move	E.S.	EXCH.	EX.
G3: and don't forget food colouring	inf	h	informing	I	Inform	119
G2: food colouring	rec	h	acknowledging	R		
G1: and icing sugar	inf	h	informing	I	Inform	120
G3: yeah icing sugar	rea	h	acknowledging	R		

Repeat

As discussed above, the girls more frequently use the act of *repeat* in their Inform exchanges, which are realised through a *dictate-repeat* act structure. *Repeat* functions to provide a positive acknowledgement or endorsement of a preceding *dictate* which occurs at I in the exchange. Thus, *repeat* is another act in which the propositional content is focused upon some sort of positive evaluation or acknowledgement of the preceding move. In other words, it is another discursive means of expressing agreement and consensus within the group. The example in Extract 3.22 is the same one cited earlier as an example of the girls using features which contribute to the co-production of written outcomes in their groups. In this example, the repeated use of *dictate* and *repeat* simultaneously serve the functions of facilitating the co-production of the written outcome and expressing agreement and consensus about the exact content and structure of that outcome.

Extract 3.22

Dialogue	Act	E.S.	Move	E.S.	EXCH.	EX.
G3: right	s	pre-h				
what's the hygiene I mean the safety rule	inq	h	eliciting	I	Elicit	3
G1: what's the safety rule em	sugg	h	eliciting	R/I		
carry the pot with two hands?						
G2: okay	conc	h	informing	R		
G1: carry	dict	h	informing	I	Inform	4
G2/3: carry	rep	h	acknow'ing	R		
G1: the pot	dict	h	informing	I	Inform	5
G2: the pot	rep	h	acknow'ing	R		
G1: with	dict	h	informing	I	Inform	6
G3: with	rep	h	acknow'ing	R		
G1: two hands	dict	h	informing	I	Inform	7

Again, it is the cumulative effect of the relatively high frequencies with which the girls systematically use these features that contributes to a stronger orientation towards agreement and consensus within their single-sex group interactions. It is not the case that the boys *never* use these features, nor is it the case that all the girls use these features *all* the time. Rather, it is the relative frequencies of usage of these features across the groups which produces a gendered effect in the discourse. It is only through the application of SFDA that these frequencies and systematic usages and patterns are revealed.

Features which indicate interactional engagement and attention to 'face needs'

The groups studied also displayed different levels of interactional engagement and attention to the 'face needs' of others in the group, according to the results of the SFDA. The term 'face' was coined by

Brown and Levinson (1987) and refers to an individual's social standing which they want others to recognise and respect. They distinguish between positive face (the desire for approval from others) and negative face (the desire to behave without being imposed on by others unnecessarily). 'Face needs' refer to both of these sets of desires and wants in conversation. Brown and Levinson also define 'face threatening acts' (FTAs) as any linguistic behaviour which has the potential to cause damage to the speaker's positive or negative face. Politeness strategies generally function to mitigate any perceived or actual threats to face which occur during conversation and some studies have considered the face needs and the use of politeness strategies in relation to gender (for example, Coates, 1996; Goodwin, 1990; Holmes, 1995). The SFDA of the classroom data collected for this study generally supports these studies and goes a little further in terms of detailing the specific types of discursive features which are used repeatedly and systematically to achieve this interactional engagement and attention to face needs.

For the girls in the study, the attention paid to meeting the face needs of others in the group was high, whereas for the boys' and mixed-sex groups, it was relatively low. This supports and quantifies previous research by Davies (2005), who found that the girls in her study facilitated a climate in which they could experiment with language and ideas in ways which did not threaten each other's face. In my own study, maintaining positive social relationships seems to be an important concern for the girls whereas it seems less important for the boys. This supports some of the studies previously cited which reported similar findings or claims based on gender and adult interaction in non-educational contexts (for example, Holmes, 1995).

The girls, on the whole, demonstrate high levels of interactional engagement by producing proportionally more acknowledging moves at R and F in their discourse than the boys' and the mixed-sex groups. As explained earlier, acknowledging moves often have an evaluative function in that they positively or negatively assess the preceding utterance in an exchange. Employing more acknowledging moves is, therefore, one way in which the girls produce more evaluation through their interaction. Acknowledging moves, particularly those which are realised by *receive* and *react*, also function to enhance the cohesion of the interaction and to show the other interactants in the group that the speaker is listening and is engaged in the discussion. The boys' and mixed-sex groups less frequently show that they are engaged in the discussion through any verbal means. *Receive* and *react* are generally supportive in that they offer positive endorsement of a preceding utterance rather than disagreeing with it. Extract 3.23 contains some examples.

Extract 3.23

Dialogue	Act	E.S.	Move	E.S.	EXCH.	EX.
G3: oh oh God	s	pre-h				
I threw it away this morning	inf	h	informing	I	Inform	84
G2: she threw it away	rea	h	acknow'ing	R		
G1: you silly cow	rea	h	acknow'ing	F		
G2: oh	m					
I have to put a price on	inf	h	informing	I	Inform	85
G3: ten pounds can I buy yours {aside}						
G1: mine's 79p {laughter}	inf	h	informing	I	Inform	86
G2: mine's gonna be 79	inf	h	informing	I	Inform	87
G3: yeah	rec	h	acknow'ing	R		
G3: mine's gonna be about 29	inf	h	informing	I	Inform	88
only joking 85	com	post-h				
G1: 87 {laughter}	inf	h	informing	I	Inform	89
G2: 87 {laughter}	rea	h	acknow'ing	R		

Employing such conversational support strategies seems important in the girls' interaction but much less important in the boys' single-sex and mixed-sex group interaction. The girls' use of acknowledging moves as a support strategy seems to facilitate the continued exchange of ideas and exploration of hypotheses within the girls' discourse. The girls' use of *receive* and *react* to realise the head of acknowledging moves at R and F may also be interpreted as a way of providing support and positive feedback for each other's utterances.

Receive

I have already discussed how the acts of *receive* and *react* function to express consensus and agreement, and are used particularly frequently in the girls' single-sex interaction. These acts (*receive* in particular) also function to show a high level of interactional engagement between the speakers. *Receive* realises a lot of what other researchers have termed 'minimal responses' (Coates, 1996, 2003; Davies, 2005; Holmes, 1995) – conversational features which do not contain much propositional content, but which serve an important social and affective function of enabling the speaker to verbally show that they are engaged and attentive to the contributions of the other speakers. Acknowledging moves which are realised by *receive* (and, to a lesser extent, *react*) do seem to have more of a social function in the girls' interaction – as *receive* does not convey any real propositional content, it functions primarily as a means of meeting the positive face needs of the interactants, as in the exchanges in Extract 3.24. *Receive* in the girls' discourse is often

Extract 3.24

Dialogue	Act	E.S.	Move	E.S.	EXCH.	EX.
G3: what they've done they've put a swiss roll at the front of it now on top on the top	inf	h	informing	I	Inform	56
G1: oh	rec	h	acknowledging	R		
- - - - - - - - - - - - -						

G3: what's that shape on em on your computer where you get that funny kinda shape	inq	h	eliciting	I	Elicit	79
like you get a square but you get this horrible shape	com	post-h				
shall I do some brackets and the lines coming to them						
G1: it's like two glasses of milk and they're like that	inf	h	informing	R		
G2: oh	rec	h	acknowledging	F		

used primarily as a minimal response – as a means of addressing the face needs of the speaker who produced the preceding informing move and of encouraging further exchange of ideas or information within the group. The *receive* produced by G2 in exchange 79, for example, does not necessarily indicate that any understanding has taken place – the act simply functions to show the rest of the group that G2 is listening and is engaged in the discussion and is encouraging further discussion to take place.

The girls' use of these acts as minimal responses provides empirical and quantitative support for others who claim that conversational features such as minimal responses and positive feedback are characteristics of all-female rather than mixed-sex or all-male talk (Coates, 1996; Holmes, 1995).

Also at the level of acts, the girls further displayed their attention to the face needs of others by systematic and repeated use of *concur* and *confirm*, a high employment of *suggestion*, a low employment of *directives* (and a minimal use of *directives* which are realised by an imperative form), and a low employment of *protest*.

Concur and *confirm*

I have already discussed how the use of *confirm* and *concur* function to indicate agreement and consensus. These acts also function to indicate interactional engagement, especially *concur* which provides a positive acknowledgement of a preceding move, rather than a stronger endorsement of it, as is the case with *confirm*. *Concur* has more of a social affective function (Holmes, 1995), in that its primary meaning is simply to show that another speaker acknowledges and accepts the previous speaker's contribution and does not disagree with it. In terms of content, it does not add much to the conversation. Extract 3.25 illustrates this feature.

Extract 3.25

Dialogue	Act	E.S.	move	E.S.	EXCH.	EX.
G1: right	fr	pre-h				
em the stuff's spilling everywhere	sugg	h	eliciting	I	Elicit	1
G2: yeah em the fridge	conc	h	informing	R		
G3: you may spill something out of a pot if not	sugg	h	eliciting	I	Elicit	2
G1: careful						
if not careful okay	sugg}					
G2: yeah okay careful	conf	h	informing	R		

G3: right what's the hygiene rule I mean the safety rule	s inq	pre-h h	eliciting	I	Elicit	3
G1: what's the safety rule em carry the pot with two hands?	sugg	h	eliciting	R/I		
G2: okay	conc	h	informing	R		

The use of *confirm* or *concur* acts at R in this example function to show that the speakers accept the preceding *suggestions* in each case as correct information and, thus, as part of the shared knowledge of the group.

Suggestion

Another way in which the girls construe a co-operative, collaborative approach in their group discussions is through their frequent use of *suggestions* to realise the head of eliciting moves at I or R/I in Elicit exchanges. This feature of the girls' interaction is consistent with the notion that the girls are less concerned with displaying their individual knowledge through their interaction and are more concerned with collaboratively creating new knowledge as a group. This supports the findings of Davies (2005), who observes girls frequently expressing uncertainty and conjecture and hedging their utterances so as not to put themselves forward as an 'expert' within the group – there is more emphasis, instead, on the creation of joint responsibility for problem-solving within the girls' groups. I would add to this that the use of *suggestions* is one means of achieving this and providing quantitative support for such qualitative findings. The girls tend to hypothesise more in their discourse, try out alternative meanings and evaluate each possibility as it occurs – all functions of the *suggestion* act. This is exemplified in Extract 3.26, in which the task which the students were engaged in involved them designing a product name and product packaging for products which had been made in a previous Food Technology lesson. One of the learning objectives of this task was for the students to decide upon a name for their product. The girls in this extract can be seen discussing various product names before one is finally agreed upon in exchange 114. In this sequence of Elicit exchanges, the girls explore and evaluate a variety of possibilities and then decide upon a final outcome (G1's 'yeah I'm gonna have that') across a short stretch of talk.

Extract 3.26

Dialogue	Act	E.S.	Move	E.S.	EXCH.	EX.
G1: rolly jam	sugg	h	eliciting	I	Elicit	111
G2: okay	conc	h	informing	R		
Cadbury's rolly jam	com	post-h				
G1: jam rolly	sugg	h	eliciting	I	Elicit	112
G2: jam rolly	s	pre-h				
that's a good one	conf	h	informing	R		
G1: jam roly poly	sugg	h	eliciting	I	Elicit	113
shall I have that						
G2: jam roly poly yeah	conf	h	informing	R		
G3: jam roly poly	sugg	h	eliciting	I	Elicit	114
jammy roly poly						
G1: yeah I'm gonna have that	conf	h	informing	R		

Not only do these sequences of exchanges consisting of the repeated use of *suggestion* at I enable the girls to explore a number of possibilities before deciding upon the final one, it also allows them to be constantly engaged in paying attention to the face needs of others in the group by not making strong assertions. As *suggestions* are less assertive than *informatives*, it is also easier to disagree with them in a non-threatening way (although the girls still do not express much disagreement in their interaction). The repeated responses to the *suggestions* at R also show a high level of interactional engagement between the group members throughout this sequence.

By contrast, the boys make relatively infrequent use of *suggestions* in their Elicit exchanges. As mentioned previously, the boys generally make less use of Elicit exchanges in general than the girls and, when they are used, they tend to be realised through a different move and act structure. Within their Elicit exchanges, the most frequent acts used to realise the eliciting move at I amongst the boys in their single-sex groups are *inquire* followed by *marked proposal*. A typical example which includes the boys' use of both of these eliciting acts is included in Extract 3.27.

Extract 3.27

Dialogue	Act	E.S.	Move	E.S.	EXCH.	EX.
B2: what's it used for	inq	h	eliciting	I	Elicit	6
B1: mixing	inf	h	informing	R		
B3: what we gonna call it though a wooden spoon?	m.pr.	h	eliciting	I	Elicit	7
B2: oh yeah	conf	h	informing	R		
B1: mixing what kinds of food all kinds of food	m.pr.	h	eliciting	I	Elicit	8
B2: what's the next one	inq	h	eliciting	I	Elicit	9
B1: a grater	inf	h	informing	R		
B2: no what's this one	inq	h	eliciting	I	Elicit	10
B2: what's this which recipes it's used for	inq	h	eliciting	I	Elicit	11

The boys' more frequent use of *inquire* and *marked proposal* contrasts with the girls' relatively higher use of *suggestion* within the acts which realise eliciting moves. Again, it is the cumulative effect of these systematic patterns which contributes to the emergence of discourse which appears to be gendered.

Features which contribute to interactional coherence

A final marked area of difference across the groups which is revealed by the SFDA is in relation to discourse features which function to contribute to interactional coherence. The interaction appears to be more coherent when the utterances are clearly linked both structurally and in terms of their propositional content. The interaction also appears to be more coherent when its content and structure is on-task, logical and easy to follow. The features which most explicitly function to create coherence are the use of organisation exchanges (Structure and Boundary exchanges) and the structures which occur *within* exchanges, particularly adherence to the multi-move IR or IRF structure.

Structure and Boundary exchanges

The SFDA statistics reveal that it is the girls in their single-sex groups who deploy Structure and Boundary exchanges the most frequently. The girls' proportionally higher employment of Boundary and Structure exchanges suggests that they are more explicitly aware of how they are structuring and constructing their discussions than the boys' or the mixed-sex groups. The girls' Boundary and Structure exchanges make explicit the progression and direction of the interaction. These exchanges often mark where certain goals of the task in hand have been attained (realised by *conclusion* at I) and which goals still have to be attained (realised by *metastatement* at I). The occurrence of Structure exchanges at regular intervals throughout the interaction thus enables the interactants to continually evaluate their discussion in terms of how it prospectively or retrospectively relates to the goals set up at the beginning of the group discussion activity. This is exemplified in Extract 3.28.

Extract 3.28

Dialogue	Act	E.S.	Move	E.S.	EXCH.	EX.
G3: now	fr	h	framing	I	Boundary	37
G2: we're not doing that one we're doing we've gotta read this together	ms	h	opening	I	Structure	38

G2: we'll read a sentence each	ms	h	opening	I	Structure	39
G1: okay then	acq	h	answering	R		
G2: it's fair then	[acq	h	answering	R]		
G2: how many is there	inq	h	eliciting	I	Elicit	40
G1: hang on a minute	s	pre-h				
right we've done that right?	con	h	opening	I	Structure	41
G2: read a sentence each	ms	h	opening	I	Structure	42
(Students reading from worksheet – 10 minutes)						
G2: right	fr	h	framing	I	Boundary	43
G3: to do	s	pre-h				
now think about designing a small cake for one of the following occasions (reads list from text)	ms	h	opening	I	Structure	44
G1: okay	acq	h	answering	R		

This extract also shows how the goals of the task are often restated in Structure exchanges. G2's utterance in exchange 38 and G3's utterance in exchange 44 re-state two of the goals that they have been set by the class teacher ('we've gotta read this together' and 'think about designing a small cake for one of the following occasions'). This helps to keep the group focused on the requirements of the task.

The following series of exchanges in the girls' interaction is an example of how, through the use of Structure exchanges, the students evaluate all of their preceding interaction in relation to the attainment of the goals of the group task and summarise what has been attained so far. Thus, the girls seem to be explicitly keeping track of what they have achieved, and what they still need to achieve, in terms of the task in hand.

Extract 3.29

Dialogue	Act	E.S.	Move	E.S.	EXCH.	EX.
G1: right em	fr	pre-h				
otherwise the cakes may not turn out perfect?	con	h	opening	I	Structure	27

G3: done	acq	h	answering	R		
G2: yeah	rec	post-h	acknowledging	F		
G1: em	m				Structure	28
makes the surface of the mixture?	con	h	opening	I		
G3: done	acq	h	answering	R		
G1: em	m				Structure	29
helps the margarine to add em this is called creaming?	con	h	opening	I		
G2: done that	acq	h	answering	R		
G1: hang on	s	pre-h			Structure	30
this is called creaming	con	h	opening	I		
G2: we've done that for number four	acq	h	answering	R		
G3: yes we have yes it's all right it's all right	rea	h	acknowledging	F		

As well as marking out clear boundaries and stages which have been completed in the discourse, the use of the acts of *conclusion* and *acquiesce* in each of these exchanges functions as a means of evaluating and assessing what has been learnt so far. Similarly, *metastatements* function to focus the speakers on the next stage of the task. The fact that the boys use these types of exchange with a much lower frequency that the girls suggests that their interaction is perhaps less organised than that of the girls, or maybe that they are using different means of organising it. The frequency of Structure and Boundary exchanges is also relatively low in the mixed-sex interaction. When they are used, it is usually by the girl speakers who are attempting to re-focus the discussion after a period of off-task talk. The following extract illustrates this:

Extract 3.30

Dialogue	Act	E.S.	Move	E.S.	EXCH.	EX.
B2: I'm starving hungry	inf	h	informing	I	Inform	22
I hate this cheese	inf	h	informing	I	Inform	23

Andrew was doing this on the floor	inf	h	informing	I	Inform	24
B1: come on come on	dir	h	directing	I	Direct	25
B2: put those away	dir	h	directing	I	Direct	26
the blue ones are the best ones	com	post-h				
G2: blue what ⇓	ret	h	eliciting	I b	Clarify	27
B2: I've got someat behind me ⇑	inf	h	informing	I	Inform	28
G2: blue what ⇓	ret	h	eliciting	I b	Clarify	29
B1: can I borrow your ruler ⇑	n.pr.	h	eliciting	I	Elicit	30
B2: course you can	inf	h	informing	R		
I've got another one	com	post-h				
G1: right	fr	pre-h				
now we have to find first design ideas	ms	h	opening	I	Structure	31

Extracts such as these suggest that girls are the 'organisers' in the mixed-sex interaction. They appear to work harder than the boys to keep the group focused on their task.

Multi-move exchanges

Interactional coherence is also enhanced by the use of exchanges which consist of more than one move. As explained earlier, in order for moves to belong within the same exchanges, there has to be a direct relation between both their propositional content and discursive function.

If that is not the case, then the moves must be split up into separate exchanges. Thus, moves which go together within an exchange tend to display a high degree of coherence. And this coherence is enhanced further if stretches of interaction consist of a series of multi-move exchanges. As noted earlier, this characteristic was much more typical of the girls' single-sex interaction than the boys' or mixed-sex interaction and was one means of construing relatively high levels of co-operation and collaboration in the girls' interactions. In conjunction with the girls' relatively higher use of Structure and Boundary exchanges, this feature also further contributed to the greater interactional coherence of their talk. This supports, quantifies and adds detail to previous studies on girls' group interactions which have found them producing higher levels of cohesiveness in their talk (for example, Davies, 2005). In Extract 3.31, the two- and three-move exchanges allow for a constant evaluation of each other's utterances to take place.

Extract 3.31

Dialogue	Act	E.S.	Move	E.S.	EXCH.	EX.
G2: what's what's fibre	inq	h	eliciting	I	Elicit	15
tell me what fibre does to you	com	post-h				
G1: it makes you more healthier	inf	h	informing	R		
G3: that's a good idea	rea	h				
fibre makes you healthier	com	post-h	acknowledging	F		
G2: does it do anything to your heart	n.pr.	h	eliciting	I	Elicit	16
G3: yeah	inf	h	informing	R		
so you don't have a heart attack	com	post-h				

G1: you know when if you get too fat if you eat too much and you have to have that thing like that sucker thing what goes round your stomach	inf	h	informing	I	Inform	17
G3: yeah ⌝	rec	h	acknowledging	R		
G2: yeah ⌋	[rec	h	acknowledging	R]		

Each eliciting move is responded to with an appropriate and relevant informing move (in exchanges 15 and 16). Acknowledging moves extend the exchanges further. When this is contrasted with a typical example of a series of single-move exchanges which are exhibited more frequently by the boys' single-sex groups, it is clear how much less coherent the conversation sounds (Extract 3.32).

Extract 3.32

Dialogue	Act	E.S.	Move	E.S.	EXCH.	EX.
B3: God man	s	pre-h				
we've only done three	inf	h	informing	I	Inform	111
B2: he's run out of space	inf	h	informing	I	Inform	112
B2: ow that hurt	inf	h	informing	I	Inform	113
B2: that's to cut cheese that is	inf	h	informing	I	Inform	114

B3: I know how to cut cheese	s	pre-h					
that's to make it bigger that's to make it smaller	inf	h	informing	I	Inform	115

From such examples, it seems that the boys perceive the objectives of the task as being individual rather than collective. This interpretation was supported through the student interviews in which one of the boys reported that:

> you can get one person doing one bit and another person doing another

This implies that students are expected to perform different tasks within the group, rather than collaboratively working on a single task. Another boy argued that:

> if two people are looking for the same if you don't find anything hopefully the other person has

Again, this implies that the students are not actually expected to be working together on a task but are, instead, engaged in separate activities which will then be collated in the group at a later point. Thus the differing levels of interactional coherence may, at least in part, be related to the perceived purpose and nature of working in groups.

It is perhaps also worth noting that the boys spent more of their discussion time engaged in 'off-task' talk than the girls did in their respective single-sex discussions. Like the boys' single-sex talk, the mixed-sex interaction was characterised by relatively high levels of off-task talk. I observed that the girls were often very quiet at the times when the boys were engaged in off-task talk. At times, they seemed almost defeated in their attempts to keep the boys focused on the task in hand, although this did vary slightly across groups and across classes. When the boys steered the conversation towards off-task talk in the interaction, the girls often withdrew from the discussion if their attempts to get the discussion back on-task were unsuccessful. These observations were supported through some of the student interviews:

Hannah: they [girls] are a lot less chatty like boys chat all the time and girls get on with it

Bradley: we ... like to talk about things like what we what we were watching and stuff like that ... and sometimes we we get in a lot of trouble

it's always like it's always like sometimes you just don't feel like working girls do get the work done and then they start talking we'll be working and talking at the same time

Hayley: I reckon boys are naughtier than girls ... they get they get less work done and they talk a lot

In these interview extracts, both the girls and boys acknowledge that the boys tend to produce more off-task talk when working in groups (either single-sex or mixed-sex) and that this results in them not completing the required work as effectively as the girls and/or being reprimanded by the teacher. It is interesting to note in the second extract, a boy observes that girls do engage in off-task talk in the classroom but only once they have completed the required task/s.

Summary – what does the SFDA reveal about gendered discourses in the classroom?

The SFDA applied to the classroom interaction data shows that there are systematic differences in the ways that the boys and girls talk when working in groups. And, in quantifiable terms, there are more differences than similarities. It is through the systematic repetition of the features which appear in the SFDA framework across the groups that produces a gendered effect whereby the girls and boys exhibit differential patterns of interaction in their group talk. This approach is consistent with the arguments made by language and gender researchers such as Hultgren (2008) and Baker (2008), discussed earlier, that 'numbers count' – it is through the identifiable, systematic production of discursive features that gendered discourses start to become apparent. When we look at specific examples, we are able to say that those examples are typical of an overall trend or pattern for that particular group of speakers. Thus, we can provide evidence of systematic patterns of language use which contribute to what may be termed 'dominant' modes of producing gender in the classroom contexts under scrutiny. Tables 3.10 and 3.11 summarise the dominant interactional patterns for the girls (Table 3.10) and boys (Table 3.11) in the study, performed through the frequent and repeated use of particular discourse features. Both tables are based on results taken from both the single-sex and mixed-sex interaction. The

Table 3.10 Characteristics of interaction systematically produced by the girls

Characteristics of interaction	Discourse features through which characteristics of interaction are realised
Sustained orientation towards the pedagogic goals of the task	• High occurrence of 'on-task' talk • High occurrence of Structure exchanges to focus discussion towards the goals of the task
Orientation towards the collaborative co-production of outcomes Downplaying of individuality and competitiveness	• High occurrence of *suggestion* at I in Elicit exchanges • High occurrence of *receive* and *react* • High occurrence of *dictate-repeat* Inform exchanges • High occurrence of multi-move exchanges
Orientation towards achieving agreement and consensus within the group	• High occurrence of *confirm, concur* and *repeat* • High occurrence of *receive* and *react* • Low occurrence of *reject* and *protest* • Low occurrence of Direct exchanges and directing moves
High levels of attention paid to the face needs of others in the group Strong orientation towards achieving interactional coherence and engagement	• High occurrence of acknowledging moves, especially *receive* and *react* • High occurrence of *suggestion* • High occurrence of *confirm* and *concur* • Low occurrence of Direct exchanges and directing moves • *Reject* and *protest* usually followed by explanatory *comment* at the post-head of the move • High occurrence of Structure and Boundary exchanges • High occurrence of multi-move exchanges

Table 3.11   Characteristics of interaction systematically produced by the boys

Characteristics of interaction	Discourse features through which characteristics of interaction are realised
Weaker orientation towards the pedagogic goals of the task	• High occurrence of off-task talk • Low occurrence of Structure exchanges to focus discussion towards the goals of the task
Emphasis on display of individuality and competitiveness	• High occurrence of Inform exchanges and informing moves • High occurrence of Direct exchanges and directing moves • High occurrence of single-move exchanges • Low occurrence of *suggestion* • Low occurrence of *confirm* and *concur* • Low occurrence of acknowledging moves, especially those realised by *receive* and *react* • Low occurrence of *dictate* and *repeat*
Stronger orientation towards conflict and disagreement within the group	• High occurrence of Direct exchanges and directing moves • High occurrence of *protest* and *reject* • Low occurrence of *confirm*, *concur* and *repeat* • Low occurrence of *receive* and *react*
Less attention paid to the face needs of others in the group Weaker orientation towards achieving interactional coherence	• Low occurrence of Structure and Boundary exchanges • High occurrence of single-move exchanges • High occurrence of Direct exchanges and directing moves • High occurrence of *protest* and *reject* • Low occurrence of *suggestions* and frequent non-response to *suggestions* • Low occurrence of *confirm* and *concur* • Low occurrence of *receive* and *react*

interaction of the girls and the boys, then, can be characterised as typically exhibiting a repeated set of discourse features (right column) which combine to form a dominant way of producing gender through their classroom talk (left column).

These gendered patterns are found to systematically occur in the single-sex interaction, as shown throughout this chapter. But they are also found in the mixed-sex interaction in which the boys and girls exhibit very similar patterns of usage of discourse features to those found in their respective single-sex interaction. However, the mixed-sex interaction, on the whole, shares more similarities with the boys' single-sex interaction, because the girls simply contribute less to this kind of group talk. The girls emerge very much as the 'organisers' of mixed-sex interaction – they do much of the work of bringing the talk back on-task when the boys are engaged in off-task talk. During much of the mixed-sex interaction, I observed that the girls generally talked less than they did in their single-sex groups and often simply got on with completing the task whilst only occasionally contributing to the group discussion. For this reason, the single-sex group discussions (of both girls *and* boys) seemed generally more successful than the mixed-sex ones, at least in terms of the talk remaining focused on the task. This may be because the students were more used to working in single-sex groups and, with the exception of a small number of individuals (who will be discussed in Chapter 4), chose to work in single-sex, rather than mixed-sex, groups whenever they were given a choice. In some of the interviews, the students explicitly talked about how working in mixed-sex groups often felt 'unnatural' to them. However, perhaps further investigation is needed to fully account for the increase in off-task talk and the girls' increased reticence in the mixed-sex interaction.

Another possible reason for the greater similarities between mixed-sex interaction and the boys' single-sex interaction could be that the boys perform a more dominant role in the classroom and therefore 'impose' their characteristic patterns of single-sex interaction onto the mixed-sex talk. If the girls assume a less dominant role, perhaps they are more accepting of the boys' patterns of interaction in the mixed-sex talk. But, again, this is a speculative interpretation which cannot be supported through the SFDA evidence alone. Further insights may be gained, though, through the incorporation of other kinds of discourse analysis alongside the SFDA and this will be explored in the following two chapters.

Although the patterns of interaction summarised in Tables 3.10 and 3.11 are not mutually exclusive, there seems to be enough statistical evidence around the frequency of usage to strongly suggest that the patterns are meaningful in terms of gender and therefore contribute to the emergence of gendered discourses. To be able to provide quantitative support for these claims about the emergence of gendered discourses is something that more qualitative post-structural approaches such as FPDA and CDA are less able to do. The results presented in this chapter are effective in being able to quantify work by researchers such as Davies who use post-structural approaches to discourse analysis to argue that particular linguistic features are used more frequently to 'contribute to an atmosphere conducive to collaborative learning' (2005: 200). Despite this, Davies does not actually provide quantitative evidence to support these claims about 'frequency'. And this is a limitation of much work on classroom interaction which adopts a post-structuralist approach. But the SFDA can provide quantitative evidence showing gendered patterns of language use in this kind of classroom interaction.

SFDA also provides a level of linguistic detail that is often missing from more qualitative studies. And the pre-coding of SFDA also helps to reduce researcher bias and removes a reliance on the analyst's subjective interpretations of the data. SFDA also provides a statistical warrant (Swann, 2002) for paying attention to gender in analysing the classroom discourse. However, there are aspects of interaction which SFDA alone cannot account for. As Swann (2002: 51) points out:

> On its own, the establishment of general patterns in the distribution of linguistic features is a limited and potentially reductive exercise and tells us nothing about how language is used by women and men in specific contexts, nor about what speakers are doing as they talk.

Therefore, in order to gain a more comprehensive understanding of the relationship between language and gender in classroom interaction, it is necessary to provide a more contextualised and detailed analysis. This is where a combination of SFDA and other approaches can be particularly fruitful. The SFDA framework itself is also not without its criticisms. For example, Seedhouse (2004) argues that the focus on single utterances as single speech acts in SFDA is problematic. Seedhouse claims that because there is no straightforward correlation between form and function in SFDA, the model does not necessarily capture the complexities of classroom interaction. He argues that SFDA misses the point that the IRF cycles, which form the basis of classroom SFDA, can perform different interactional and pedagogical work according to the context in which they are operating. This claim is based on the notion that SFDA models are inherently acontextual. However, many advocates of SFDA would dispute this claim, arguing that utterances only have meaning in relation to other utterances, therefore the classification system is based on contextualised understandings of utterance functions. Moreover, and as will be shown throughout the remainder of this book, SFDA is not an approach which has to be used in isolation – it can be used in conjunction with more explicitly context-focused approaches to discourse analysis, one of the key effects of which is to validate all of the approaches being used.

Taking these issues into account, I would suggest the following as some limitations of SFDA:

- There is a lack of focus on individual similarities and differences between speakers.
- SFDA is not able to account for a fluidity of identities and subject positions throughout the progression of interaction (and it treats gender and the gendered discourses that emerge from the interactional analysis as relatively stable and fixed).
- SFDA does not pay close attention to instances in the interaction where gender (and/or sexuality) is explicitly evoked. SFDA treats all interaction the same in terms of its contribution to the production of gendered discourses. But there may be places where more explicit attention is being paid to gender by the participants. SFDA does not allow for such instances to be more 'heavily weighted' in terms of their contributions to gendered discourses.
- Due to its focus on identifying general patterns and trends, SFDA does not allow for the detailed consideration of instances of counter-hegemonic discourses, any challenges to the dominant modes of interaction for girls and boys, or an examination of any 'marginalised' voices which may emerge in all or part of the interaction.

In order to address these limitations of SFDA, it is necessary to draw on different methods of analysis, most notably those which are designed specifically to interrogate and examine the issues above. Post-structuralist approaches, with their emphasis on the local and qualitative, are perhaps best suited to addressing such issues, so it is to those approaches that I turn in the next chapter.

4
From Structural to Post-structural: Critical Feminist Approaches

In this chapter, I move from analysing classroom talk in purely structural terms to incorporating post-structural approaches. Specifically, this chapter explores how the methods of feminist post-structuralist discourse analysis (FPDA) and critical discourse analysis (CDA) can expand our understandings of classroom discourse by examining the social meanings which are constructed through the particular discursive patterns revealed by the SFDA presented in Chapter 3.

Post-structural understandings of gender and education tend to focus on discourse, therefore linguistic approaches to discourse analysis can be particularly useful for describing the precise linguistic processes which realise particular social discourses. Post-structuralist approaches to gender and education place underlying assumptions of identity at the centre of their enquiry. Analysis focuses on the kinds of identity formations which take place, the norms, values and in/equalities contained within particular ideologies, and the importance of local institutional sites in the production of gendered identities. Post-structuralist accounts of schooling allow for more fluid, dynamic, uncertain and contestable formations of gender and sexual identities. Whilst some researchers (Connell, 1995, 2006; Epstein, 1998) have focused predominantly on the discursive constructions of masculinities in schools, others have paid more attention to the discursive production of femininities or both femininities and masculinities (Davies, 2006; Francis, 1998, 2000; Hey, 1997; Reay, 2006; Skelton, 2001; Walkerdine, 1990).

Unlike SFDA, both FPDA and CDA move away from focusing predominantly upon the structural details of interaction and resist notions that meanings are embedded within textual structures. CDA, for example, sees meanings, including gendered meanings, as interactional accomplishments between texts, their immediate situational contexts

117

and their broader socio-political contexts (see, for example, Caldas-Coulthard, 1996; Lazar, 2005; Wodak, 2001, 2008). CDA also focuses more explicitly upon accomplishments of power in the classroom (for example, Bergvall, 1996; Sunderland, 2002). Explorations of gender and power in the classroom may not only focus upon the teacher's power, but may also examine power relationships between the students. This is illustrated in some of the data extracts in this chapter. I will first provide brief explanations of CDA and FPDA, before applying both frameworks to the data.

Critical discourse analysis (CDA)

Proponents of CDA argue that it is a diverse approach containing different 'strands' of analysis, which arguably may include the kinds of SFDA seen in the previous chapter. Wodak and Meyer (2001) note that there is no monolithic CDA, rather it can incorporate different elements and analytic approaches, depending on the data, context and purpose of study. But what all types of CDA share in common is a concern with ideologies and power and the ways in which they are achieved, reinforced and also contested through language (and other semiotic resources). Whatever form of detailed linguistic analysis is used within a CDA approach, it always works towards a socially transformative goal. This chapter incorporates selective elements of Fairclough's systemic-functional approach (1995, 2001, 2003) to CDA in its investigation of how the classroom is a political site for the negotiation and enactment of gender identities and power relations. This approach, I argue, works well alongside SFDA. Having already used SFDA to identify structural patterns in the discourse which contribute to the discursive construction of gender, sequences of classroom dialogue are additionally analysed using CDA to reveal how linguistic features such as vocabulary and particular grammatical structures can also contribute to the construction and/or subversion of gender ideologies.

CDA is rooted in critical linguistics, and early work, informed largely by Marxist theory, tended to be concerned with the effects of capitalism, social class and power relations. Such work was criticised by some language and gender scholars (Cameron, 2001; Lazar, 2005) for downplaying gender issues and failing to consider how feminist theory could usefully be incorporated into CDA as a means of interrogating gendered power relations. This led to the development of a body of work termed 'feminist critical discourse analysis' (Lazar, 2005) and it is this strand of CDA which most directly informs the analyses presented in this chapter. Unlike the other approaches used in this book, CDA is explicitly concerned with social injustice, power struggles and in/equalities and with examining the role that discourse plays in constructing, reifying and contesting these issues. According to Cameron (2001: 123–4), CDA is concerned with the 'hidden agenda of discourse'. She explains:

> ... the central claim of CDA is that the way certain realities get talked or written about – that is, the choices speakers or writers make in doing it – are not just random but ideologically patterned. These choices do much of the work of naturalising particular social arrangements which serve particular interests, so that in time they may come to seem like the only possible or rational arrangements ...

In relation to gender, the 'hidden agenda' tends to be concerned with the way language is used to construct ideologies around gender which are constitutive of unequal power relations between social actors and serve the interests of those in power. Those ideologies are 'naturalised' in that it seems as though they are naturally occurring rather than discursively constructed. This works not through single or occasional instances of particular kinds of language use, but through the repeated and systematic patterning of language. In analysing these patterns, Cameron urges us to pay attention not just to the surface features of language (*what* is said or written) but to more subtle underlying features, presuppositions and patterns (*how* certain things are said or written). For this reason, the kind of linguistic analysis used in CDA needs to be systematic and able to identify repeated patterns across stretches of text. It is only through repetition that particular ideologies become naturalised through discourse.

It is the uncovering of ideological representations and enactments of gender, then, which lie at the heart of feminist critical discourse analysis (FCDA). Drawing on the work of Althusser (1971), Fairclough (2003: 9) describes ideologies as 'representations of aspects of the world which can be shown to contribute to establishing, maintaining and changing social relations of power, domination and exploitation', and claims that we both shape, and are shaped by, ideologies, including ideologies of gender. Lazar (2005) states one of the key aims of feminist CDA as being to show that social practices which may appear to be neutral and natural are actually gendered in ways which sustain a patriarchal social order in the wider socio-political context. She argues that dominant relations of power systematically privilege men as a social group and disadvantage and exclude women. The work of feminist CDA is to uncover how this is achieved discursively, with the idea that understanding is a pre-cursor to social transformation.

My own use of feminist CDA in this chapter is largely underpinned theoretically by Foucault's work on discourse, gender, sexuality and identity. This aspect of Foucault's work is potentially empowering, as it implies that hierarchical gender relations, whereby men dominate women, are not stable but can be challenged and changed by manipulating the way individuals interact with one another. Rather than seeing language and identity as static and unchangeable, Foucault encourages us to view both language and identity as 'a multiplicity of discursive elements that can come into play in various strategies' (1990: 100). Foucault describes discourse as language in action, claiming that discourse can be understood as a series of events or 'statements' that set up relationships with other statements. These dialogic relationships between statements can be a site of struggle and Foucault argues that it is the struggle over power relations which creates what we perceive as reality. For Foucault, different discourses do not simply reflect different realities but play an active role in creating realities, identities and relationships. This supports a broader post-structuralist view of discourse as a 'socially constitutive signifying practice' (Lazar, 2005: 11). Within CDA, Fairclough (1995) explains how the relationship between discourse and the social is a dialectal one so that discourse both constitutes, but is also constituted by, social practices and structures.

However, Foucault is careful to argue that, although there are an infinite potential number of discourses available, certain discourses have evolved throughout history into dominant or 'hegemonic' (a term attributed to Gramsci) discourses whilst others have become marginalised. Therefore, the potential fluidity of discourse and gender is, in reality, constrained to some extent by broader social structures. The knowledges, behaviours and meanings embodied in dominant discourses are those which emerge as permissible or desirable in society. In this way, they develop into culturally dominant ideologies about what kinds of knowledge are valid and what behaviours and meanings are permissible. Dominant discourses accrue power, which means they are difficult to challenge. The less they are challenged, the more they become normalised – they take on the appearance of being naturally occurring and stable, rather than transient and temporarily constructed through ever-shifting contexts of interaction. These hegemonic discourses are imbued with power and have the appearance of being commonsense and natural.

Dominant discourses promote the idea that there is one absolute truth – what Foucault refers to as a 'politics of truth' (1984: 74). Dominant discourses about gender in Western society, for example, have been through a naturalisation process so that it appears natural and true that men should exhibit behaviour and knowledge which are perceived as masculine and women should exhibit behaviour which is perceived as feminine. These dominant gender discourses put ideological constraints upon what is socially and culturally acceptable as masculine and feminine behaviour – they work to limit the potential meanings about gender which may be expressed and created, by pushing some meanings into the margins. The effect of this normalisation process is that if men behave in a way that is not considered masculine, or if women behave in a way not accepted as feminine, within dominant discourses about gender, such individuals are perceived as behaving 'unnaturally' and, as a result, risk being constructed as abnormal or socially deviant in terms of their gender identity. This whole normalisation process simultaneously works to conceal the very fact that it is fabricated rather than natural. However, whilst marginalised gender discourses are suppressed and subjugated, they still potentially offer sites where dominant practices and discourses can be contested, resisted and challenged. Lazar (2005) notes that hegemonic structures themselves are never static and are, therefore, always susceptible to challenge and resistance. In order for any sort of social hegemony to be maintained, it must be able to adapt over time to social changes. This creates a tension between hegemonic structures as powerful and resilient but, at the same time, fragile and open to contestation. Approaches which are more structuralist in their orientation (such as SFDA) are less able to allow for the possibility of such diverse discourses. These are the arguments which underpin much work on feminist CDA which has emerged in recent years. As Lazar (2005: 9) explains:

> The task of feminist CDA is to examine how power and dominance are discursively produced and/or resisted in a variety of ways through textual representations of gendered social practices, and through interactional strategies of talk.

This is precisely what the CDA-informed data analysis presented in this chapter aims to do in relation to the 'interactional strategies of talk' found in the classroom. CDA is well-suited to being used within an ethnographic approach as both linguistic ethnography and

CDA acknowledge the impartiality of the analyst. As Litosseliti and Sunderland (2002: 21) explain:

> If language choices are sociologically and ideologically shaped, then analysts' own understandings and interpretations of social interaction are also inextricably partial...A critical (feminist) discourse analysis by definition then cannot remain descriptive and neutral, since the interests guiding it aim to uncover or make transparent those social processes and mechanisms than can perpetuate injustice, inequality, manipulation and (sex) discrimination...

Hence, self-reflexivity is an important component of CDA, just as it is in linguistic ethnography and the approach of FPDA discussed later in this chapter. In explicitly adopting a political stance, Lazar (2005) argues that this enables a dialectal relationship between theory and practice in CDA – what she terms a 'praxis-oriented approach' (2005: 5). This term refers broadly to scholarship that explicitly makes analyst biases part of its argument and is the case with feminist CDA. Lazar goes on to further support this stance by stating that no research is entirely objective and that 'all knowledge is socially and historically constructed' (2005: 6). What CDA does is to overtly recognise and make explicit what the biases actually are, and to use that self-reflexivity to support the arguments made through its application. In relation to gender, Lazar argues that this helps to produce a critique of existing social structures and inequalities around gender which can then be used as the basis for political action and social transformation.

In its application, CDA draws on various linguistic analytic frameworks (such as pragmatics, conversation analysis and systemic-functional grammar) and focuses its analysis on a range of linguistic features (for example, lexis, clauses/sentences/utterances, conversation structures, structures of genre). I argue in this chapter that CDA can successfully draw on SFDA as an analytic framework and, in doing so, can focus upon the systematic patterning of types of utterances in order to show how the repetition of certain discourse patterns is instrumental in the construction and constitution of gendered power relations in the classroom.

Fairclough's CDA framework

I draw on Fairclough's (1995, 2001) CDA framework for approaching the data collected for this research. In his framework, Fairclough argues that there are three dimensions of discourse which can be analysed in any text when using CDA. He refers to these three dimensions as *description, interpretation* and *explanation,* and his definitions of each are as follows:

Description is the stage which is concerned with formal properties of the text.

Interpretation is concerned with the relationship between text and interaction – with seeing the text as the product of a process of production, and as a resource in the process of interpretation...

Explanation is concerned with the relationship between interaction and social context – with the social determination of the processes of production and interpretation, and their social effects. (Fairclough, 2001: 21–2)

In the present study, the description stage refers to analysis of the formal properties of the classroom dialogue. As mentioned above, there are various formal linguistic features which can be focused on at this stage. Fairclough tends to draw predominantly on systemic-functional grammar during this stage in his own analysis of (mainly written) texts (which focuses on a text's lexico-grammar), although other descriptive frameworks may also be used. I argue that SFDA may appropriately be used within the description stage of CDA as it focuses on discursive patterns and structures in the utterances which constitute the interactional data. SFDA is restricted only to the description stage when used within a broader CDA framework. By itself, it does not incorporate a critical consideration of either the processes or the social conditions of production and interpretation involved in the classroom interaction. This is one of the key ways in which CDA can add further dimensions to the findings yielded through the application of SFDA. By self-reflexively drawing on knowledge of the wider social context in which the interaction takes place, further insights may be gained into how exactly gender is discursively produced. This is what I aim to do in this chapter. I also consider some aspects of the lexis used in the interactional data, focusing particularly on how gender- and sexuality-specific concepts are lexicalised. Fairclough (2001: 96) argues that ideological struggles are often encoded in the lexical choices made in both spoken and written data. A notably high usage of words which fall into the same semantic field – what Fairclough refers to as 'overwording' or 'over-lexicalisation' – can particularly highlight the specific ideological preoccupations in a text. I found several examples of these kinds of lexical choices being made around the concepts of gender and sexuality in the classroom data, which I discuss later in this chapter.

Feminist post-structuralist discourse analysis (FPDA)

Having described CDA, and explained why it is potentially useful for analysing the data in conjunction with the SFDA presented in the previous chapter, I now turn to the other 'post-structuralist' approach which is used in the research – FPDA. There is a great degree of overlap between CDA and FPDA, which is why I have chosen to deal with them within the same chapter as this seems an effective way of avoiding unnecessary repetition. Also, as I embarked on the analysis of data using each approach, I found that it was difficult to separate out the two approaches completely and that, in fact, both analyses worked better when used in conjunction with one another. However, there are some differences between the two approaches, which is why I am introducing them separately before applying them simultaneously to the data.

Baxter (2002a, 2002b, 2003, 2008) describes FPDA as a 'supplementary' approach in that it values a multi-perspective view and should be used in conjunction with other methods. In this way, it may simultaneously complement and undermine other methods of discourse analysis, revealing interesting areas of interaction between competing terms, methods and sets of ideas that allows for more multiple, open-ended readings of a piece of analysis, ultimately creating divergent forms of knowledge. Baxter (2008: 245) defines FPDA as follows:

> an approach to analysing intertextualised discourses in spoken interaction and other types of text. It draws upon the poststructuralist principles of complexity, plurality, ambiguity, connection, recognition, diversity, textual playfulness, functionality and transformation.

Like CDA, FPDA moves away from focusing predominantly on the structural details of interaction and resists the notion that meanings are only embedded within textual structures. And like CDA, FPDA is post-structural but has a less overtly political agenda than CDA. Whilst CDA work on gender has an avowedly ideological agenda and a commitment to focusing on social problems and working on behalf of oppressed groups, FPDA downplays this element in its approach. Rather than focusing upon issues around power and explicitly advocating an emancipatory agenda, FPDA does not presume, in an *a priori* way, that women as a social group category are necessarily going to emerge as powerless. Instead, it views female subject positions as complex, shifting and multiply located. There are competing discourses of gender in any given context, including the classroom, and the interplay between discourses means that speakers can continually fluctuate between subject positions on a matrix of powerfulness and powerlessness. Having a degree of *agency*, individuals can recognise how and through which discourses they are being 'positioned', and can then take up or resist particular subject positions.

Importantly, FPDA aims to 'release the words of marginalised or minority speakers' (Baxter, 2002a: 9) and entails giving space to marginalised or silenced voices in localised interactions. CDA does this too, but FPDA often places more emphasis on this aspect of its analysis. Baxter's analyses have focused, for example, upon certain girls who say little in classroom settings. This ultimately allows for a greater richness and variety of debate, discussion and freedom to speak from all social groups, not just those who are heard more often and are, in that sense, considered to be more dominant. This means that FPDA is ultimately concerned with equality (like CDA), but this concern arises from an epistemological perspective rather than an ideological one. As a methodological approach, FPDA is best suited to small-scale, ethnographic case studies in which the complexity of competing and continually changing gender discourses can be captured, at least temporarily. CDA and FPDA both tend to adopt methodologies which are more sympathetic to linguistic ethnography in which a knowledge and understanding of context is crucial to interpreting the data. Specific analytical methods include an analysis of what Bakhtin (1981) terms 'polyphony' (competing voices) in discourse, and denotative and connotative analyses. These methods of analysis are applied to sequences of classroom discourse in this chapter, revealing how speakers constantly change subject position and engage with competing discourses of gender. Importantly, FPDA is not simply concerned with identifying discourses, but focuses more on how discourses interact, how they variously position speakers in relation to other discourses and how speakers shift between subject positions. Baxter (2002a), for example, examines how competing gender discourses are sometimes produced in the context of public speaking in the classroom. Comparisons are made between what this kind of analysis reveals, and what both structural approaches, such as those explored in Chapter 3, and other kinds of post-structural analysis such as CDA, can reveal. In applying FPDA alongside CDA, and incorporating the use of SFDA at the denotative level of description, I explore how FPDA can complement the other types of analysis used in the book with the ultimate aim of enhancing our understandings of gender and classroom interaction.

A key component of Baxter's FPDA procedure is the distinction between denotative and connotative analysis (drawing on previous work by Barthes, 1977), and this provides a focus for the analysis presented in this chapter. According to Baxter, denotative analysis focuses on features which include the amount of talk/turns produced by each speaker, the physical and spatial context of the conversation, factors that appear to contribute to the negotiation and control of the floor, and some basic characterisation of the speakers based on the researcher's knowledge of them. Denotative analysis is supposed to provide an 'uncontroversial' and non-evaluative account of what is happening in the data. In this sense, it is similar to the description level of Fairclough's CDA framework. And just as SFDA can be fitted into the CDA description level, it could perhaps also operate as a form of denotative analysis within FPDA. Connotative (FPDA) analysis is interpretive in that it moves beyond mere description to identify emerging social 'discourses' in the data, and the specific conversational features which point to the emergence of these. This kind of analysis focuses more critically upon the contextualised emergence of (multiple) gendered discourses, competing discourses and the interplay between subject positions. The connotative analysis may also consider polyphony in the interactional data – how competing discourses (some dominant and some marginalised) may emerge. For example, Baxter identifies the use of humour to construct some speakers as confident and popular and as a means of gaining peer approval, which leads to the emergence of the 'peer approval discourse'. And she notes that the speakers' own unelicited references to gender contribute simultaneously to the construction of a 'gender differentiation discourse'. In Baxter's study, interview data is used alongside transcribed extracts of classroom discussion in the connotative analysis. Connotative analysis also lends itself well to analysing the discourse produced by, and surrounding, participants who do not often get a chance to speak – in other words, those who are in some way 'marginalised' in the classroom context under scrutiny. This, of course, is dependent on the analyst's own knowledge and interpretations of which speakers are marginalised – information which is obtained via the broadly ethnographic approach being used throughout the research.

In sum, FPDA provides a supplementary approach which seeks to add another dimension to existing approaches and to address some of their limitations. It provides a framework which is, in some ways, more fluid than that of CDA, and enables a more explicit examination of how participants may move between dominant and marginalised discourses, draw on the linguistic resources associated with both, and be multiply positioned in and through the discursive contexts under scrutiny. Importantly, FPDA stresses that individuals have agency – they are able to recognise, take up or resist positionings. Within a CDA framework, a greater emphasis is often placed on social structures which position individuals within matrices of power. A starting point for CDA is usually a set of social problems or issues, whereas this is not necessarily the case for FPDA. Through its use of interview data alongside transcripts of spoken interaction, FPDA also seeks insights into people's perceptions of dominant and marginalised ideologies. These same principles will be used to analyse the data extracts presented in this chapter.

Organisation and presentation of analysis

Because FPDA and CDA are being deployed simultaneously in the analysis of data, I will briefly explain how the analysis will be presented in this chapter. To simply split the chapter into two broad sections on CDA and FPDA would have resulted in unnecessary repetition, especially at the descriptive level of CDA and corresponding denotative level of FPDA. Therefore, I have chosen to use the frameworks and sub-headings more closely associated with FPDA as a means of organising the chapter. These include sections on gender differentiation and collaborative talk discourses, peer approval discourses, marginalised voices, and the interplay between subject positions. Elements of CDA are then incorporated into relevant sections. In particular, I incorporate CDA into those sections which deal with connotative analysis of specific data extracts, and the final sections on marginalised voices and the interplay between subject positions, as these are the places where CDA is best suited to offer the most useful insights. The main differences between approaches emerge at the levels of explanation in CDA and connotative analysis in FPDA, and these differences can easily be written about within the same sections of analysis. Whereas FPDA is well-suited to analysing how particular gendered discourses emerge through the classroom interaction, CDA can offer further insights into how those discourses are hierarchised and how they may reify, or sometimes contest, hegemonic discourses and ideologies of gender which circulate in the wider social context. At the level of explanation, CDA can add to FPDA a more explicit consideration of the social conditions of production and the social effects that these conditions have on the discursive production of gendered identities and subjectivities. Perhaps the most interesting tension between CDA and FPDA is the relative emphases placed by each on the role of structure and agency in relation to the discursive production of gender. Whereas both approaches acknowledge that both structure and agency play a role, CDA tends to place more emphasis on the social structures which constrain the production of identities, whereas FPDA tends to highlight individual agency a little more. However, when used together, rather than creating a tension which could not be resolved, I found that these different emphases worked to produce a more detailed and comprehensive account of the processes at work in the data.

Unlike Baxter, I will draw more on the interactional patterns which emerge from the SFDA and will examine the discursive effects which such patterns have. It is hoped that this will illuminate some of the complementary ways in which the two types of analysis can be used. I first consider how the interactional patterns previously identified by the SFDA can further contribute to the gendered discourses of collaborative talk and gender differentiation. I then go on to examine specific instances as well as SFDA patterns which contribute to peer approval discourses. Like Baxter, I then focus on extracts in which the speakers produce unelicited references to gender and examine the kinds of discourses produced in these situations. Finally, I examine the discourse produced by and around some of the 'marginalised' participants, and the interplay between subject positionings which emerges through the FPDA analysis. As in Baxter's study, interview data are used alongside some of the classroom transcripts.

'Gender differentiation' and 'collaborative talk' discourses

In her FPDA-based study of classroom discourse, Baxter analyses whole-class teacher-led discussions in secondary English lessons. The aim of her research was to investigate whether girls were considered as 'effective' as boys when speaking in public settings such as whole-class discussions or debates. In doing so, Baxter identifies what she terms 'significant moments' in the discourse and conducts a detailed FPDA of these moments. Baxter's subsequent analysis leads her to identify three prevailing interactional strategies (or what she terms 'discourses') in her data: peer approval, collaborative talk, and gender differentiation. Similar discourses have also been identified in other FPDA studies of classroom interaction in other contexts. For example, Sunderland (2004) uses post-structuralist discourse analysis to identify a range of gendered discourses in the foreign language classroom. In a study of gender and student group classroom discussion, Davies (2005) uses FPDA to examine how girls use the same discursive strategies to simultaneously create a sense of unity and group solidarity and to enhance their learning. Although using FPDA, Davies notes that it is the 'sustained' (2005: 204) way in which the girls use particular discursive resources in their group talk that leads to the emergence of gendered discourses. Although Davies does not explain how such features can be quantified and evidenced as 'sustained', I suggest that combining FPDA with more quantitative approaches such as SFDA is one way of achieving this. The same analytical procedures are used to analyse the data in this chapter. The application of Baxter's FPDA framework to a different kind of classroom interaction – student-led group discussion – and different types of lessons – Design and Technology as well as English – should help to assess the overall effectiveness of the framework, as well as revealing the details of how particular gender discourses are enacted in the localised contexts under scrutiny.

Baxter's identification of a 'gender differentiation' discourse is primarily based on what the teacher and student participants say in the interviews about the differences that they themselves perceive between the teachers' treatment of boys and girls, and their perceptions of the different kinds of behaviour exhibited by students. In her study, Baxter notes the extent to which both the students and teachers constructed and naturalised their classroom experiences according to constructs of gender differentiation. In other words, gender categories were perceived and constructed in binary terms, and this whole process was naturalised. Baxter supports this idea through examples of classroom discourse in which the gender differentiation discourse is seen to emerge alongside two other dominant emergent discourses of peer approval and collaborative talk. Baxter notes how, in her study of English classes, the teacher often explicitly articulated the 'rules' of collaborative talk before an oral activity took place. These rules were based around abilities in listening to each other, taking turns and co-operating with each other. Girls, especially, were able to follow these rules of collaborative talk more closely than boys. It is interesting that this same discourse of collaborative talk emerged both in the English and the Design and Technology classes in my study. The discourse also emerged even when the teachers had not explicitly stated or re-iterated the rules – they simply asked the students to work in groups without providing any further specific guidance on how they should structure their talk. In my study, the gender differentiation and collaborative talk discourses were strongly supported through the SFDA. SFDA was less able to quantify the emergence of a peer approval discourse, yet this discourse did emerge through the FPDA and CDA, mainly through the use of particular gender-related lexis, rather than through the frequency of using particular types of utterances, as is the case with SFDA. For this reason, I deal with the discourses of gender differentiation and collaborative talk in this section. I then discuss the peer approval discourse in the following section.

What FPDA alone does not reveal is how frequent these discourses are in the data, nor does it provide a systematic analysis of the structures of interaction that contribute to the production of the discourses, along with the content of what is actually said and by which speakers. The SFDA presented in the previous chapter can yield this kind of information from the data and so supports the FPDA in that it shows that the discourses purported to emerge through FPDA happen frequently and systematically across reasonably large amounts of classroom interaction. The SFDA also reveals how the discourses which emerge in the FPDA or CDA are realised structurally in terms of how the interaction is organised and how relative frequencies of particular elements of the interactions cumulatively contribute to the emergence of discourses. In using FPDA alongside SFDA, we can see that the SFDA itself strongly suggests a gender differentiation discourse, simply because there appear to be more differences than similarities in the way the linguistic categories are deployed by the girls and boys. We do not need to look at extracts of the data themselves to see that there are clearly demarcated differences in the frequencies with which particular linguistic features are deployed. But SFDA does not reveal the detail and possible complexities of what is actually happening in the interactions in which those features are being used by the speakers. This is where an approach such as FPDA, with its emphasis on close linguistic analysis of contextualised extracts of data, can 'fill in' the information which is missing from SFDA when used as a singular approach. The discussion of the next few extracts illustrates how FPDA can further our understanding of how particular gendered discourses emerge from the boys' and girls' differential use of the linguistic categories identified in the preceding SFDA.

In the previous chapter, the SFDA revealed quantitative differences in the frequencies with which particular linguistic features were used by the boys and girls in the study. The analysis also produces a warrant for focusing more on differences than similarities because the differences are far more numerous than the similarities. In FPDA terms, these structural differences in the interaction contribute to the production of a 'gender differentiation' discourse as the interaction happens. But

SFDA is still required to tell us precisely which features produce this discourse. The most marked differences between the boys and girls which emerged from the SFDA were:

- Girls' more frequent use of Structure and Boundary exchanges
- Girls' more frequent use of *dictate-repeat* Inform exchanges
- Girls' more frequent use of acknowledging moves, especially those realised by the acts of *confirm, concur, receive, react* and *repeat*
- Boys' more frequent use of Inform exchanges, especially single-move Inform exchanges
- Boys' more frequent use of Direct exchanges and directing moves
- Boys' more frequent use of *protest* and *reject* acts

Note that 'more frequent' is always relative to the frequency with which the same feature is used by the other types of groups.

These same features also contribute to the emergence of a 'collaborative talk' discourse which is taken up more noticeably by the girls in the study. The denotative analysis in this section is presented slightly differently from Baxter's. Mine incorporates a description of the SFDA as well. Whereas Baxter's denotative analysis comments on features such as the length and quantity of turns taken by each speaker, my analysis incorporates a description of the types of turns taken using the SFDA categories. Thus, we can already begin to see how elements of SFDA and FPDA can be amalgamated to produce a more detailed description of classroom interaction. For this reason, I have presented the data extracts in this section in the same way as they are presented in the preceding chapter – with the SFDA elements included in the right-hand columns. This is different from Baxter's FPDA, in which the dialogue is presented without any accompanying analysis lines – the analysis is presented in the discussion which follows or precedes each extract. Whereas Baxter's extracts contain line numbers, mine are numbered not by line but by exchange. This does not affect the analysis – it is simply a different way of referring to particular parts of the dialogue.

In Extract 4.1, a group of girls are in a Food Technology lesson. During the first part of the lesson, the teacher spent some time talking to the whole class about how to produce effective designs for cakes. She then instructed the class to work in groups to produce their own designs. Each group was given a worksheet containing a series of instructions concerning the task. The teacher told the class to read through the worksheet in their groups and then follow the instructions to produce a design. Extract 4.1 occurs just after the class have organised

Extract 4.1

Dialogue	Act	E.S.	Move	E.S.	EXCH.	EX.
G3: now	fr	h	framing	I	Boundary	37
G2: we're not doing that one we're doing we've gotta read this together	ms	h	opening	I	Structure	38
G2: we'll read a sentence each	ms	h	opening	I	Structure	39
G1: okay then	acq	h	answering	R		
G2: it's fair then	[acq	h	answering	R]		
G2: how many is there	inq	h	eliciting	I	Elicit	40
G1: hang on a minute	s	pre-h				
right we've done that right?	con	h	opening	I	Structure	41
G2: read a sentence each	ms	h	opening	I	Structure	42
(Students reading from worksheet – 10 minutes)						
G2: right	fr	h	framing	I	Boundary	43
G3: to do	s	pre-h				
now think about designing a small cake for one of the following occasions (reads list from text)	ms	h	opening	I	Structure	44
G1: okay	acq	h	answering	R		

themselves into (self-selected) groups and started the task. The extract is a typical example of Structure exchanges being used more frequently by the girls, as revealed through the SFDA. What SFDA does not reveal is what exactly happens when the girls use such exchanges, and what the cumulative effect of this relatively high usage of Structure exchanges may be. These are questions which both CDA and the supplementary approach of FPDA may be able to address more adequately.

In Extract 4.1, a descriptive or denotative analysis shows a sequence of mainly Boundary and Structure exchanges being used by this group of girls. At the beginning of the extract, G3 closes the previous transaction and starts a new one by producing a Boundary exchange. This is immediately followed by a Structure exchange which functions to prospectively structure the discourse. This Structure exchange, and the one that follows it, is initiated by G2. Within Structure exchange 39, she states 'we'll read a sentence each' as the opening move, suggesting that the reading activity be shared amongst the group. This is agreed upon by G1 in the answering move which follows. G2 then produces an Elicit exchange but the eliciting move at I is not responded to. Instead, what follows are two more Structure exchanges initiated by G1 and G2 respectively. And what is proposed in these exchanges is agreed upon by all group members. Although G2's eliciting move in the Elicit exchange is not responded to, this does not appear to cause any problems either in terms of the social cohesion of the group or the progression of the interaction. Following this extract, I observed that the girls moved through the reading activity and the ensuing group design task fairly quickly. This extract shows that the floor is shared fairly equally between all group members and everybody contributes not just to the discussion as a whole, but to the initiation of exchanges. After reading through the worksheet, another Boundary exchange is produced to mark a transition from the reading task to the design task. This Boundary exchange is produced by G2. G3 then initiates the following Structure exchange. In addition to the use of these Boundary and Structure exchanges, we can also see from the denotative analysis that there are several instances of the use of 'we' which also signals collaboration and a sense of group cohesion (see, for example, Coates, 1996 and Reay, 1991 for further discussion of the use of 'we' by female speakers).

This denotative analysis is helpful because it adds another dimension to the previous SFDA. What the SFDA reveals is that girls use more Structure exchanges than boys. What it does not show is the girls' democratic and egalitarian approach to the use of these types of exchanges, in that no one individual dominates these exchanges, or even dominates the Initiation (I) moves which function to initiate the exchanges. The SFDA stops short of focusing upon what each individual group member is doing during the interaction, but FPDA can provide us with this information, even at the denotative stage of analysis. A connotative analysis (in FPDA terms) or interpretation (in CDA terms) suggests that the discourse of 'collaborative talk' is important for the group, at least in this particular setting. There is an explicit need for the floor to be shared so that this is seen as 'fair'. These girls place a high value upon taking an egalitarian approach to group work where each group member contributes fairly equally and there is no apparent 'leader'. The implication therefore, is that a more hierarchical approach to this kind of group work may be valued less positively.

A similar connotative analysis emerges from the girls' use of certain types of Inform exchanges, as seen in Extract 4.2. In this extract,

Extract 4.2

Dialogue	Act	E.S.	Move	E.S.	EXCH.	EX.
G2: the bin behind the door	dict	h	informing	I	Inform	20
G3: bin the bin	rep	h	acknowledging	R		
G2: the bin ⇑	[rep	h	acknowledging	R]		
G1: by a fridge	dict	h	informing	I	Inform	21
G2: bin bin should should have em the top on	dict	h	informing	I	Inform	22
G1: should have the	rep	h	acknowledging	R		
G1/3: top on ⇑	[rep	h	acknowledging	R]		
G2: em and the rule is always?	inq	h	eliciting	I	Elicit	23
G3: always keep the top on always	dict	h	informing	R		
G1: keep	dict	h	informing	I	Inform	24
G3: keep	rep	h	acknow'ledging	R		
G1: the	dict	h	informing	I	Inform	25
G3: the	rep	h	acknowledging	R		
G1: top on	dict	h	informing	I	Inform	26
G3: top on	rep	h	acknowledging	R		
G2: on yeah ⇑	[rep	h	acknowledging	R]		

a different group of girls, in a different Food Technology lesson, is trying to produce a list of safety rules for working in a kitchen. Again, the class teacher has spent the first part of the lesson explaining some general principles of safety in the kitchen and has provided some examples. She has then asked the students to work in self-selected groups in which they are given a picture of a kitchen where several safety rules are being broken. Each group is asked to discuss the picture to identify which rules are being broken and to produce a written list of the rules. Extract 4.2 occurs about half way into the discussion.

A denotative analysis of this extract shows the girls engaging in a sequence of a particular type of Inform exchange which did not occur at all in the boys' single-sex or mixed-sex interaction, according to the SFDA. These are the Inform exchanges which are realised by the acts of *dictate* at I and *repeat* at R in the informing and acknowledging moves respectively. These types of exchanges only occur when the students are engaged in the process of collaboratively producing a written text. Clearly, the boys' single-sex and mixed-sex groups were also required to produce written texts as a part of their group tasks during the research period, but they did so in a much more individualistic way. The written texts produced by the boys' groups, in particular, tended to be similar in terms of their content, but different in terms of the actual wording, presentation and so on. Extract 4.2 also shows that no one person in the group constantly initiates the exchanges – the initiations are produced by different speakers (although G1 does seem to fall into the role of 'initiator' more in the final three exchanges). Again, there is no disagreement expressed within this extract. The *repeat* acts which realise the acknowledging moves all function to express agreement and consensus.

In terms of the connotative analysis, there is, again, a sense of a collaborative conversational floor and a general feeling of consensus amongst the group. This further contributes to the emergence of a 'collaborative talk' discourse. Furthermore, there is an additional sense that any textual outcomes which emerge from the discussion should be constructed collaboratively and should, therefore, be the same for each group member. This is not the case for the boys in the study, especially in their single-sex groups. The boys were observed to be more concerned with producing individualised written outcomes. In fact, as discussed in the preceding chapter, there were occasions where the boys were so concerned with producing individualised outcomes that they accused each other of 'copying' if they perceived another group member as attempting to engage in any kind of collective text production. One such example,

Extract 4.3

Dialogue	Act	E.S.	Move	E.S.	EXCH.	EX.
B2: I've got eighteen now eighteen I've got eighteen	inf	h	informing	I	Inform	77
B1: you got eighteen fourteen I've got	s inf	per-h h	informing	I	Inform	78
what you copying me for	inq	h	eliciting	I	Elicit	79
B2: I don't need to copy look how many I've got I've got eighteen	inf com	h pos-h	informing	R		

already presented in Chapter 3, is again included in extract 4.3 to illustrate this point.

Examples such as these suggest that the boys in the study place a relatively low value upon collaborating in order to produce collective written outcomes, whereas this kind of activity is more highly valued by the girls, at least in this context. Although single extracts are produced and analysed here, the SFDA in the previous chapter does show that this is a consistent and systematic pattern across the groups in the study. This contributes not only to the girls' discourse of collaborative talk, but to the overall discourse of gender differentiation which emerges from these patterns of interaction.

If we add a more critical dimension to the FPDA connotative analysis, by considering the analysis in terms of wider social and institutional norms of gendered behaviour, we could argue that the girls' focus on collaborative talk and their emphasis on egalitarian values function as a means of downplaying issues of power and status within their groups. Because power is more closely associated with dominant forms of masculinity, and it is only boys who are expected to perform these forms of masculinity in the school context, it may be expected that the interactional practices which the boys engage in are more likely to involve struggles around power. Such struggle inevitably involves competition, so this may provide an explanation as to why more explicitly competitive discourses are produced by the boys, especially in their single-sex interactions. And their higher use of certain discursive features identified through the SFDA provides them with the means of enacting such practices. Therefore, the findings from the SFDA operate at the level of description. But we need to consider the wider discursive context in order to interpret and explain those findings. The boys' greater emphasis upon competition and power struggle is further realised through their use of different types of Inform exchange than those employed more frequently by the girls. This is exemplified in the following extract.

Extract 4.4 is taken from a Food Technology class in which the students have been set the task of producing a 'star profile' (a type of

Extract 4.4

Dialogue	Act	E.S.	Move	E.S.	EXCH.	EX.
B3: what	s	pre-h				
I'm doing the equipment list before I do the star profile ⇓	inf	h	Informing	I	inform	13
B4: I'm doing Bakewells ⇑	inf	h	informing	I	Inform	14
B2: I am ⇓	inf	h	informing	I	Inform	15
B3: I'm doing pizza again I am ⇑	inf	h	informing	I	Inform	16
B1: I'm doing mini pizza	inf	h	informing	I	Inform	17
B3: oh I made eleven right my mom had six	inf	h	informing	I	Inform	18
B1: I made em I made twelve I made twelve I had about six and my nephew had two and I don't know where the rest went	inf	h	informing	I	Inform	19

structured brainstorming activity) for designing and producing a particular food item of their choice. The class are evidently used to producing
star profiles, as the teacher does not need to explain what they are in
order for the students to start the task. The teacher instructs the students
to work in self-selected groups and each group is asked to engage in discussion to produce a star profile. Extract 4.4 occurs about two minutes
into the task.

As explained in Chapter 3, although the girls in the study used more
Inform exchanges consisting of a *dictate* (I)-*repeat* (R) structure, the boys'
use of Inform exchanges as a whole was higher than that of the girls
in their respective single-sex groups. How, then, do the boys' Inform
exchanges differ from those produced by the girls? First, a denotative
analysis of Extract 4.4 shows that the exchanges tend to be shorter, often
consisting of only one move at I, and that is not responded to in any way
by the other group members. The extract shows a sequence of single-
move Inform exchanges in which the boys simply produce a series of
statements about what they are doing or how they think something
should be done. These contributions are, therefore, quite individualised.
This is further corroborated by the frequent use of 'I' in the extracts,
which emphasises the individual nature of each group member's contributions; see Coates (2003, 2007) and Reay (1991) for further discussion
of this feature.

A connotative analysis of this extract suggests that, although the floor
seems to be shared fairly equally with no one group member dominat-
ing the discussion, the interaction still sounds very competitive because
the contributions are so individualised. Although we do need to be careful not to over-simplify and over-generalise the connotative analysis by
claiming that boys are always competitive – see, for example, work by
Cameron (1997), Hewitt (1997), Leap (1996) and Swann (2003) which
discusses how interaction between male friends can contain elements of
both competitiveness and collaboration – the fact that the SFDA reveals
that the boys systematically engage in this kind of interactional practice cannot be ignored. The SFDA, importantly, reveals what is markedly
absent in the interaction, as well as what is present. The low occurrence
of acknowledging moves is marked in the boys' single-sex interaction
when we compare it with that of the girls. Not only do the boys produce
very few positive evaluations or endorsements of each other's utterances, they frequently fail to produce any kind of evaluative utterances
(in the form of acknowledging moves) at all. This further contributes
to the competitiveness of their discourse. However, the SFDA does not

address the question of why the boys are so concerned with producing such individualised contributions which almost act as a kind of running commentary on what each group member is doing as they are undertaking the task in hand. Again, adding a CDA dimension to the connotative level of the FPDA suggests that the apparent competitiveness of the boys' interaction may be reflective of, or an enactment of, power struggles which reify the dominant discourses of masculinity operating in this context. The boys seem to be using these kinds of interactional resources as a means of trying to assert status or be 'one-up' (Tannen, 1993) in the group.

These meanings associated with this kind of interactional pattern seem particularly evident in Extracts 4.5 and 4.6. These extracts are taken from a Textiles Technology lesson in which the class have been instructed by the teacher to work in groups to discuss ideas and then produce a written list of 'containers' which may be made from fabric. The teacher has explicitly encouraged the groups to list as many items as possible.

Extract 4.5

Dialogue	Act	E.S.	Move	E.S.	EXCH.	EX.
B2: I've got eighteen now eighteen I've got eighteen	inf	h	informing	I	Inform	77
B1: you got eighteen fourteen I've got	s inf	pre-h h	informing	I	Inform	78
what you copying me for	inq	h	eliciting	I	Elicit	79
B2: I don't need to copy look how many I've got I've got eighteen	inf com	h post-h	informing	R		
- - - - - - - - - - - - - - - -						
B2: I've got twenty-three anyway	inf	h	informing	I	Inform	88

Extract 4.6

Dialogue	Act	E.S.	Move	E.S.	EXCH.	EX.
M2: oh yes	s	pre-h				
I've got another one and another one	inf	h	informing	I	Inform	96
M3: teddy bear teddy bear	sugg	h	eliciting	I	Elicit	97
M2: yeah teddy bear	conf	h	informing	R		
M1: twenty-four	inf	h	informing	I	Inform	98
M4: yeah I've got more than you	inf	h	informing	I	Inform	99

In terms of a denotative analysis of these two short extracts, the speakers in each case produce a series of predominantly informing moves which express how many items each speaker has produced on his (individual) list as the task progresses. Although there were many occasions during the study when the boys easily drifted off-task during their discussions (much more so than the girls), on this occasion they remain focused. It seems as if the very competitive nature of the task itself, focused on producing as many items on a list as possible within a set amount of time, functions to motivate these boys. In terms of a connotative analysis, the boys, again, seem to be systematically drawing on certain interactional features to create competition within their group. And that competition is constitutive of the power struggles which are an inherent part of the dominant discourses of masculinity operating in this context. When we compare these extracts from the boys' groups with a similar extract taken from a girls' group, this highlights the gender differentiation discourse which emerges from the systematic production of the different kinds of interactional patterns by the boys and the girls.

Extract 4.7 is similar to the two extracts discussed above in that the girls' group are, rather uncharacteristically, engaged in producing a kind of 'running commentary' on what each individual is doing in a practical sense as the interaction happens. Extract 4.7 is taken

Extract 4.7

Dialogue	Act	E.S.	Move	E.S.	EXCH.	EX.
G3: oh oh God I threw it away this morning	s inf	pre-h h	informing	I	Inform	84
G2: she threw it away G1: you silly cow	rea rea	h h	acknowledging acknowledging	R F		
G2: oh I have to put a price on G3: ten pounds can I buy yours {aside}	m inf	h	informing	I	Inform	85
G1: mine's 79p {laughter}	inf	h	informing	I	Inform	86
G2: mine's gonna be 79 G3: yeah	inf rec	h h	informing acknowledging	I R	Inform	87
G3: mine's gonna be about 29 only joking 85	inf com	h post-h	informing	I	Inform	88
G1: 87 {laughter} G2: 87 {laughter}	inf rea	h h	informing acknowledging	I R	Inform	89

from a Resistant Materials Technology lesson in which the class have been designing packaging for products made in lessons earlier in the term. The class have been asked to include specific information in their designs, including the price of the product, and this is what the group in Extract 4.7 are discussing. In this case, the group are working on individual designs and have not been instructed to produce one collaborative design in the group. They just happen to be discussing their work with each other as they are doing it, which the teacher generally permits in this kind of lesson. Extract 4.7 occurs a few minutes after the class have started to work on their tasks and involves a group of girls who are seated around the same table and have been engaged in discussion about their work since they started it.

On a denotative level, what is different about this group of girls' use of a sequence of Inform exchanges is that more of the exchanges contain an acknowledging move at R (and F) than is found in the boys' interactions. The acts which realise these acknowledging moves (*receive* and *react*) are positive evaluations of preceding moves. They either take the form of 'yeah' (exchange 87) or repetition of the whole or part of the preceding utterance (exchanges 84 and 89). Therefore, this series of exchanges involves not only a commentary on what progress each group member is making, but accompanying positive acknowledgements and endorsements of this progress from other group members. On a connotative level, this further contributes to the general tendency towards consensus and the collaborative talk discourse which emerges as characteristic of the girls' single-sex interactions. The continual acknowledgement of each other's utterances demonstrates high levels of mutual engagement and social cohesion within the group which we see to a much lesser extent in the boys' and mixed-sex groups. Again, if we add a more explicitly critical dimension to this analysis, we could say that the dominant discourses of femininity operating in this context consist of a set of practices which emphasise the values of social cohesion, equality, consensus and collaboration, and that the girls' systematic production of certain interactional practices reifies and re-produces this discourse. Although this discourse may be beneficial in the classroom context in terms of enabling the girls to complete the tasks more effectively, its value in professional domains has been questioned (see, for example Baxter, 2002a; Holmes, 1992; Holmes and Stubbe, 2003; Kendall, 2003 for discussions of gender and talk in the workplace). However, if girls are seen to challenge the dominant discourses of femininity in any way, as will be seen later in this chapter, there is a danger of being marginalised by the rest of the class. The same applies to the boys in their challenging of dominant discourses of masculinity. As we will see later, FPDA is well-suited to account for the interplay between dominant and non-dominant discourses.

Another key difference between the boys' and the girls' groups which emerged from the SFDA presented previously was the boys' comparatively high use of Direct exchanges. Again, whilst SFDA is useful for drawing out this systematic difference and showing how it contributes to the cumulative construction of a gender differentiation discourse, it falls short of being able to offer explanations about what exactly happens in those parts of the interaction where these kinds of exchanges take place. One example is included in Extract 4.8. This extract involves discussion between three boys in a Food Technology lesson. This is the same lesson, task (discussion of kitchen utensils and their uses) and group of boys as presented in Extract 4.4.

Extract 4.8

Dialogue	Act	E.S.	Move	E.S.	EXCH.	EX.
B2: draw it	dir	h	directing	I	Direct	97
draw the spatula	com	post-h				
B1: yeah you do	rej	h	behaving	R		
B3: draw the spatula	dir	h	directing	I	Direct	98
B2: I can't see it all the way over there	rej	h	behaving	R		
B3: look it's got	s	pre-h				
a hole in it	inf	h	informing	I	Inform	99
{laughter}						
B3: boys boys Alex look	s	pre-h				
it's got one there	inf	h	informing	I	Inform	100
B1: Alistair get on with it	dir	h	directing	I	Direct	101
B2: I can't draw	rej	h	behaving	R		
B3: Alex stop being rude	dir	h	directing	I	Direct	102

A denotative analysis shows that Extract 4.8 consists of a series of Direct exchanges with two Inform exchanges occurring in the middle of the extract. B2 starts by telling the group to 'draw the spatula', in exchange 97. Rather than other group members obeying this command, B1 then retaliates with 'yeah you do', suggesting that B2 himself should draw the spatula. B3 then tells B2 to draw it. B2 refuses by saying 'I can't see it all the way over there'. The talk then starts to drift off-task as the boys start playing with the utensils. B1 attempts to stop B2, the main culprit, from playing with the utensils and to turn his focus back to the task in hand by producing another directing move – 'Alistair get on with it'. Again, B2 (Alistair) rejects this directing move by saying 'I can't draw'. B3 then contributes another directive to B1 to 'stop being rude' (exchange 102). So this extract consists of a series of directing moves, none of which are followed or responded to positively by the other group members. Different speakers contribute different directing moves – no one group member contributes all of them, so the floor appears to be shared fairly equally.

A more critical, connotative analysis suggests that the boys enjoy giving directions to each other but not necessarily following them. I noticed that the same boys did not seem to have similar problems in following directives issued by any of the class teachers. The boys were also generally well-behaved, although they were not particularly high achievers. It seems then, that it is only in the peer group discussions that these boys seem to display resistance when someone else in the group tries to give orders to everyone else. This also happened in the mixed-sex groups – in fact, in the mixed-sex interaction, the boys resisted following the orders both of each other and of the girls (on the relatively rare occasions when the girls produced directing moves). In other words, the boys were seen to systematically reject the subject position of one who passively follows the orders of one of his peers. It is acceptable to follow the orders of the teacher perhaps because they are subjectively positioned as an authoritative figure in this context. But the peer relationship which characterises the group interaction is supposed to be between social equals. However, using CDA to incorporate our knowledge of the wider social context, social equality does not appear to be a part of the dominant discourses of masculinity operating in this context and this may, therefore, provide an explanation as to why struggles over status and hierarchy seem to emerge so strongly in the boys' interaction. For these boys, it is simply not socially acceptable to allow oneself to be positioned as passive and that may be why it is reflected in the discursive practice in which they systematically engage of simultaneously producing and resisting *directives*.

Having used FPDA, and aspects of CDA within the connotative level of analysis, to provide a more nuanced and detailed analysis of how discourses of gender differentiation and collaborative talk emerge through the classroom interaction, we can see how this approach is useful for providing concrete, contextualised examples to illustrate some of the claims made based on the statistical findings of the SFDA. However, as discussed in Chapter 3, it is important to remember that approaches such as FPDA (and, to a certain extent, CDA) can only really focus on what is present in the data. In the case of gender, it is important to also consider what may be absent from the discourse compared to what is present (or at least more visible and/or used more frequently) in the interaction of the groups of the opposite sex. For example, FPDA by itself may not be able to identify the boys' relatively low usage of *dictate-repeat* Inform exchanges, Structure exchanges and so on. It is only by comparison with the girls' discourse, in which these particular features are shown through the SFDA to be used more frequently, that we may begin to consider why the *absence* of such features in the boys' discourse may significantly contribute to the production of their gender as much as the features which are used with relative high frequency. Likewise, the girls' relatively low use of features such as Direct exchanges may contribute to the discursive construction of their gender just as much as the features which are used more frequently and are therefore highly visible in their interactions.

'Peer approval' discourses

Another key finding of Baxter's classroom study is the emergence of what is termed a 'peer approval discourse'. Drawing on previous work by Francis (1998), Baxter defines this discourse as denoting 'the ways in which students' relations with each other are organised and expressed in terms of notions of 'coolness', popularity, personal confidence, physical attractiveness and sexual reputation, friendship patterns, sporting prowess and so on' (Baxter 2003: 92). A similar peer approval discourse is identified in my data, even when the students are working in groups and their talk is not overheard by the whole class. As in Baxter's study, the peer approval discourse is often most notably produced by the 'popular' boys in each class and is based upon and constructed partially through the use of humour. What constitutes female popularity is actually quite different, and Baxter notes that the girls and boys in her study were not positioned on an equal basis in terms of the peer approval discourse. However, Baxter's study focused on whole-class, teacher-led interaction. It is notable, therefore, that a similar discourse emerged in my own study, which focused predominantly upon group interaction between students.

In my study, the emergence of a peer approval discourse in group discussion seemed slightly more complex than in Baxter's teacher–student interaction research. There seemed to be two oppositional discourses of masculinity operating in the classes I observed and recorded. One of these dominant discourses was primarily concerned with emphasising academic attainment and success. I refer to this as an 'academic achiever' discourse and it is closely aligned with the 'conservative masculinity' identified by Connell (1987, 1995) which contains characteristics such as intellectual, professional and financial success and is more closely associated with middle-class, rather than working-class, masculinities. The other dominant discourse identified in my data is one which appears to be concerned with devaluing academic achievement and gaining prestige through overtly rejecting the school system. This is more closely aligned with 'lad' masculinity (following Willis, 1977 and drawing on other work such as Epstein, 1998; Head, 1999; Mac an Ghaill, 1994) and the kind of 'hegemonic masculinity' defined and explored by Connell (1987, 1995). Both of these dominant discourses of masculinity are concerned with gaining power and status over others in the group. The 'academic achiever' does it by displaying his individual academic knowledge and competing with others' knowledge and intellectual ability. The 'lad' does it by explicitly displaying his *lack* of knowledge and emphasising instead other skills associated with hegemonic masculinity, such as physical strength, the ability to disrupt lessons and disturb the teacher, his ability to tell jokes and make fun of other class members. According to Willis (1977) and Connell (1995), 'lads' develop an explicitly oppositional masculinity which does not conform to the school's requirements and does not involve competition through academic work. None of the boys in the study were observed to perform 'academic achiever' and 'hegemonic' discourses of masculinity simultaneously, but they did shift between them within and across lessons. The acceptability of being able to shift between these discourses supports the FPDA principle that gender identities are fluid and negotiable.

Hegemonic masculinity discourses seem to function primarily as a means of boys gaining power and status when they do not have the means to do so through academic achievement. In the classes observed, hegemonic masculinity seemed to be valued more highly by the boys than the more conservative academic achiever masculinities. And the performance of hegemonic masculinity by the boys seemed to result in them gaining the highest amount of peer approval, both from other boys and also from the girls. The specific linguistic means through which the boys performed hegemonic masculinity included high levels of off-task talk and boasts about bad behaviour in their single-sex interaction but also in the mixed-sex groups. It also over-lapped with the emergence of a gender differentiation discourse dis-cussed in the previous section – the boys often used the same discursive resources (in SFDA terms) to create gender differentiation and to per-form hegemonic masculinity as a means of gaining peer approval. This included those discursive features discussed in the previous section (for example, the features which contributed towards a greater orientation towards competitiveness and individuality, higher degrees of conflict and disagreement, a relative lack of interactional coherence and less attention paid to the face needs of others in the group). There are many examples of boys constructing this peer approval discourse in the data, but I have chosen to cite two examples in which both gender and sexu-ality are explicitly evoked by the speakers. In the introductory chapter, I discussed examples in which young people explicitly talked about the interrelationship between gender and sexuality in relation to their expe-riences of school. But the SFDA in Chapter 3 was not able to account for this interrelationship in any way, whereas CDA and FPDA are bet-ter suited to being able to explore this important dimension of gender and schooling. From this point on, I will simply present the dialogue without the accompanying SFDA columns, as the rest of the analysis presented in this chapter is informed less by the SFDA and focuses more on the content of the talk and some elements of lexis and grammar.

In Extract 4.9, the boys are in a Textiles Technology lesson and they have been set the group task of making a collage of different kinds of fabric containers. In order to carry out this task, each group has been given a number of magazines and catalogues in which they can identify and cut out the images required to make their collage. Extract 4.9 occurs about five minutes into the activity.

Extract 4.9

1	Alistair:	she's got fat legs
2		she's too young to be a model got too much
3		make-up on
4	Alex:	that's you
5	(LAUGHTER)	
6	Tom:	what are they
7	Brendan:	let's have a look
(Teacher intervention – 30 seconds)		
8	Brendan:	she's fit
9		nice arse there

10	(LAUGHTER)	
11	Alistair:	oh I'm cutting that one out
12	(LAUGHTER)	
13	Brendan:	how about her
14		oy Alistair
15	Alex:	Alistair's looking through the catalogue for
16		his mom and dad
17	(LAUGHTER)	

In FPDA terms, the boys in this extract work to position themselves as both hegemonically masculine and unquestionably heterosexual. This is achieved through the objectification and derogation of women. According to Connell (1987,1995), this is an essential component of hegemonic masculinity. Speakers can only produce hegemonically masculine subjectivities if heterosexuality is a part of this. However, within a FPDA framework, it is important to remember that these subjectivities are always temporary, fluid and unstable. In fact, this extract sounds very much like the boys are putting on a performance of their sexuality in order to gain each other's approval. Their performance of heterosexuality almost sounds exaggerated. Examples such as these, in which such an exaggerated performance of sexuality seemed to be occurring, were rare in the data collected. When I observed this group of boys, for most of the time they did not engage in these kinds of exchanges. So when they do occur, they appear as very marked, especially as they explicitly evoke both gender and sexuality simultaneously.

From a CDA perspective, the heterosexual display exhibited by boys here is imbued with power. The over-lexicalisation of women's body parts functions to reduce the concept of 'woman' simply to her physical body and appearance. The use of evaluative language (fat legs, nice arse, got too much make-up on) is also reflective and constitutive of a dominant subject position in which boys somehow have the 'authority', and are 'legitimised', to say what women's bodies should and should not look like. The comments in which this kind of language occur are encoded grammatically as declaratives (*informatives* within the SFDA framework) – as assertions which are not hedged through any modality and, therefore, are presented as statements of fact. The boys in this extract, then, are temporarily engaged in the very explicit 'policing' of women's and girls' bodies. The whole extract is characterised as humorous. In Baxter's study, the peer approval discourse is also largely constructed through the boys' use of humour. Specifically in relation to sexuality, Kehily and Nayak (2006) have also observed how humour is used in the discursive construction of heterosexual display and homophobia in order to gain peer approval amongst boys. There was much laughter throughout Extract 4.9. Humour is created partly through Alex equating Alistair with one of the female models in the picture they are looking at ('that's you'). The evident juxtaposition of Alistair, who continually constructs himself, and is constructed by others, as hegemonically masculine, with a biological female creates such an impossible subject position that a high degree of humour is generated within the group just by this comment. But the comment also offers a possibility for resistance and challenge. Through producing this comment, Alex actually questions Alistair's status not just as a hegemonically masculine boy, but as a boy full-stop. Alistair is actually silenced following this comment, so perhaps the challenge to the identity he was trying to construct for himself was successful, at least temporarily. Following the laughter, the class teacher intervenes for 30 seconds in order to reprimand the group and try to get them back on-task. This is unsuccessful, as the boys immediately continue to discuss the women in the pictures (from line 8).

Importantly, what this extract also shows, in addition to being an example of a peer approval discourse, is how gender and power are dependent on heterosexuality. The heterosexual display that the boys are engaged in is, arguably, as important as the way 'women' are discursively constructed as powerless. In fact, the two are inextricably linked, as Ellis and Forrest (2000: 85) argue:

> ... heterosexuality has become the central resource of the capitalist, nationalist order as conservative visions of the heterosexual, 'nuclear' family as the basic building block of society imply. It provides the means for managing rights of succession and the transfer of capital and power, and the foundation for creating a belief in a natural national family.

In fact, the heterosexual nuclear family is also explicitly evoked at the end of this extract ('Alistair's looking through the catalogue for his mom and dad'). In this case, heterosexuality is not just performed through exaggerated performances of physical attraction; it is also constructed through evoking an idealised (two parents of opposite sex) heterosexual family unit. Thus, in this short extract, both a gender differentiation discourse (based around compulsory heterosexuality) and a peer approval discourse (produced through a humorous and exaggerated display of heterosexuality with the humour occurring at women's expense) are produced simultaneously.

In the next extract, gender is again explicitly evoked by the speakers. At this point during the discussion, the talk has drifted away from focusing upon the activity in hand to being 'off-task'. The boys are discussing who is the 'hardest' in the group. Being 'hard' is, in itself, a key component of the hegemonic masculinity operating in this context.

Extract 4.10

1	Lee:	Alistair's harder than you
2	Nick:	I've done all that
3	Lee:	I've done all that
4	Nick:	what you doing
5	Lee:	kicking your head in
6	John:	shut up you woman
7		everyone Lee's a woman
8	Nick:	yeah Lee's a woman
9	Lee:	pass us that rubber John
10	Nick:	look it's a $\neq$
11	Lee:	I dare you to scream to whistle down there
12	John:	no
13	Lee:	give me that rubber
14		give me Ahmed's rubber
15	John:	Lee is an idiot
16		you have to colour it in Sir said you idiot

[Gap of approximately two minutes]

17	Lee:	let's have a look at yours
18		give it here give it here and I'll give you that one one
19		each one
20		Ahmed what's you say
21	John:	Nick's a woman yeah

The first part of Extract 4.10 (lines 1–16) is a very obvious display and negotiation around hegemonic masculinity. The content of the conversation itself is focused on who is the 'hardest' member of the group. Being the 'hardest' is seen as one of the most effective means of gaining peer approval. In the previous chapter, the SFDA has already revealed the frequent use of *directives* by the boys in their single-sex interaction, along with the relative lack of interactional coherence produced cumulatively through the frequent use of single-move exchanges.

Both of these features are evidenced here. Incorporating a critical dimension, the systematic repetition of these discourse features produces a sense of competitiveness in the interaction and reinforces the ideology of boys as individualistic and competitive. The ideology of hegemonic masculinity also characterises boys as physically and verbally aggressive and we can see how this aspect is encoded and reinforced through some of the lexico-grammar used in this extract, for example, 'Alistair's <u>harder</u> than you', 'shut up' and 'kicking your head in'. A critical analysis would interpret this extract as the boys using language to reinforce the norms and values associated with hegemonic masculinity, and to re-assert hegemonic masculinity as dominant in this context. And it is the performance of this dominant form of masculinity which results in peer approval for the boys. This is achieved both through particular elements of the lexico-grammar and through the structure of the discourse itself (use of *directives* and so on).

Second, gender is constructed in hierarchical terms in this extract. The term 'woman' is clearly used as an insult implying that the concept 'woman' is not something which is valued highly by this particular group of speakers at the point at which this discussion is taking place. Lee is referred to firstly as a 'woman' and then as an 'idiot'. Hence the term 'woman' becomes associated with 'idiot'. Lee is positioned by the others as less powerful in this instance because he is aligned with femininity. And the very fact that the term 'woman' is being used in a derogatory way implies that women are devalued in terms of power, an insight which can only be gained by incorporating a critical dimension to the analysis and drawing on knowledge of the wider socio-political context in relation to gender. Kehily and Nayak (2006) have also commented on the 'expelling' of femininity from the self onto others amongst boys in their classroom talk. In their study, they found that verbal gaming rituals, similar to those observed in Extract 4.10, were used amongst boys as an important route for the performance of 'macho' masculine identities and the simultaneous subordination of other forms of masculinity. The term 'man' is not used in a parallel way by the girls in the study. Although the girls occasionally engaged in bickering with each other, they rarely engaged in any verbal insulting or name-calling. However, in some of the interviews with the young LGB-identified people, some of the girls discussed how the term 'lezza' (or similar terms) was used as an insult between girls, and directed at girls from boys. Because 'man' (or equivalent terms) is associated with power and status, this largely precludes them from being used as a term of abuse. However, an alternative strategy for girls to use is to draw on the hierarchies of femininity operating in the school context, in which heterosexual femininities are more highly valued than non-heterosexual ones. This is a point I shall return to in Chapter 5.

It is important to remember that FPDA would acknowledge that peer approval is only one discourse amongst a plurality of potential subject positions circulating in this school context. We should not assume that this same discourse is re-produced by all students in the class, or indeed in the school, nor that the specific students involved in this extract would necessarily produce this same discourse all the time. However, when FPDA is used alongside SFDA, what emerges is compelling evidence that certain discourses do dominate in this environment, and we can quantify this. Moreover, FPDA in conjunction with CDA reveals what happens when individuals produce forms of resistance to the dominant modes of gender identification. Again, because SFDA is able to quantify interactional patterns, this helps to validate the claims made by FPDA and CDA about particular discourses being dominant and others being marginalised, whilst retaining an acknowledgement that these discourses may be continually changing and under (re-) or (de-) construction.

Peer approval discourses among the girls did not appear to emerge as strongly as they did among the boys, especially in single-sex group interaction. Peer approval among the girls appeared to be based simply on their adherence to producing collaborative talk and consensus in their groups. They often gave explicit verbal approval to each other, especially concerning each other's academic work, through the frequent use of SFDA features such as informing and acknowledging moves giving a positive evaluation (most notably *confirm*, *concur*, *receive* and *react*). Unlike the boys, the girls did not appear at any point to seek peer approval through the use of heterosexual display, verbal play or humour (although laughter did occur in their group discussions). For the girls, it was more the case that peer approval was achieved through participation in collaborative talk.

Marginalised voices

As discussed earlier, FPDA also focuses on sequences of dialogue which do not fit the overall discursive patterns which dominate classroom interaction. FPDA differs from both SFDA and CDA in that it encourages us to focus on voices which appear to be marginalised or exceptional in some way. This is an important aspect of classroom interaction which would be missed if only applying SFDA. Interestingly, when any of the girls systematically use the same interactional features as the boys frequently do (which is relatively rare), the result is not peer approval but marginalisation. Thus, we can begin to see how the peer approval discourse overlaps with a discourse of gender differentiation. There were some students in the study who appeared to be marginalised by other class members, at least on some occasions. In SFDA terms, the way they interacted with other students often did not conform to the dominant patterns of interaction according to their gender. The SFDA itself does not necessarily reveal this, as it only focuses on the most visible and marked patterns of interaction. But it is important also to consider those individuals who produced interaction which seemed to differ from the general patterns and frequencies observed. This is another concern of FPDA. Baxter encourages a consideration of what may be termed 'marginalised voices', as these are often sites of resistance and challenge to dominant gender ideologies. It is, therefore, useful to consider in more detail exactly what these marginalised voices are contributing and how they are being received. In this study, four students seemed to stand out in terms of being perceived as 'different' in some way, according to the rest of their class. I refer to these individuals as Damian, Kim, Jeremy and Francis.

Damian

The main aspect of Damian's behaviour which I noted as being different from the rest of the boys was his willingness to voluntarily work in mixed-sex groups with girls. When given a choice, the rest of the boys (and girls) generally elected to work in single-sex groups. When Damian chose to work in a mixed-sex group, he was invariably the only boy. When Damian engaged in group discussion with the girls, it was the girls' characteristic ways of interacting (based on the frequencies revealed through the SFDA) which prevailed and did not seem to be altered in any way through the involvement of a boy in their group. Thus, Damian was evidently conforming to using discursive features in similar ways to the girls in their single-sex interactions. In fact, when I looked closely at the way that Damian interacted with boys, this was quite different from the way he interacted with the girls. He generally adopted the dominant interactional characteristics of either the boys or the girls, depending on which group he was in, and therefore demonstrated that he was able to draw on a wide range of interactional resources associated with the girls and boys in this class. On the occasions where the teacher made the class work in mixed-sex groups (of equal numbers of boys and girls), it was usually the boys' dominant mode of interaction which prevailed, meaning that the girls had to adapt to this or simply remain silent. Damian was the exception to this pattern of behaviour in that he seemed happy to accommodate the interactional norms more typically demonstrated by the girls.

On several occasions, Damian's gender and sexuality were brought into question by other boys in the class. Although there is no evidence showing a direct link between the way Damian interacts in mixed-sex groups and the boys' questioning of the acceptability of his masculinity, the rest of the boys were observed to frequently construct Damian as 'different' in terms of his gender and sexuality. One such instance is included in Extract 4.11. In this example, the students are not working on a group task. They are involved in a practical Textiles Technology lesson and are simply chatting with each other while they are working on a design task. During this general chat, Damian starts singing to himself.

Extract 4.11

1	Alistair:	who's singing like a girl
2	Alex:	Damian
3	[Gap of approximately 20 seconds]	
4	Ahmed:	I'm not
5		you are queer though
6	Damian:	I'm not
7		I'm not gay
8	Ahmed:	where's your boyfriend

Here, Damian is accused of 'singing like a girl' and is then labelled as 'queer' by Ahmed as a means of insulting him by constructing his gender identity as deviant and unmasculine. A connotative analysis suggests that the activity of 'singing', in this localised context, is one which appears to be associated with femininity. When I observed this interaction taking place, I heard Damian singing to himself as he was conducting the practical activity that had been set for the class by the teacher. In other words, his singing was not an explicit 'performance' for the benefit of others in the groups or the class. He was simply singing to himself, almost absent-mindedly. Therefore, Damian was not deliberately putting on a female voice or doing anything to explicitly mark out his activity as 'feminine', yet this is how it was perceived and discursively constructed by the other boys in his group. Damian is immediately labelled a 'girl' and Alistair's tone of voice when he produced this assertion strongly implied that this was not seen as a good thing by the rest of the group. Not only is Damian constructed as feminine, but his girl-like status is ascribed a low cultural value. It simply does not conform to the dominant values of hegemonic masculinity which seemed to be highly valued by the majority of the boys in the class. Thus, Damian is subjectively positioned as low status and marginal by the other boys in the group.

The subsequent labelling of Damian as 'queer' is consistent with Connell's (1995) argument that compulsory heterosexuality is inevitably tied up with hegemonic masculinity. Damian's gender is constructed as feminine, thus, not conforming to the principles of hegemonic masculinity operating within this context. As a result, his heterosexuality is brought into question. At no point during the research did Damian appear to reveal to any members of the class that he was actually gay. In fact, in Extract 4.11 he vehemently denies the accusation. Therefore, the other boys' labelling of him as queer does not appear to be based on any actual evidence of homosexual desires or practices. It simply arises from the perception of Damian as non-hegemonic in terms of his gender.

Another observation of Damian's linguistic behaviour which I found interesting was the fact that there appeared to be no direct link between Damian frequently choosing to work with the girls and accommodating to their dominant mode of interaction, and the labelling of him as 'queer' by the other boys in the class. But the labelling of him as 'queer' and 'gay' could partly be the cumulative effect of Damian's frequent interaction and collaboration with girls, which none of the other boys ever seemed to do. Previous studies (Davies, 2006; Duncan, 1999) suggest that boys, perhaps rather ironically, often prefer to distance themselves from girls as a means of constructing and consolidating their hegemonic masculinity (of which heterosexuality is a crucial component). But Damian chooses to align himself with girls, therefore constructs himself as a 'not-boy'. Through resisting the dominant ideologies of gender operating in this context, he constructs an almost impossible subject position for himself. His gender becomes 'unintelligible', a point which will be returned to in the next chapter. It is likely that Damian's apparent resistance, regardless of whether or not this is conscious or deliberate, is perceived as a threat to the values of hegemonic masculinity adhered to by the other boys. If Damian's gender were to be 'legitimised' in any way, the dominant ideologies of masculinity would begin to lose their power. In CDA terms, the dominant hierarchies and ideologies of gender must be maintained in order for existing power relations between the boys and girls to be upheld. Any practices culturally associated with femininity must continually be devalued, and any boy adopting those values must be 'punished' by being marginalised in order to maintain the status quo. Importantly, what Damian's behaviour shows is that ideologies are inherently unstable. The very fact that Damian is seen as a threat highlights how unstable those ideologies actually are. I will discuss this in greater detail in Chapter 5, where I argue that incorporating elements of queer theory into the analysis can offer further insights into the discursive processes at work.

Kim

Kim is another individual (in the same class as Damian) who was perceived as different by the rest of the class. Kim was one of the lowest achievers in the class and was frequently in trouble for misbehaviour. Although she seemed to have a good relationship with the other students, and participated in single-sex group discussions when the class were asked to do so, she also often chose to work alone for much of the time. On several occasions, I observed her choosing to physically separate herself from other class members, and work in a quiet corner of the classroom, as long as the teacher permitted this. In Extract 4.12, Kim is engaged in conversation with John. John is one of the dominant boys in the class, and frequently exhibits many of the key characteristics of hegemonic masculinity. In this extract, Kim and John are not working on a group task – they are simply chatting as they are getting on with their work which, in this case, involves designing a product in a Textiles Technology lesson. In this extract, both Kim and John are discussing instances where they have been 'put on report' for bad behaviour.

Extract 4.12

1	John:	what was you put on report in the first place for
2	Kim:	truanting
3	John:	that's what I was put on report for
4		I went truanting
5		I was on report for about a whole term right and em
6		Lee Barman Lee Barman was on report for two weeks
7	Kim:	what did Michael do to get on report
8	John:	just just
9	Kim:	he got put on report and the next day he was taken off
10		it

In this extract, John almost seems to be boasting about being on report. In fact, this seems to contribute to his position as one of the most dominant boys in his class. Throughout this conversation, he seemed to be impressed that Kim had been put on report, even though, as a girl, this is not perceived or constructed as the kind of behavior which results in being seen as a high status girl in this context. Later in this same conversation, John explicitly states that Kim is 'one of the naughtiest girls in Year 8'. Interestingly, Kim challenges this assertion.

Extract 4.13

1	John:	you're one of the naughtiest girls in Year 8 ain't you
2	Kim:	who
3	John:	you
4		why do you be naughty
5	Kim:	I'm not that naughty
6	John:	how many detentions have you had
7	Kim:	twenty-one
8	John:	twenty-one?
9		remember last year when Mr. Saunders came down to
10		our classroom
11	Kim:	someone fainted in our class the other day

In Extract 4.13, Kim tries to downplay how 'naughty' she is. In line 11, she initiates a topic change, perhaps as a means of diverting the conversation away from the discussion about her behaviour. During the conversation, I observed that Kim seemed to become increasingly uncomfortable about talking with John about her poor behaviour. In this extract, Kim's behaviour is perceived as different from that of the other girls in the class. John explicitly asks 'you're one of the naughtiest girls' and not 'you're one of the naughtiest people' as if the kind of behaviour Kim frequently engages in is not expected of girls but is expected of boys. In the student interviews, Kim and another girl in the same class – Elizabeth – were both referred to as being 'one of the lads'. They were constructed as being different from the rest of the girls in the class by their association with the boys more than the girls. It may be that the girls perform a marginalised gender at the cost of losing their connection with other girls in the class. By performing gender in a non-dominant way, these girls risk not being accepted by other girls because they do not perform a dominant feminine discourse, and risk not being accepted by the boys because they are performing a dominant masculine discourse with a female body. This, in itself, is inconsistent with the dominant gender ideologies about sex and gender operating in this classroom context. The boys may see this as a threat to their social status. Kim may, therefore, choose not to perform a more marginalised gender with the other girls so that she does not lose them as friends.

As with Damian, the very fact that Kim's behaviour is discursively constructed as deviant suggests that the dominant ideologies of gender operating in this context are unstable and in constant need of re-iteration and re-construction in order to maintain their status and legitimacy, a principle upheld by CDA. Kim's non-hegemonic behaviour, as with Damian's, is perceived as a threat, otherwise it would not be interrogated in the way that it is by other students. What is clear from this critical analysis of Kim's subjectivity, and that of Damian discussed above, is that all participants in these classroom settings are complicit in maintaining existing gender relations and ideologies. The participants are not passive recipients of those ideologies, but they actively re-produce them through performing and policing gendered behaviours. Although Kim and Damian may be seen to be resisting those ideologies, and constructing alternative subject positions for themselves, the consequences of doing this are evidently risky. Ultimately, both Kim and Damian try to deny that they are 'different' and resist the positioning of them by the rest of the class as marginal. Hence, Kim tries to deny that she is 'one of the naughtiest girls in Year 8' and Damian denies that he is gay. The immense pressure to conform to dominant gender ideologies is overwhelmingly evident in this respect. Both FPDA and CDA offer us ways of seeing different subject positions around emergent gender identities being discursively constructed. Both approaches can show how individuals shift between subject positions that are accorded different degrees of power by socio-cultural factors such as gender and sexuality (and race, ethnicity and so on) and other competing discourses such as peer approval. The analyses suggest that individuals have some degree of agency but this can vary considerably according to how powerfully positioned they are overall across the discourses circulating within the classroom context. Whilst FPDA is potentially liberating in that it does not restrict the potential discursive constructions of gender which may be produced in any given situation, CDA more explicitly draws our attention to how those different possible constructions are actually highly constrained. And they are constrained by the participants themselves, as well as through mechanisms which may be operating in the wider social context beyond the immediate school environment. In order to illustrate these arguments further, I turn to two more students who were habitually constructed as 'different' by their peers.

Jeremy and Francis

Jeremy and Francis were observed to behave differently from the rest of the boys in the class. This was also perceived by the other students in the class. However, the ways in which they were constructed as marginal were quite different from Damian or Kim. Jeremy and Francis appeared to be close friends and usually chose to work together whenever they had a choice. Furthermore, they frequently separated themselves from the rest of the class and chose to work as a pair on their own during lessons, rather than joining a larger group. They often moved to the edge of the classroom to work. They are both high academic achievers (relative to the rest of the class) and are generally well-behaved. Both boys were tolerated as academic achievers by the more 'hegemonically masculine' boys in the class, as long as they did not attempt to interact or associate themselves too much with them. Francis, however, seemed to be tolerated more when he was not with Jeremy. This may be because he is often involved in activities which are seen as characteristic of hegemonic masculinity outside the classroom, such as football. Thus, his gender appeared to emerge differently in different contexts. The use of FPDA enables us to arrive at this explanation precisely because it allows for the fluidity of gender and acknowledges that gender is always emergent and contingent. This important aspect of Francis's emergent and dynamic gender identification is not something which could be captured through SFDA alone. Therefore, elements of CDA and FPDA are necessary for providing a fuller picture of the complex ways in which gender emerges through the interactions which take place. The interplay between subject positions is an issue I will return to in the next section.

In denotative SFDA terms, the other boys in the class often directed information-seeking eliciting moves towards Jeremy or Francis even if they were not working in their group. In Extract 4.14, Jeremy is constructed as an 'academic achiever' by the other boys ('you should be asking Jeremy'). Jeremy, however, attempts in lines 8 and 10 to downplay this 'high achiever' status which has been ascribed to him.

Extract 4.14

1	Alistair:	how do you spell wallet
2	Jamie:	wall-et
3	Bradley:	you should be asking Jeremy
4		trainers how do you spell trainers
5	Jamie:	spell wallet
6	Alistair:	wallet

7		you know how to spell wallet don't you
8	Jeremy:	no
9	Alistair:	he does
10	Jeremy:	no I don't

Extract 4.15 also shows the boys directing their questions towards Jeremy and Francis as a means of gaining the required information to complete the task in hand.

Extract 4.15

1	Lee:	Jeremy
2		what's two twenty-eights
3	Jeremy:	two twenty-eights is fifty-six
4	Bradley:	do you want to know what two twenty-eights
5		are
6	Jeremy:	fifty-six
7	Ahmed:	two twenty-eights
8	Jeremy:	two twenty-eights are fifty-six

[Gap of approximately 2 minutes]

9	Lee:	Jeremy Francis
10		what's twenty-five divided by three
11	Francis:	eight point one
12	Lee:	eight point one?
13	Francis:	yeah

Jeremy in particular does not feature much at all in the interaction when he is not providing the information required by the other boys in the group. It is as though he is only permitted to interact with the group because he can provide the group with the answers or information they need to complete the task. Boy academic achievers such as Jeremy are tolerated as long as they have a purpose in the boys' interaction and as long as their social status is lower than that of the other (hegemonically masculine) boys in the group. What these FPDA analyses of Damian, Kim, Jeremy and Francis all show is that both the girls and the boys can perform marginal or resistant gender discourses in this classroom, but they do so at great social risk. In performing a gendered identity which emerges as resistant to dominant ideologies, they are often excluded from interactions with other students who more consistently perform their gender in ways which conform to the dominant gender discourses circulating in the context under scrutiny. Thus, whilst the FPDA highlights the subject's agency, the incorporation of a CDA perspective, importantly, draws attention to the wider social structures which constrain the choices and possibilities available concerning the production and performance of gender.

Interplay between subject positions

As discussed earlier, one of the principles of FPDA is that gender identities are emergent, fluid and multiple. The gendered subject positions which discursively emerge through spoken interaction can, therefore, change across lessons or even during the course of an interaction within the same lesson. But the close attention paid to contextualised and localised examples of interaction which typifies FPDA is well-suited to examining gender from this perspective. I have already discussed above how Francis's gender identity emerged differently depending on the context he was in, and how his gender therefore emerged as dynamic rather than stable. Of course, the example of Francis is not an isolated one. According to FPDA, the gender identities of all participants are always fluid and constantly under construction. However, in Francis's case, the fluidity of his gender was particularly marked. I now turn to two more examples where this interplay between different gendered subject positions was marked more explicitly than at other times during the interactions. Moreover, in these examples, it is not simply that the gender identity of the speaker in question shifts during the course of the interaction, but instead multiple identities seem to emerge simultaneously. And what emerges is not simply an interplay between subject positions which have equal currency in this particular classroom context, but an interplay between positions which are discursively constructed as powerful and powerless. This is an important aspect of any sort of post-structural analysis. According to Walkerdine (1990: 3), for example, girls (and arguably boys) are 'produced as a nexus of subjectivities, in relations of power which are constantly shifting, rendering them at one moment powerful and at another powerless'. Thus, the connotative FPDA analysis presented after each extract contains much overlap with a critical discourse analysis in that it focuses more explicitly on the interrelationship and interplay between gender and power relations in the interaction. In Extract 4.16, I argue that one of the girls, Jane, is simultaneously constructed as powerful and powerless within a short stretch of interaction with one of the boys in the class. This example is taken from a Food Technology lesson in which the students are required to produce a list of safety rules for working in a kitchen.

Extract 4.16

```
1     Bradley: you know this you know this
2              do you have to copy it out
3              you know this
4              do you have to write out write out all that Jane and
5              match them up
6     Jane:   yeah do that
[Gap of approximately 30 seconds]
7     Bradley: Jane after the first one would you put that by it
8              make sure all knives are clean
9     Jane:   em make sure all ingredients and all materials are
10             all within the use by date
```

In this example, Jane is positioned by Bradley as knowledgeable because he is asking her for instructions and answers. She is almost being positioned as the 'teacher'. The teacher subject position is authoritative and knowledgeable and therefore can, at least potentially, be seen as one which holds power in a situation such as this one where having the requisite knowledge to be able to complete a task successfully is valued. Jane picks up this subject position with no evident resistance – she immediately supplies the expected responses to Bradley's requests for information. In this sense, Jane is simultaneously being constructed as relatively powerless. Bradley is the one who initiates the exchanges, controls the topic of conversation, and places Jane is a position in which she is required to supply the information that he wants. Of course, Jane could refuse to do so, but this might have resulted in an altercation. Jane simply supplies the information which has been demanded of her. A similar example is included in Extract 4.17. In this short exchange, different speakers are involved but essentially the same thing happens.

Extract 4.17

```
1     Nick:   Lucy Lucy
2              what are we meant to do again
3     Lucy:   put design ideas on there
4     Nick:   for that?
5     Lucy:   yeah
```

Here, Lucy is, like Jane, positioned as powerful because she is being asked for some sort of instruction and knowledge. She is constructed by Nick as having the knowledge that he requires, which temporarily places her in a powerful subject position over him. However, the same act simultaneously positions Lucy as relatively powerless in relation to Nick because the discourse structure places her in a position where she is obliged to provide the required response without sounding confrontational. These kinds of examples are interspersed throughout the girls' single-sex interaction as well as in the mixed-sex discussions. However, a difference which emerges when looking at the SFDA is that all of the girls involved do both the asking and the being asked. The exchange initiations are not dominated predominantly by one speaker, as they tend to be in the mixed-sex interaction. In the mixed-sex interaction, I noticed that it was only the boys who asked the girls for instructions and answers. The girls did not ask the boys – they only supplied them with the answers. And the boys tended not to ask each other. The only exceptions I observed were when the boys asked Jeremy and Francis, as discussed above. In these instances, Jeremy and Francis were, like the girls, simultaneously positioned as powerful and powerless. From a CDA perspective, knowledge is often 'commodified' in the classroom as it holds power in this context (Foucault explicitly equates knowledge with power in a general sense, but this relationship is particularly salient in educational contexts). Jeremy and Francis were positioned as powerful in that they held 'knowledge' as a valuable commodity. But they simultaneously were placed in positions in which they were obliged to 'hand over' this commodity when required by others. Moreover, Connell (1995) argues that possessing knowledge and intellectual ability is a component of 'conservative masculinity' rather than 'hegemonic masculinity'. Conservative masculinity may be a powerful gender discourse in certain contexts, but in the school context studied here it is hegemonic forms of masculinity which seem to emerge as the most highly valued. Thus, Jeremy and Francis are constructed as relatively powerless in that their conservative masculinity is not as highly valued as hegemonic masculinity. However, it is important to remember that hegemonic forms of masculinity are not necessarily static and stable. A combination of FPDA and CDA seems useful, then, in terms of accounting for how powerful ideologies emerge and are perpetuated in the classroom, but also how those ideologies are unstable and may be contested. Whilst FPDA provides a framework which enables the explicit acknowledgement and analysis of the interplay between multiple gendered subject positions, CDA is more careful to focus on how those subject positions may be constrained.

Summary

As in Baxter's FPDA study of teacher-led interaction in English class-rooms, my own application of a combination of FPDA and CDA to student group discussions has also revealed discourses of gender differentiation, collaborative talk and peer approval. But my own analyses using these qualitative approaches are additionally supported through the use of quantitative SFDA at the level of descriptive (CDA) or denotative (FPDA) analysis. What the SFDA provides is quantitative support to show that these discourses are *systematically* and *repeatedly* produced in the interactional data. Furthermore, the very emergence of the SFDA patterns around gender strongly suggests that the subjects in the study do not have complete agency and control over the way they choose to perform their gender. This, in turn, necessitates some kind of critical analysis of the wider prevailing power structures operating in the context under scrutiny which function to limit and constrain individual agency. Therefore, the use of CDA alongside FPDA also emphasises, importantly, how the emergent gender discourses entail a power dimension which functions mainly to perpetuate existing gender and sexuality relations and structures. And this critical dimension offers an explanation as to why the SFDA patterns and structures emerge so strongly. However, the use of FPDA simultaneously shows how multiple gender discourses can emerge, and that there can be interplay between them, which illustrates the important point that gendered discourses, no matter how much they seem to reify existing power structures, are open to contestation.

FPDA and CDA, then, offer alternative accounts of the data at the interpretation and explanation levels of CDA, and at the connotative level of FPDA. Rather than simply trying to evaluate which interpretation has the most validity, I argue that we should simply value the fact that these two similar approaches to discourse analysis, when used in conjunction with one another, can offer a more insightful analysis than when each is used on its own. A key limitation of both approaches, as discussed in Chapter 2, is that they often rely on isolated instances and are not able to quantify the claims made about selected examples. What I have tried to show in this chapter is that SFDA can be used *within* CDA and FPDA frameworks (at the level of description in CDA and in the denotative analysis in FPDA) in order to provide this quantification and to show how the gendered discourses which CDA and FPDA claim emerge in the interactional data actually do so systematically.

Another limitation of both CDA and FPDA is that, although both are informed by aspects of critical and feminist theories, relatively little attention is paid in either approach to the apparent interrelationship between gender and sexuality. As we have seen from some of the examples in this chapter, when participants explicitly evoke gender in their discussions, they often simultaneously evoke sexuality. This happens particularly around the boys' peer approval discourses and in the marginalised gender discourses that are produced by both the girls and boys. In discussing these examples using CDA and FPDA, I have already begun to critically interrogate the relationship between gender and sexuality. However, I found that the theories underpinning CDA and FPDA were rather limited in terms of the insights they could offer to explain this rather special relationship. Why is it that gender and sexuality seem so intricately tied together? In order to answer this question, and a range of other issues concerning language, gender and sexuality, I found that I had to turn to the contributions of queer theory, and it is this approach that I discuss in the next chapter.

5
Beyond Identity: Queer Theory

Having considered how innovative combinations of SFDA, FPDA and CDA can offer more fruitful analyses than adopting a single approach, this final analysis chapter considers the further incorporation of perspectives which highlight the political significance of what the previous analyses reveal. The analyses presented and discussed in Chapter 4 show how CDA and FPDA can offer differing interpretations of the same data (although there are similarities in the interpretations offered by each approach as well), but those interpretations are not necessarily incompatible. In this chapter, I argue that incorporating elements of queer theory can further our understanding of how ideologies of gender and sexuality are constructed, negotiated, maintained and challenged by the students in their spoken interaction. In doing so, I draw on previous work which has explored the uses of queer theory in analysing gender, sexuality and language (Bucholtz and Hall, 2004; Leap, 2008; Morrish and Sauntson, 2007; Sauntson, 2008). Queer theory is helpful for achieving this because it takes 'normality' itself as its main object of investigation. Rather than presenting gender as an *a priori* category – as something which is already there waiting to be 'discovered' – queer theory interrogates the underlying preconditions of gender identity, and how these may be enacted and formulated in discourse. This principle led to the development of queer linguistics. Hall (2003: 366) defines 'queer linguistics' as 'a field that explicitly questions the assumption that gendered ways of talking are indexically derived from the sex of the speaker'. It is primarily concerned with how heterosexual normativity is discursively (re)produced and sometimes resisted through specific linguistic practices. In this way, queer linguistics is premised upon some (but not all) similar principles to FPDA but it also seems to sit quite comfortably alongside CDA with its political and emancipatory agenda. However, it may not sit so comfortably alongside SFDA and indeed

166

the relatively apolitical principle of FPDA, which, although revealing in terms of the discursive construction of gender, does not espouse a particular political agenda from the outset. Through the detailed analysis of data extracts, this chapter will explore such tensions and possibilities for complementarity.

Within queer theory, Butler's (1990, 1993, 1997, 2004) theories of performativity are of crucial importance for enabling us to question socially sanctioned concepts of normality in relation to gender and sexuality. This chapter considers how notions of 'normal' and 'abnormal/marginal' genders are negotiated and constructed in both the classroom interaction and interview data, and how students and teachers define and police the boundaries of gender normality. Queer theory presents a unified view of gender and sexuality in that it recognises that cultural ideologies of gender normativity are bound up with assumptions of heterosexuality. This is a key tenet of queer theory which distinguishes it from the other approaches used throughout the book. We started to see this in some of the examples discussed in Chapter 4 and in the conversations with LGB-identified young people discussed in the introductory chapter. In this chapter, I argue and illustrate how the methods of analysis used throughout the book can be used alongside queer theory to critically examine the discursive constructions of 'normal' and 'queer' gender and sexuality in the classroom settings under scrutiny. I show how incorporating some of the principles of queer theory into the types of analyses already used can help to uncover the ways in which heterosexuality is naturalised and how other forms of sexual and gender identity are 'queered' in classroom interaction. Again, using aspects of queer theory in conjunction with the analytical frameworks of SFDA, FPDA and CDA is not straightforward and carries with it a set of tensions and contradictions which are sometimes difficult to resolve. I explored some of these tensions and contradictions in Chapter 2, and attempted to offer some ways of potentially resolving them. In this chapter, some of these ideas will be tested out in the data analysis. I argue that confronting such analytic and methodological tensions is more fruitful than ignoring them, and acts as a means of moving the field of gender and language research forward, in terms both of its theory and methodology. Indeed, some recent work in gender and language has utilised aspects of queer theory selectively in conjunction with more overtly feminist approaches to develop more practical and concrete systems of discourse analysis (for example, Bucholtz and Hall, 2004).

Throughout the chapter, I will discuss ideas and examples in which the related concepts of 'homophobia' and 'heterosexism' frequently emerge. For this reason, it is perhaps useful to provide explanations of what these terms mean. I take the following definitions from the *No Outsiders* group, a team of practitioners and researchers who have conducted extensive action research into homophobia and heterosexism in UK primary schools. These are not the only possible ways of defining homophobia and heterosexism, but they encapsulate the key issues involved:

> Homophobia/biphobia/transphobia: these terms refer both to outright expressions of prejudice, dislike or distaste towards lesbian, gay, bisexual, trans and gender variant people and also to the silencing or ignoring by individuals and institutions of these people's identities or existence. Like institutional racism, institutional homophobia, biphobia and transphobia operate in schools as ways of marginalising non-heterosexual and non-gender normative identities. (*No Outsiders*, 2010: xiii)

> Heterosexism: the way in which heterosexuality is assumed to be the only normal form, and therefore the superior form, of sexuality, and the presumption that everyone is heterosexual unless otherwise stated. (*No Outsiders*, 2010: xiii)

Homophobia and heterosexism are related in that they are mutually perpetuating. In the *No Outsiders* project, the researchers found that both of these related processes were pervasive in UK primary schools but, significantly, that it was possible to begin to challenge and deconstruct them through planned interventions. In the present study which focuses on the secondary school context, I use queer theory to explore whether similar or different findings emerge through the linguistic analysis of classroom interaction and interview data. In the rest of this chapter, I will firstly explain some principles of queer theory, with a particular focus on Butler's work on the interrelationship between gender and sexuality. I will then outline some previous work that has been carried out on sexuality and schooling, and in the area of language and sexuality. In the latter sections, I will consider how elements of queer theory may be firstly applied to some of the interview data, and then to the classroom interaction data.

What is queer theory?

The term 'queer' became popularised in the 1990s but its meanings remain quite diverse. It can be used simply as a shorthand term for 'lesbian and gay' and has historically been used in certain contexts as a term of abuse directed towards those who identify as non-heterosexual. Intellectually, it refers to that which interrogates identity and resists binary categorisation. Queer theory has been influenced by the work of Butler (1990, 1997, 2004), Fuss (1991), Sedgwick (1990), Foucault (1972, 1990) and Althusser (1971). Although purportedly not restricted to the domain of sexuality and gender, a key line of development of queer theories can be traced back to the homophile,[1] feminist, and lesbian and gay liberation movements of the 1950s, 1960s and 1970s. Jagose (1996) describes how homophile movements were generally characterised by being conservative and integrationist, whilst gay liberation movements were seen as more radical with their agenda of challenging and overturning existing social relations and institutions. Although queer theory shares some characteristics with gay liberation, it also partly arose out of a critique that gay liberation still espoused a commitment to some kind of 'natural' or essential sexual identity, one which could only be understood in terms of power and oppression.

Feminism, particularly lesbian feminism, has been influential in revealing how oppressions surrounding sexuality are intricately tied to oppressions surrounding gender. Rich (1993), for example, explores how practices which function to naturalise heterosexuality and pathologise lesbianism simultaneously function to privilege heterosexual masculinity. She describes heterosexuality as 'a political institution which disempowers women' (1993: 227) and proposes challenging and denaturalising heterosexuality by arguing that it is more 'natural' for women to align themselves with other women and for men with other men. Wittig (1993) also proposes that the categories of gender ('women' and 'men') are political categories which are complicit in the maintenance of heterosexuality. But, unlike Rich, Wittig places lesbianism outside the categories of gender by arguing that 'the refusal to become (or to remain) heterosexual always meant to refuse to become a man or a woman' (1993: 105). Thus, to refuse heterosexuality is the most direct way to refuse male economic, ideological and political power. However, both authors share a commitment to challenging and destabilising what Rich terms 'compulsory heterosexuality' and it is this aspect of lesbian feminism which has informed queer theory. Butler (1990), for example, develops this notion in her claim that heterosexuality is naturalised by the performative repetition of normative gender identities. We have already seen this performative repetition taking place through the kinds of language systematically used by the students in this study. And we have seen how students' identities are immediately interrogated and marginalised if they do not conform to those dominant modes of repetition.

However, queer theories differentiate themselves from gay liberationist and (lesbian) feminist models by resisting their commitment to notions of a coherent lesbian or gay subject and community. Jagose (1996) notes that the non-specificity of 'queer' protects it from criticisms made of the exclusionary and essentialising tendencies of referring to identity categories such as 'lesbian' and 'gay'. But, as discussed earlier in this book, and as seen in much work on gender and language which purports to be adopting any sort of 'post-structural' approach, this shift away from 'identity' can be problematic in terms of conducting concrete analyses of gender and language. Even when gender (also sexuality) is not conceptualised as an *a priori* category, the very fact that already-established gender categories are evoked in the analysis (masculinity and femininity) functions to re-instate those forms of identity which are associated with gender without actually questioning where they come from or why they are being evoked in the first place. Despite its resistance to using pre-discursive identity categories, I argue that queer theory is actually better placed to explain how those identity categories come to have such salience and are difficult to challenge not just socially but in analyses of linguistic interaction. I explore this aspect of queer theory in more detail in the next section.

Gender and sexuality: 'knots that must be undone'

Butler suggests that the categories of gender and sexuality have been 'causally entangled in knots that must be undone' (1998: 225–6) and readings of queer theory often reveal apparently contradictory positions regarding gender and sexuality. On the one hand, gender and sexuality cannot be separated, yet on the other, it is sometimes necessary to separate them in academic enquiry. This point is supported in other works within queer theory (Sedgwick, 1990) and linguistics (Cameron and Kulick, 2003). A point noted by Butler (1998), Sedgwick (1990) and Rubin (1984) is a peculiarity of the relationship between gender and sexuality, as opposed to gender and any other social variable. Rubin (1984) has claimed that although sexuality and gender studies have historically constituted different avenues of enquiry, they frequently overlap and influence each other, lending them a unique relationship. In a development of Rubin's position, Sedgwick argues that although there is potential to create some 'analytic distance' between gender and sexuality, they are inextricable in that one can only be expressed in terms of the other. On a fundamental level, one can identify and construct oneself as a lesbian by expressing sexual desire for and/or identification with other women, where 'women' is socially understood as a gender category or as a biological sex category. One does not say, for example, that one is 'white' or 'working class' because one desires or identifies with women. Gender is not an integral resource in the enactment of other forms of social identity in the way that it is in the enactment of sexual identity. Work by Cameron (1997), Coates (2007), Leap (1996), Morrish and Sauntson (2007, 2010) and others has shown that the semiotic resources associated with gender categories are deployed as a means of constructing sexual identities in and through discourse. Such work suggests that there is a clear relationship between gender and sexuality, that the two are not experienced separately, and cannot be separated for the purpose of analysis. McElhinny (2003) argues that the very idea of two genders is conflated with a presumption of heterosexuality. These arguments can be applied specifically to the school context. Epstein (1994) has argued that schools are particularly highly marked in terms of them functioning as sites for the reproduction of normative gender and its associated heterosexuality. She states that 'schools provide a site for practising heterosexuality within the context of developing conventional gender roles' (Epstein, 1994: 5). Drawing on earlier work by Thorne (1993), Eckert (1996) has also commented that secondary schools are particularly marked sites for the production of heterosexual identities (more so than primary schools, which are normatively asexual). According to Eckert, the transition into a heterosexual social order in secondary school brings boys and girls into an engagement in gender differentiation and encourages boys and girls to view themselves as 'commodities' in a heterosexual market. Thus, schools are places where students not only learn what is prescribed by subject curricula, but they learn the norms and rules associated with dominant ideologies of gender and sexuality in order to commodify themselves in a predominantly heterosexual marketplace.

Of course, it is important to be wary of over-simplifying the relationship between gender and sexuality and of uncritically conflating the two terms. We should take heed of Cameron and Kulick's (2003: 53) useful summation that 'Sexuality and gender may be interdependent, but they are not reducible to one another.' However, it seems clear that the study of gender and language would undoubtedly benefit from investigating the 'knots that must be undone' in terms of gender and sexuality. Linguistically based work which explicitly examines sexuality alongside gender has suggested that sexuality is produced in relation to particular material conditions and relations of power and has revealed some of the ways in which people deploy the semiotic resources culturally associated with gender to perform sexual identity in discourse. Moreover, people frequently draw on ideologies of gender essentialism to understand and construct sexual identities for themselves and others. For example, Morrish and Sauntson's (2007) analysis of 'coming out' narratives reveals that references to gender are commonly deployed in such texts as a means of enabling the narrators to organise and understand sexual identities. Both queer theory and queer linguistics are, therefore, careful to point out that what Spivak terms 'strategic essentialism' (cited in Landry and MacLean, 1996: 204–5) is sometimes a useful organising concept for social actors in their processes of identity construction (see also Bing and Bergvall, 1998).

In Butler's more recent work, she is careful to highlight notions of constraint rather than claiming gender can be simply performed at will (a common misreading of Butler's work). Whilst retaining a commitment to queer notions of performativity, Butler defines sexuality as 'an improvisational possibility within a field of constraints' (2004: 15) and argues that both gender and sexuality are mobilised and incited by social constraints as well as extinguished by them. These constraints often come from essentialised social ideologies of gender and sexuality. Butler also notes that performative accomplishments of hierarchised genders are also often compelled by social sanction and taboo. The result of this hierarchisation is that idealised or hegemonic masculinities and femininities stereotypically associated with heterosexuality are ranked higher than the marginalised genders typically associated with homosexuality. Drawing on the work of Connell (1995) and Kiesling (2002) as well as Butler, Coates (2003, 2007) notes that heterosexuality is an integral identifying component of the most powerful genders – 'hegemonic' masculinity and femininity – in society. Moreover, powerful ideological mechanisms for linking gender to biological sex are crucial for maintaining hierarchies of gender. When performances of gender are enacted in the social world, those very performances become subject to interactional practices which place the performance within a gender hierarchy that is constantly under construction.

A corollory of the arguments above is that hierarchies of gender are produced by heterosexuality and challenged by homosexuality and certain forms of 'non-normative' heterosexual practice. Halberstam's work on female masculinity (1998), for example, is important for revealing how masculinity, as a gender category, is not just the domain of men, but can also be performed by women, sometimes more effectively. Furthermore, she claims, it is often women who 'police' the boundaries and properties of what constitute acceptable forms of masculinity in society. Connell (1995) also makes the point that it is entirely possible to talk about masculinity in relation to women's lives as well as those of men.

Specifically in relation to school environments, we can examine how hegemonic masculinity and compulsory heterosexuality come into play in a range of contexts and processes involved in schooling, including classroom interaction. Dominant ideologies about gender embody the notion that, for a feminine or masculine gender to be considered 'normal' and socially acceptable, the gender performance must conform to the unwritten rules and norms of heterosexuality. Mac an Ghaill (1994) has observed how male students at school frequently perform their masculinities not only through the overt subordination of female students, but also through the homophobic bullying of other male students who are not seen to be performing their masculinities in the same way as the majority of male students who consider themselves to be the dominant group. He also observes how allegedly 'gay' behaviour among boys is frequently associated with femininity in order to traduce the former. Skelton (1997), in an examination of the relationships between 7 to 11-year-old boys, also explores the ways in which anti-homosexual behaviour and harassment features heavily in the way the boys in the study enforced a culture of hegemonic masculinity at school. Skelton observes that the dominant form of masculinity in school is that of the 'hard man' and the performance of this dominant kind of masculine gender involves demonstrating sexual power over female students and the constant affirmation of heterosexuality.

We can already see from this empirical work that performances of gender are inextricably tied to sexuality. This research is particularly important in the current environment in which the problematic issue of homophobia in British schools is starting to receive much more critical and political attention. There is an increasing awareness that issues around homophobia, and sexual diversity more broadly, can only be fully addressed in conjunction with a critical interrogation of gender. Conversely, many of the issues around gender which continue to pervade the school environment can only be addressed alongside a consideration of the way sexual diversity is dealt with in the school context. I now turn to examine some recent work in education which has taken sexuality, rather than gender, as its starting point.

Studies of sexuality and schooling

Over the past few years, a small but growing body of research has emerged which has examined the circulation of sexuality discourses in the school environment (Atkinson *et al.*, 2009; DePalma and Atkinson, 2009; Duncan, 1999; Epstein, 1994; Epstein and Johnson, 1998). As it is sexuality, rather than gender, which provides the focus and starting point for queer theory, it is perhaps useful to examine research which has investigated issues around sexuality and sexual diversity in relation to education, even that which does not specifically focus upon language. Much of this research has been informed, either explicitly or implicitly and to varying degrees, by aspects of queer theory. As discussed previously, some of this research inevitably ends up addressing issues around gender in relation to sexuality and is, therefore, important for further setting the context for the analyses presented later in this chapter.

Previous research has found that discourses of heteronormativity and homophobia are prevalent in almost all aspects of the school environment. Homophobic bullying is the second most common form of bullying after body size/weight and has detrimental effects on students' well-being, safety and academic achievement (Pearson, Muller and Wilkinson, 2007). Based on surveys of thousands of teachers and lesbian, gay, bisexual and transgendered (LGBT) young people, the reports produced by the gay rights organisation Stonewall (Guasp, 2009; Hunt and Jensen, 2007) show that homophobia and heteronormativity are pervasive across all types of schools in the UK. These findings are a great cause for concern about the environments which LGBT young people experience in UK schools, and the impact of this on all aspects of their school lives, including their safety and health, self-esteem, academic performance and attainment. All forms of homophobia clearly have a serious negative impact on the experience of school and on attainment, and severely undermine any sense of equality of rights and access to a safe and positive environment in which to learn. Importantly, it is not only the LGBT students who are affected by homophobia in schools, but everyone hearing homophobic language or witnessing/ experiencing homophobic behaviour is affected. The pervasiveness of homophobia in schools is a particularly significant issue at the time of writing, given the recent increases in homophobic hate crimes in the UK. In 2010, there was a 12 per cent increase over the previous year in reported hate crimes based on the victim's sexual orientation (statistics published by the Association of Chief Police Officers).[2] Other studies and reports have highlighted a worryingly high suicide (and attempted suicide) rate for LGBT-identified teenagers, and a range of mental and emotional health problems (see, for example, the final report of the *Children and Adolescent Mental Health Services* review, 2010 and the *Prevalence of Homophobia* survey conducted by Oldham NUT).[3] Therefore, it is important to address issues of sexuality in schools in order to begin to consider how these wider social problems around sexuality may be challenged and redressed.

The prevalence of homophobia and heteronormativity in British schools has also been identified and explored in research by DePalma and Atkinson (2009), Duncan (1999), Epstein and Johnson (1998), Forrest (2000), Morrish and Sauntson (2007), O'Higgins-Norman (2009) and Youdell (2005). Forrest (2000) notes how non-heterosexual identities are unusually invisible in the school context, which is potentially confusing for young people. There is an obvious contradiction between the visibility of lesbian and gay cultures outside school and their invisibility in school. Forrest argues that this contradiction, in itself, can send out strong messages about sexuality to young people in school which are overwhelmingly concerned with constructing non-heterosexual identities as 'deviant' or 'abnormal' in some way. The effects of this on all young people, and indeed on all adults involved in their education, has been well-documented. The detrimental effects of homophobia in schools on young people's mental health have been examined by Pearson, Muller and Wilkinson (2007) in the USA. Pearson, Muller and Wilkinson provide an overview of various research which has repeatedly found that same-sex-attracted youth achieve lower academically than their other-sex-attracted counterparts. They also note that same-sex-attracted youth are at a higher risk in general of mental health problems which can lead to disengagement from the learning process and social withdrawal, both of which impact negatively on academic achievement. As we have already seen in Chapter 1, some of the LGBT-identified young people interviewed as a part of the research presented throughout this book also reported on their own disengagement from learning and varying degrees of social withdrawal.

Duncan (2006) has also examined the prevalent use of the term 'gay' as an insult in schools. He observes that 'gay' is mainly used to denote boys who do not possess enough of the qualities fitting the ideal male stereotype of the dominant peer group. In the schools that Duncan visited, hypermasculinity had a hegemonic status within the school culture. The use of 'gay' as an insult was a key way of policing masculinity in the schools and was thus used more as a means of policing boys' performance of gender than as an accurate way of referring to known or 'out' homosexuals. Epstein (1998) also found the term 'gay' being used to refer to boys who were academically successful or who were simply seen as enjoying school work. In her study, she found that some boys rejected the perceived 'feminine' of academic work as a defence against being called 'gay'. This clearly has potentially significant effects on the academic achievement of boys, a point I will return to in the final chapter.

In a UK-based study of secondary schools, Youdell (2005) similarly notes how heteronormativity is linked particularly to sex and gender. Youdell focuses her study on 15- to 16-year-old girls and, drawing on the work of Butler (1990, 1993), examines how their sexed, gendered and sexualised selves are constituted. She claims that the girls' subjectivities can be thought of as 'constituting constellations' that create both possibilities and constraints for 'who' the students can be in terms of their sexuality. Airton (2009) also argues that gender is a problem which is linked to homophobia in schools. She observes that gender non-normativity and queerness is often conflated in the school environment. Therefore, one way of tackling the problem is to increase gender diversity. She argues that academics and educational practitioners should not simply be talking about anti-homophobia and anti-heterosexism, but should be discussing what she terms 'pro-gender diversity' as something which could benefit everyone in schools, not just same-sex-attracted students. It seems, then, that gender is often seen as a key process which is closely linked to discourses of heteronormativity and homophobia in schools. This is a key position taken by many researchers in this field (for example, DePalma and Atkinson, 2009; Duncan, 1999; *No Outsiders*, 2010) and it is one which is advocated in my own research.

Given the range of issues around gender and sexuality and schooling that this previous research raises and addresses, the remainder of this chapter considers how elements of queer theory might usefully be deployed in examining how these issues are played out in spoken classroom discourse. Classroom discourse is one site within the school in which wider social discourses, such as sexual diversity, heteronormativity and homophobia, may be enacted, reinforced or sometimes challenged. I now turn to consider more explicitly the role that language may play in these processes.

Performativity, gender, sexuality and language

Until recently, queer theories have sat at the margins of linguistics with their main applications occurring within social theory and literature (for example, Hall, 2003; Sedgwick, 1990). One possible reason for this is that queer theories do not espouse any particular methodology applicable to the study of language. An oft-cited criticism of queer theory is that its uses and applications are limited both within and outside the academy, given its largely theoretical nature. Linguistics, by its very nature, demands a certain methodological and analytical rigour which queer theories, by *their* nature, do not offer. However, certain publications have considered how selective aspects of queer theory may be used alongside other approaches and methodologies to further our understanding of gender and language in educational and other contexts (see, for example, Bucholtz and Hall, 2004; Campbell-Kibler *et al.*, 2002; Livia and Hall, 1997; Morrish and Sauntson, 2007). And, as stated previously, in this book I specifically argue that selective aspects of SFDA, CDA and FPDA can be used alongside queer theory in order to enhance our understanding of how gender and sexuality operate in relation to language in classroom contexts.

Gender and language research has also too often been guilty of colluding in the privileging of heterosexuality over other forms of sexuality (see McElhinny, 2003, for a more detailed account) and queer theory may help address such issues. Gender and language-related research which focuses upon social actors who do not identify as heterosexual has often occurred at the margins of the field (for example, as token chapters in edited collections and the occasional journal article), whilst work which takes language and homosexuality as its primary focus has incorporated fuller discussions of heterosexuality and gender. Research which adopts the latter focus is beginning to reveal how a dual focus on gender and sexuality within linguistics can enhance our understanding of both.

Like FPDA, queer theories try to resist producing their own totalising discourses. Butler points out that 'normalising the queer' would indeed signal its end. Historically and intellectually, then, it may at first be quite difficult to see how queer theories, with their emphasis on non-specificity and the erasure of identity, may be reconciled with feminist theories, with their more overtly political agenda focused around recognisable, if constantly shifting, identities. Indeed, much current work in the field of gender and sexuality across a range of disciplines has sought to resolve this conundrum – how is it possible to retain a commitment to a political and emancipatory agenda whilst, at the same time, resisting notions of 'identity' as something which is fixed, stable and inevitable? Although it is not the aim of this chapter to attempt to address this complex theoretical question, I will try to show how queer theory may be used to offer explanations for particular instances in the data which may be missed by the other approaches employed throughout this book.

Butler's (1990) theories of performativity and appropriations of language styles are crucial to understanding queer perspectives and have been applied to some gender and sexuality work (Livia and Hall, 1997; Morrish and Sauntson, 2007, 2010). It is mainly Butler's work which will be utilised in the analysis of data in this chapter. Butler's claims about identity, of which gender is an integral component, have been influential both in queer theories and approaches to the study of language, gender and sexuality. According to Butler, identity is not fixed or inherent in the individual or society, but is rather fluid, shifting in different contexts of interaction. In Butler's notion of performativity, identities do not pre-exist, but rather are brought into being by a series of 'citational' acts – including linguistic acts – which are understood to produce those identities. In this performativist paradigm, Butler argues that 'gender is a kind of imitation for which there is no original' (1990: 6) and posits that gender is something we 'do', not what we 'are'. Gender is thus a 'construction that regularly conceals its genesis' (Butler, 2006: 63) in that the same discursive practices which are deployed to construct gender simultaneously conceal the very fact that gender is nothing more than a fabrication. Within a performativist paradigm, different contexts of interaction will produce subtly different gendered identities – a tenet shared by FPDA and CDA.

Under the influence of Butlerian queer theory, recent work in gender and language continues to problematise the binary divide of genders, sexes and sexualities. Issues surrounding how men and women might resist expectations about their gendered linguistic performances, questions about agency and volition, and explorations of the relationship between gender and sexuality all owe a great deal to Butler's theoretical work. In linguistics, Livia and Hall (1997) were the first scholars to use the term 'queer' to refer generally to non-normative performances of resistance. Chapters in their volume consider linguistic applications of performativity in gay, lesbian, bisexual and transgendered contexts. What is revealing about this, and subsequent sexuality and language work, is that it becomes evident that in making performative statements about sexuality we inevitably make performative statements about gender, and vice versa. This issue was discussed in the introduction to this book and has emerged in aspects of the analyses presented in preceding chapters. Thus, once we begin to examine real-life language practices, gender and sexuality interact to such an extent that it becomes impossible to completely separate them in linguistic analysis. This is a key issue which emerges from the data analysis presented in the following sections.

Queer theories are not without their criticisms. One key criticism of queer theory is its loss of specificity, rendering it 'apolitical' (see, for example, Hennessy, 1993; Walters, 1996). In this respect, it may be useful to draw on queer theory alongside other approaches which are characterised by more explicitly emancipatory agendas, such as CDA. Another criticism is that the term 'queer' still carries negative connotations for many lesbians and gays who would, therefore, wish to resist the term, even in an academic context. A further concern is that many self-identified 'queers' have oppressed gender non-conformists within their own communities (Livia, 2002, for example, has noted the oppression of butch-identified women within lesbian communities), and there is a danger of re-rendering invisible already oppressed groups which have previously fought for visibility. Some have claimed that it would, therefore, be more helpful to consider queer theories alongside feminism (Bucholtz and Hall, 2004; Livia and Hall, 1997), and I would add that in terms of applications to linguistic analysis, it is useful to use queer theory alongside other forms of analysis such SFDA, CDA and FPDA. If queer theory is utilised selectively, in conjunction with other analytical approaches which are more explicitly informed by feminist lines of enquiry, perhaps it can provide an effective contribution to developing understandings of relationships between gender, sexuality and language in classroom, and other, contexts. To examine the extent to which this approach could be successfully applied is one of the key aims of this chapter.

Gender and sexuality in the interview data

Queer theory is particularly useful for those parts of the data in which sexuality was either explicitly mentioned or invoked, or when conceptualisations of gender in terms of 'normality' and 'deviance' were the topic of discussion amongst the speakers. If the explicit evoking of gender by speakers functions as a warrant (Swann, 2002) for focusing on gender in the data analysis, as has been explored in the preceding chapter, then perhaps the same principle can be applied to sexuality. In the data collected, there were several instances where sexual identity categories were explicitly evoked by the speakers, and these will be considered later in this chapter. Although other post-structural approaches such as CDA and FPDA are helpful for analysing the ways in which gender is discursively constructed in particular contexts, and how those constructions are temporary and can shift both contextually and temporally, what is missing from both approaches is an explicit consideration of how gender identities are inevitably tied up with sexuality identities. Analysis of a number of extracts will attempt to illustrate the interconnectedness of gender and sexuality in both the classroom talk of the students and in the critical reflections of some teachers and young people in the interview data. Some extracts of the classroom talk, most notably those which were used to explore the issue of 'marginalised' voices in the classroom, have already been presented in Chapter 4 and analysed using the frameworks of CDA and FPDA. The very process of marginalisation, which applications of both CDA and FPDA draw attention to, implies that there is a kind of 'normality' which is always under construction (and also under threat of being contested, resisted and challenged) in classroom settings. The addition of an analysis which is informed by queer theory enables us to interrogate this normality specifically in relation to gender and sexuality. In the extracts of 'marginalised voices', there was frequent mention of terms explicitly relating to gender and sexuality, suggesting that the students themselves also perceived this ideological link. And by contrast, the interrelationship between gender and sexuality is not just a theoretical construct – it is experienced as a material reality for the students. The same finding also occurred in some of the interview data, as discussed below.

A number of problematic issues around the way gender and sexuality were discussed (or not discussed) in classroom settings were highlighted by a number of teachers and young LGB-identified people who were interviewed. Three key linguistic issues surrounding sexuality emerged from this interview data:

First, the school environment was largely characterised by a pervasive silence surrounding issues to do with gender and sexual diversity. Issues around homosexuality, bisexuality and transgender were rarely discussed openly or positively in any aspect of the school context.

In the following extracts, both young people (Extracts 5.1–5.3) and teachers (Extracts 5.4 and 5.5) comment on the silence surrounding sexuality in general, and homosexuality in particular, during classroom discussions (English in Extracts 5.1 and 5.2 and Personal, Social and Health Education/ sexual health in Extract 5.3), and in other aspects of the school environment, such as the school's general policies and approaches to bullying (Extract 5.4). In all extracts, 'I' is the interviewer.

Extract 5.1 – Young person interview

1	I:	did she [English teacher] ever raise issues about
2		sexuality as part of the teaching you know part of a
3		text that you were looking at or
4	Carl:	no
5	I:	no okay
6	Carl:	sometimes what she was sometimes it's like the
7		movies that we watched
8		once there was a gay person in it [I: yea] and
9		everybody knew he was gay and they was like 'ooh
10		he's gay'
11	I:	so that wasn't kind of raised as something to discuss
12	Carl:	no
13	I:	no okay what about issues to do with sexuality more
14		generally I mean
15		were issues around heterosexuality ever raised did
16		that come up in discussion or did that come up in
17		analysing a text or a film
18	Carl:	yea
19	I:	they did yea
20	Carl:	yea cuz they was all about men and women [I: yea
21		yea] men being with women
22	I:	okay
23	Carl:	there was nothing about any gayness or anything

Extract 5.2 – Young person interview

1	Amy:	em I er I remember reading what's the book called
2		brilliant book 'The Color Purple'
3	I:	oh yea
4	Amy:	fabulous book I stayed up all night reading it [I:
5		mmm] thinking this you know em when they they got
6		em like a dialogue in books that's kind of done in an
7		accent [I: yea] and you come down the next morning
8		and you kinda talk in that accent [both laugh] it was
9		one of those books for me [I: yea] but er even with
10		that it wasn't really mentioned [I: really] which to me
11		was like surely surely that's a huge [I: yes] part of
12		this book
13	I:	yea
14	Amy:	but maybe it maybe it's because I was still you know

15		I was still quite young I don't know really but [I: yea
16		yea] that was only mentioned in passing

Extract 5.3 – Young person interview

1	Todd:	I would suggestions I would make to them I would
2		em that you should have people but cuz you get like
3		sexual health but it's only on straight people [I: yea]
4		it was so annoying cuz I was like I don't really I
5		know all of like straight stuff [unclear] but I wanted
6		to know about the gay stuff

Extract 5.4 – Teacher interview

1	Ann:	it surprised me a little bit because the school does
2		have a strong anti- bullying [I: yes] policy and posters
3		everywhere and students who are trained in
4		anti-bullying and staff who've been out on
5		anti-bullying training
6	I:	mmm
7	Ann:	but I don't know how much erm how much is
8		covered in that training about sexuality issues and
9	I:	right
10	Ann:	certainly none of it is fed back to staff en masse

Extract 5.5 – Teacher interview

1	Pat:	I think a lot of girls don't even realise that [laughs]
2		that there is such a thing you know [I: yea] among
3		girls you know I think whereas boys I think are much
4		more aware of it aren't they
5	I:	yea well male homosexuality's a lot more visible
6	Pat:	yea yea that's right
7		so I think em yes I mean I wouldn't say it was a huge
8		issue here at all and I think that's because it's a girls'
9		school
10	I:	yea
11	Pat:	I think it's very very hidden

It is interesting to note that, in Extract 5.5, Pat explicitly evokes gender by suggesting that homosexuality is even more hidden in her school because it is a single-sex girls' school. She suggests there may be differences between boys and girls in terms of their levels of awareness of homosexuality, with boys having a greater awareness. In FPDA terms, another gender difference discourse is invoked here, but it is one which intersects with sexuality, as that is the topic being discussed at the time.

Second, in contrast to the first point, the use of homophobic language was reported as being commonplace in schools, including in classroom discourse itself. This presents a contradictory experience for school students in that they are routinely exposed to homosexuality outside the school, and homophobic language is routinely used within the school, yet homosexuality is largely invisible in the 'formal' aspects of schooling. This point has been explored in greater detail by Epstein and Johnson (1998), who observe that sexuality is both 'nowhere and everywhere' in schools. Both the teachers and young people in my research noted the pervasive use of the term 'gay' as an insult (even the teacher who worked in the single-sex girls' school noted this, despite saying that issues around homosexuality were largely invisible in that particular school). And all of the young people reported having been on the receiving end of verbal homophobic abuse, to varying degrees. Sometimes this abuse came from teachers, as well as from other students.

In Extract 5.6, a teacher comments on the pervasive use of the term 'gay' as an insult in his school. He also comments on the difficulty of challenging the use of this word. He notes that the students do not always use the word to mean 'homosexual', but it is often simply used to negatively evaluate something or someone without necessarily implying anything about their sexuality. This supports the findings of Hunt and Jensen (2007) and Duncan (2006).

Extract 5.6 – Teacher interview

1	Neil:	em the most obvious one as I said the other week is
2		children using the word 'gay' as an insult or
3		pejorative term and it's very difficult I find to combat
4		it not from my point of view but it's become such a
5		socially accepted word that it ceases to mean
6		'homosexual' any more [I: mmm] and the children
7		don't even see it as meaning that [I: no] it's just
8		become that accepted

However, terms used with the deliberate intent of being homophobic towards those who are either 'out' as LGB, or who are perceived to be LGB, also seem to be widespread in the school environments of those interviewed. As expected, this was noted particularly by all of the young people interviewed. They all cited instances of being referred to using homophobic language, some more frequently than others. Two examples are included below in Extracts 5.7 and 5.8.

Extract 5.7 – Young person interview

1	Carl:	every time we had an assembly if there was an award
2		ceremony and he had to go up and get a certificate or
3		anything they'd all shout out em em hide your arse or
4		watch your arse something like that
5	I:	right
6	Carl:	and nothing nothing was said by any of the teachers
7	I:	okay
8	Carl:	everybody's laughing and teachers do nothing they
9		just go 'shhh'

Extract 5.8 – Young person interview

1	Joel:	all they do right I've experienced bullying and stuff
2		like that in school but it was when because because I
3		wasn't like out or anything like that and em but I still
4		got like 'you poof' and all that crap like that [I: yea]
5		and it makes you feel uncomfortable because you
6		don't wanna say 'yea and what' because then they'd
7		know

Such examples of homophobic language function to reinforce compulsory heterosexuality in the school environment. This works by constructing anyone who is not heterosexual (or who is perceived by others to be non-heterosexual) as deviant, over-sexualised, threatening and predatory (as evidenced through examples like 'hide your arse' and 'watch your arse'). Carl perceives teachers as being complicit in this sort of homophobia through their failure to challenge such language. Both Carl and Joel discuss how they experienced negative emotions (discomfort, fear, and so on) as a result of this kind of verbal homophobic abuse. In fact, in other places during their interviews, they both talk about how these negative feelings ultimately led to their increasing disengagement from school. Both of them explained how they actually left the schools in which they experienced the homophobia, and Carl left school completely to be home-tutored. This supports previous US-based findings by Pearson, Muller and Wilkinson (2007) and UK-based findings by Hunt and Jensen (2007). But these examples of homophobic language use not only function to police compulsory heterosexuality – they simultaneously function to construct and reinforce the notion of the homosexual closet. Fuss (1991) describes the closet as consisting of two binary states of 'in' and 'out' which exist alongside each other. Both Fuss (1991) and Butler (1990) argue that 'outness' is dependent on being 'in' for its definition – in other words, the meanings are relational. Therefore, coming and being 'out' actually reproduces (rather than challenges) the notion of the closet. Paradoxically, though, staying 'in' also (re)constructs the closet by reinforcing homosexuality as 'hidden', as opposed to heterosexuality which is a highly visible norm. For Fuss and Butler, then, the performative speech act which reinforces the closet is silence. But, as Morrish and Sauntson (2007) argue, that same silence can also function as a performative indicator of homosexuality simply because heterosexuality is not expressed through the speech act of silence. We can see this in Extract 5.8 in particular. Although Joel is 'out' to the interviewer, he reflects on being simultaneously in the closet, but also recognised by others as homosexual, at school. His silence concerning his homosexuality means that he is recognised (or at least suspected) by others as being homosexual (hence the labelling 'you poof'). But that same silence also reinforces a compulsory closet for Joel when he is at school.

Other researchers have discussed how boys in particular often deploy homophobic language as a means of affirming their own heterosexuality and hegemonic masculinity (Coates, 2003; Duncan, 1999; Epstein and Johnson, 1998). If boys do not engage in using homophobic language, they could be considered to be supportive of non-heterosexualities – a characteristic which is not considered to be an accepted form of hegemonically masculine behaviour. Therefore, if they want to perform hegemonic masculinity (which most boys do because it carries the highest peer prestige for boys), then they are compelled, or 'constrained' using Butler's term, to engage in such linguistic behaviour. So the use of homophobic language in these examples is inevitably tied up with the hierarchies of constraint operating around gender in the school context. This leads to the final issue concerning sexuality that emerged from the interview data:

Third, whilst homophobic language was sometimes a direct attack on someone's sexuality, more often it was used by students to police the boundaries of normative gender.

This supports the work of Duncan (2006), Epstein (1994), Epstein and Johnson (1998), Hunt and Jensen (2007) and the work of the *No Outsiders* project (2008, 2009, 2010) who all similarly found evidence of a close relationship between homophobia and the policing of hegemonic gender. In Extract 5.9, also cited in Chapter 1, Amy (a young lesbian) discusses how her perceived gender non-normative behaviour (playing football with boys) resulted in her receiving homophobic verbal abuse ('oy lezza').

Extract 5.9 – Young person interview

1	Amy:	I never really had any trouble I'd always made friends
2		very easily [I: yea] em I always er achieved
3		academically [I: yea] em teachers liked me everything
4		was fine er until I was playing football and we I
5		remember being on the pitch and I was playing
6		against all the boys which you know was fairly
7		normal really [I: yea] and er somebody called out 'oy
8		lezza' [I: right] and it tends to be with those kinds of
9		names those kinds of connotations it sticks like
10		superglue [I: yea yea] and it it just escalated from
11		there really to to the gradual name-calling[I: okay] er
12		of course everyone won't sit next to you cuz you're
13		the lezza

It is important to note that, at this point in her life, Amy explained that she was not identifying as anything other than heterosexual, although she did come out as a lesbian some years later. She states that at the point at which these reported incidents happened she did not have much awareness of her own sexuality at all. Therefore, she perceives the homophobic abuse as arising mainly as a result of her non-normative gender behaviour. This is another example of how homophobic language (and physical bullying in Amy's case) are repeatedly used as key means of policing normative gender in the school environment. Anyone who does not conform to the hierarchies of constraint operating around gender in their particular school context is positioned as 'queer'. Thus, constructions of certain (highly restricted) types of gender performance as normative are continually reinforced. This is illustrative of what Butler refers to as 'a stylised repetition of acts' (1990: 140) – particular ways of performing gender are constructed as normative over time because they are more visibly and systematically repeated through particular linguistic and other symbolic means. Amy's engagement in activities such as football are not systematically repeated by girls, therefore fall outside of what is considered normative for her biological sex. In fact, it provides an example of 'female masculinity' as discussed by Halberstam (1998). Any perceived form of masculinity performed through a female body is rendered illegitimate or 'unintelligible', to use Butler's term. As Butler (2006: 68) explains:

> Performing one's gender wrong initiates a set of punishments both obvious and indirect, and performing it well provides the reassurance that there is an essentialism of gender identity after all.

Amy reflects that a result of her experiences is a 'punishment' that takes the form of social exclusion by the peer group ('everyone won't want to sit next to you cuz you're the lezza'). Significantly, Amy also reports that she was liked by teachers and was achieving academically until the homophobic abuse began. Although she does not say it explicitly, there is an implication that this was no longer the case after the abuse began. In fact, later in the interview, Amy does explain how her academic achievement started to fall and, ultimately, she left school to be home-tutored. Amy's experience highlights the risks involved, not just in being out as lesbian, gay or bisexual in the school environment, but in simply transgressing gender norms, even in a small way. It is hardly surprising, then, that the hierarchies of gender constraint are so marked and strictly policed in school contexts.

In Extract 5.10, we find a slightly more complex example. Here, Tad (a young gay man) reports that his participation in a dance class with a group of girls led to more positive feelings around his own gender and sexuality. Unlike Amy, Tad had come out as gay at school at the point at which these reported events took place.

Extract 5.10 – Young person interview

1	Tad:	luckily I had em in the school which I was being
2		bullied in a teacher who was gay and she worked with
3		physical education and she made it more comfortable
4		for me [I: right] to even be in that environment and in
5		fact she did something really remarkable as I was so
6		uncomfortable with the boys in their changing room
7		and stuff because they taunted me [I: mmm] you
8		know saying things like 'oh [unclear] he's looking at
9		me' er and it got a bit bad so I was removed from PE
10		but I wanted to join in with something different I
11		loved hanging around with girls then because that's
12		when I felt more comfortable [I: mmm] because I
13		couldn't join in with their the girls' activities they
14		opened up a sort of group where it was dance [I:

15		right] and me and the I was the only exception of a
16		boy to be allowed for a dance lesson
17	I:	right
18	Tad:	yea and that was a good move and I thank that teacher
19		very much
20	I:	yea
21	Tad:	you know I wish I could see her again I'd thank her
22		very much for sort of opening up that opportunity for
23		me and I wish there was more tutors like her
24	I:	mmm
25	Tad:	it shouldn't take em a gay or a lesbian teacher to
26		make that movement

Earlier in the interview, Tad had discussed how he had frequently been the victim of much verbal homophobic bullying at school and this had been particularly bad during PE lessons, and especially in the boys' changing rooms. This is not unusual, as an increase in homophobic behaviour in single-sex environments (and especially during sport and PE lessons) has been noted by Epstein and Johnson (1998) and Duncan (1999). Amy, at another point in her interview, also talks about how the amount of homophobic language levelled against her increased in the girls' changing rooms during Physical Education (PE) lessons. In Tad's experience, an out lesbian teacher (which, in itself, was an unusual occurrence!) removed him from PE lessons and started up an extra-curricular dance class which she encouraged him to join (he was not permitted to simply join the girls during their PE lessons). Tad accepted this offer and joined the dance group, in which he was subsequently the only boy. Like Amy, Tad reflects that he felt 'more comfortable' in this predominantly female environment. But, whereas Amy came to experience homophobia from the boys she played football with, Tad did not experience homophobia from the girls in the dance class. Findings from Hunt and Jensen (2007) suggest there is a greater tolerance for gay men and boys from women and girls. There is no threat of sexual advancements and they can be seen as 'one of the girls'. But for Amy, being 'one of the boys' means that she cannot be seen as an object of sexual attention and objectification – a subject position which is discursively constructed as normative for girls. So, whereas Tad can construct an 'intelligible' subject position for himself within the girls' dance class as an 'honorary girl', Amy is not able to do so with the boys as this would pose too much of a threat to hegemonic masculinity which, ideologically, is supposed to be the domain of boys and men only. According to Halberstam (1998), when girls (or women) enter the ideological domain of men, domains which are infused with power, the 'female masculinity' which is exhibited in such cases threatens to reveal the relationship between masculinity and power as unstable and contestable. It threatens to reveal the very notion that masculinity can only be performed by biological males as nothing more than an ideological fiction. Boys and men are probably acutely aware of the fragility of their hold over masculinity and the power that comes with it. Therefore, it is hardly surprising that any performance of female masculinity, as in Amy's case, is met with resistance.

Of course, we may question whether the teacher in question was right to simply remove Tad from the environment in which he was experiencing the most homophobia and, therefore, in which he felt the most uncomfortable and threatened. It could be argued, instead, that the environment of the changing room itself needed to be changed in ways that would reduce the homophobia experienced within it. Challenging those who directed homophobic language against Tad, rather than removing Tad himself from the environment, may be seen to be more productive in terms of contributing to changing the overall culture of the school in terms of sexual and gender diversity. As DePalma and Jennett (2007) suggest, a reduction in homophobic abuse is more likely to occur through systematic social change rather than simply by preventing or responding to individual or particular acts of violence. But at least Tad experienced his removal from PE lessons as something positive and felt that it contributed to increasing his happiness and well-being at school. Importantly, Tad states that 'it shouldn't take a gay or a lesbian teacher' (line 25) to initiate change in the school environment. Presumably, the teacher who removed Tad from PE and invited him to join the dance class had a level of empathy and understanding of Tad's situation because of her sexuality. But Tad expresses an important need for all teachers, regardless of their sexuality, to have an awareness of issues around sexuality that may emerge in their classes, and to know how to handle them appropriately.

From these examples, and from some of the previous research discussed earlier, there appears to be a tension between the silence surrounding sexual diversity in the school environment on the one hand, and the pervasive use of homophobic language to police both gender and sexuality, sometimes simultaneously. The recordings of classroom discourse also contain instances which support some of these findings. In particular, the instances where both gender and sexuality are explicitly evoked are interesting to consider in light of these points made in the interviews, and from a queer theory perspective. Below, I focus again on some of the extracts which were considered in the previous chapter using FPDA and CDA.

Gender and sexuality in the classroom discourse

In the previous chapter, I presented analyses of a number of classroom discourse extracts in which gender was explicitly evoked by the speakers. This functioned to signal that, in these particular parts of the discourse, the students themselves were foregrounding something to do with gender construction through their conversational interactions. In some of these examples, sexuality was also evoked, sometimes directly alongside gender. This happened particularly in relation to students who were constructed as 'marginal' or 'different' in some way either by themselves or others, or both. I will now re-consider these students and some of the interaction they engage in by adding a queer theory perspective to the analysis already conducted in Chapter 4 (Extracts 4.10–4.14). I will then similarly re-consider extracts of data in which students appear to be engaging in explicit heterosexual display.

Damian

On a number of occasions throughout the research project, Damian's gender and sexuality were both the subject of debate and ridicule, even though Damian never gave any explicit indication that he identified as anything other than heterosexual. Damian's sexuality was often brought into question and constructed as 'different' by the other boys in the class, although not by any of the girls. In Extract 5.11 below, which I previously analysed in Chapter 4 using FPDA and CDA, Damian is firstly accused by another boy in the class of singing 'like a girl'. A short while later, there is a discussion about Damian's alleged homosexuality, which he denies.

Extract 5.11 – Young person interview

1   Alistair: who's singing like a girl
2   Alex: Damian
3   [Gap of approximately 20 seconds]
4   Ahmed: I'm not
5   you are queer though
6   Damian: I'm not
7   I'm not gay
8   Ahmed: where's your boyfriend

In this extract, Damian is firstly accused of 'singing like a girl' and then labelled as 'queer' by the other boys in the group. Singing is an activity which is perceived as feminine and therefore unmasculine (as masculinity and femininity are, ideologically, premised upon mutual exclusivity). A boy performing feminine-associated behaviour in the school classroom cannot go unchallenged by the other boys, otherwise they may also be seen to advocate such behaviour. As Davies (2006) points out, any behaviour which is considered weak, dependent and feminine by boys must be continually expelled in order to continue to performatively accomplish the dominant modes of masculinity. Therefore, Damian's singing has to be policed through the act of calling him 'queer' and ejecting him from the highly-valued category of heterosexuality. The label of 'queer' constructs his gender identity as deviant and unmasculine which, by default, enables the other speakers to imply that their masculine gender identity is unquestionably hegemonic and heterosexual. This supports Connell's (2006) claims that compulsory heterosexuality is inevitably tied up with hegemonic masculinity and queer theory's principle that gender and sexuality are inextricably linked.

This extract illustrates how powerful the hierarchies of gender constraint are in this classroom context. Damian performs his gender in a particular way (by singing allegedly 'like a girl'), but then his gender is immediately constructed as non-normative, not as a result of him expressing or showing any sort of physical affection or attraction to another boy, but simply because he starts singing to himself. This apparently innocuous act is constructed as challenging the principles of hegemonic masculinity operating within this classroom context. Along with this, I observed several occasions where Damian chose to work with a group of girls rather than with a group of boys, when given the option by the class teacher of self-selecting who to work with. As a result of these perceived non-normative acts, Damian's heterosexuality is called into question. Examples such as this also support findings from Hunt and Jensen (2007) that verbal homophobic bullying occurs even when the student in question does not identify as gay. And Duncan (1999) additionally found in his study that verbal abuse against boys also occurred if a boy demonstrated any kind of friendship with a girl or girls that was not seen to serve a sexual and/or exploitative purpose. Damian interacted with groups of girls simply because he wanted to – from my observations, analysis of discourse and interviews, there did not appear to be any other motivation for Damian working with the girls – he simply wanted to be friends with them. In Damian's case, the verbal bullying comes from the other boys in the class (who he also appeared to be friends with) because there is a perceived non-conformity to the dominant gender ideologies operating within the particular context in question. This has also been found in the work of Kehily and Nayak (2006) – in their study of boys and the use of humour in the classroom, they found that boys and young men who did not cultivate a 'hypermasculinity' through their interaction with other boys became subject to homophobic abuse. Although the FPDA and CDA account of Damian's discourse presented in the previous chapter is effective in uncovering the ways in which he is sometimes marginalised in the classroom as a result of his non-normative gender behaviour, it does not consider the implications for the subsequent homophobic bullying which takes place as a result of this behaviour, nor does it explicitly consider how processes of gender marginalisation are often tied in to issues of sexuality in the classroom. A queer theory dimension is needed here in addition to FPDA in order to fully interrogate the processes through which 'normality', in relation to gender and sexuality, is being discursively constructed, re-iterated and policed in this particular context. FPDA shows us how gender is discursively produced in localised interaction, but it does not necessarily offer a complete explanation as to how ideologies around sexual identity form an integral part of the policing of those constructions of gender. Queer theory, in particular the work of Butler, encourages us to see how the possible subject positions available to speakers (as identified through FPDA) are actually hierarchically constrained in ways that render some identities 'intelligible' and 'unintelligible' in terms of *both* gender and sexuality. In fact, hierarchies of constraint around gender are policed and maintained through heteronormativity and homophobia and hierarchies of constraint around sexuality are policed and maintained through the restrictions placed on what is considered to be normative gender behaviour. Moreover, these kinds of exchanges, which contain evidence of homophobic language, were never challenged either by the class teacher or by other students in the class during the whole of the research period. Challenges never occurred even when such language was clearly overheard by other people in the room. The failure to challenge this kind of language suggests that it was acceptable in this environment, and supports the quantitative findings of Hunt and Jensen (2007).

Kim

Whilst a combined FPDA and queer theory analysis of some of Damian's interaction illustrates the strict policing of hegemonic masculinity and heterosexuality between the boys, the same labelling as 'queer' for girls who do not display dominant forms of feminine behaviour does not occur. In Chapter 4, I discussed Kim's linguistic behaviour and the subsequent constructions of her by the rest of the class as a 'different' in that she was seen as deviating from the dominant forms of femininity in some marked way – by being 'naughty'. I discussed the following two extracts using a combination of FPDA and CDA, in the previous chapter. These analyses were useful for, firstly, drawing attention to Kim as a 'marginalised voice' in the classes observed in the study and, secondly, for offering a method of analysis which focused on the linguistic processes through which Kim was constructed as occupying a marginalised gendered subject position in her class. It is Kim's 'naughty' behaviour which is marked in the interaction and questioned by John in Extract 5.13. Even though the same behaviour is more frequently exhibited by the boys in the study, at no point is it interrogated in this way, suggesting that the type of behaviour is an acceptable characteristic of dominant hegemonic masculinity, but is placed outside the margins of what is considered to be acceptable feminine behaviour.

Extract 5.12

1	John:	what was you put on report in the first place for
2	Kim:	truanting
3	John:	that's what I was put on report for
4		I went truanting
5		I was on report for about a whole term right and em
6		Lee Barman Lee Barman was on report for two weeks

Extract 5.13

1	John:	you're one of the naughtiest girls in Year 8 ain't you
2	Kim:	who
3	John:	you
4		why do you be naughty
5	Kim:	I'm not that naughty
6	John:	how many detentions have you had
7	Kim:	twenty-one
8	John:	twenty-one?
9		remember last year when Mr. Saunders came down to
10		our classroom
11	Kim:	someone fainted in our class the other day

However, Kim's 'failure' to measure up to the required standards of acceptable feminine behaviour in this context does not result in her sexuality being open to debate, whereas Damian is labelled as 'gay' and 'queer' whenever he engages in behaviour which is perceived to be outside the margins of hegemonic masculinity. This suggests there may be more possibilities for the girls in this class to perform different kinds of gendered behaviour without necessarily becoming subjected to homophobic bullying as a result. It is difficult to explain exactly why this is the case, although Epstein and Johnson (1998) have suggested that girls may receive less homophobic bullying than boys simply because their sexualities are more invisible than those of boys. They also suggest that because masculinity is associated with power it may be acceptable (or at least understandable) for girls to try to perform masculinity in order to access this power. But, as femininity is not associated with power, there is no legitimate reason for a boy wanting to substitute his privileged access to the resources of masculinity with a performance of femininity. Thus, Epstein and Johnson (1998: 168–9) argue:

> ...the behaviour of 'tomboys' within the primary context is much more acceptable than the behaviour of 'sissies'. This, we would suggest, is because for a girl to be more like a boy can be interpreted positively, while for a boy to be more like a girl is, almost invariably, seen as problematic because being a girl is, in some sense, disreputable.

However, this was clearly not the case for Amy discussed earlier, or for some of the other young lesbian and bisexual women interviewed who also reported being subjected to homophobic abuse even before they had come out at school. It is, perhaps, difficult to explore this contradictory finding fully given that it comes from two distinct data-sets (classroom interaction and interviews). And just because the recordings of Kim did not capture her receiving any sort of bullying behaviour as a result of her perceived non-normative gender, this does not mean that it did not happen.

Classroom discourse and heterosexual display

Another way in which queer theory is useful for analysing and explaining certain aspects of the data is its application to sections of dialogue in which the students seem concerned with producing very explicit and highly marked displays of heterosexuality. In other words, it can be used to help interpret instances where homosexuality is noticeably absent or silenced in the discourse, as well as when it is explicitly evoked. Meyerhoff (2004), for example, argues that 'illocutionary silencing' can be important to analyse in discourse. Drawing on Austin's (1962) distinction between locutionary speech acts (what is said) and illocutionary acts (what is done when something is said), Langton (1993) makes a similar distinction between locutionary and illocutionary silencing. Meyerhoff develops this idea by suggesting that women are sometimes simply unable to satisfy the felicity conditions required to perform particular speech acts, because of the gendered structuring of society. The effect of this is that they are constantly thwarted from producing particular speech acts. This same principle can be applied to the silences which routinely occur around homosexuality. As noted in the previous chapter, these 'illocutionary silences' around homosexuality happened on a number of occasions in the boys' conversations, although these were not observed to occur at all amongst the girls. This suggests that there may be slightly different hierarchies of gender constraint operating for girls and boys in the school context and the accompanying methods of policing gender normativity may also be different.

Again, I present below some examples analysed using FPDA and CDA perspectives in the previous chapter in order to illustrate more clearly how the inclusion of a queer theory dimension can offer further insights into the discursive processes at work. In Extract 5.14, the students in the class have been asked to work in groups to produce a collage of containers which are made out of different kinds of fabric. Each group has been given a selection of magazines and catalogues which they are discussing and cutting pictures from.

Extract 5.14

1	Alistair:	she's got fat legs
2		she's too young to be a model got too much
3		make-up on
4	Alex:	that's you
5	(LAUGHTER)	
6	Tom:	what are they
7	Brendan:	let's have a look
(Teacher intervention – 30 seconds)		
8	Brendan:	she's fit
9		nice arse there
10	(LAUGHTER)	
11	Alistair:	oh I'm cutting that one out
12	(LAUGHTER)	

13	Brendan:	how about her
14		oy Alistair
15	Alex:	Alistair's looking through the catalogue for
16		his mom and dad
17	(LAUGHTER)	

As discussed in Chapter 4, there is much objectification of women taking place through this conversation. The boys make comments on body parts (legs and arse) in quite a sexualised way. They are eager to express their attraction towards the women in the pictures ('nice arse', 'let's have a look', 'oh I'm cutting that one out') in ways that sound exaggerated – Alistair likes the model in the picture so much that he wants to cut it out of the magazine. Thus, they make very explicit expressions of heterosexual attraction in these few lines. In FPDA terms, they position themselves here as unquestionably heterosexual through the objectification and derogation of women/girls. As Connell argues (1995), this is an integral characteristic of hegemonic masculinity. And, as Coates (2003, 2007) has found, in linguistic terms, hegemonic masculinity can only legitimately be discursively produced if it is understood that the speaker is heterosexual.

But Alistair is also critical of a (presumably different) model's appearance in lines 1 and 2, commenting that she has got 'fat legs', is 'too young to be a model' and has got 'too much make-up on'. Ironically, by stating what he does *not* find attractive about the woman in the picture, he reinforces the construction of his heterosexuality by showing that he has discerning taste in particular types of women and is able to evaluate their 'attractiveness', albeit in purely physical terms. The FPDA of this extract presented in the previous chapter suggested that the denotative meaning was Alistair's expression of what he did not find attractive about this particular woman. But the connotative, interpretive meanings were more to do with him expressing a right to police what is considered hegemonically attractive about women, and the kinds of female bodies which are ascribed positive values (presumably, those which are not fat). And adding a CDA dimension would interpret this in the context of wider social and power relations related to gender. As a boy, Alistair is exerting his right to say what is acceptable and unacceptable, attractive and unattractive, about women's bodies. Therefore, he reproduces a dominant ideology of men/boys having the power to 'police' women's bodies and sexualities. What queer theory adds to both of these previous analyses is an emphasis on the fact that it is heterosexuality which is being overtly marked, and perhaps even exaggerated here. Through visibly expressing *heterosexual* attraction, the boys are simultaneously erasing the possibility of any homosexual attraction. They do this as a means of constructing both their gender and sexuality as normative in order to increase peer approval. As heterosexuality is an integral component of hegemonic masculinity, it is important that the boys explicitly mark out their heterosexuality in order to be considered 'normal' in terms of their gender, and vice versa. As Duncan (1999) observes, boys' peer status is increased through heterosexual practices, or alluding to them. The final line of the extract also evokes a traditional heterosexual family structure through its reference to 'mom and dad'. Thus, both heterosexuality and heteronormativity are made visible to the point of exaggeration in this extract, whilst other forms of sexual identity are rendered silent and invisible. Moreover, it is a specific form of heterosexuality which is being condoned and reinforced in this extract. What is reinforced is a form of heterosexuality in which males exert power over females, not a form of heterosexuality in which relations between male and female are based on equality, mutual respect and so on.

A key feature of this extract is that it is clearly humorous. There is much laughter accompanying the talk and the tone of the dialogue does not appear to be threatening or aggressive. Kehily and Nayak (2006) suggest that this is a common feature of talk among boys at school and that heterosexual masculinities are often organised and regulated through humour. This humour often takes the form of ritualised verbal insults, which seems to be evident in Extract 5.14. Kehily and Nayak suggest that humour is frequently used to expose, police and create gendered and sexualised hierarchies. Both women/girls and also men/boys who do not conform to the dominant heterosexual codes of masculinity are often the target for such humour. They argue that boys' ritualised use of humour 'affirms hyper-heterosexual versions of masculinity and acts as regulatory reminders, and performative rehearsals, for the desirable behaviour of the male peer group' (Kehily and Nayak, 2006: 142). We can clearly see Alistair, in particular, trying to cultivate this 'hypermasculinity' for himself.

Follwing Alistair's critical comments about the appearance of the woman in the picture, Alex then makes a joke that Alistair is actually like the woman that he is talking about ('that's you'), resulting in much laughter from the group. The boys' labelling of each other as 'women' as an insult, and to create humour, is prevalent in the data. The term 'woman' is clearly a derogatory one amongst the boys. The following extract, which was also discussed using FPDA and CDA in Chapter 4,

contains further examples of the term 'woman' being used as a term of
ridicule and abuse amongst the boys.

Extract 5.15

1	Lee:	Alistair's harder than you
2	Nick:	I've done all that
3	Lee:	I've done all that
4	Nick:	what you doing
5	Lee:	kicking your head in
6	John:	shut up you woman
7		everyone Lee's a woman
8	Nick:	yeah Lee's a woman
9	Lee:	pass us that rubber John
10	Nick:	look it's a $\neq$
11	Lee:	I dare you to scream to whistle down there
12	John:	no
13	Lee:	give me that rubber
14		give me Ahmed's rubber
15	John:	Lee is an idiot
16		you have to colour it in Sir said you idiot

[Gap of approximately two minutes]

17	Lee:	let's have a look at yours
18		give it here give it here and I'll give you that one one
19		each one
20		Ahmed what's you say
21	John:	Nick's a woman yeah

In Chapter 4, I noted how Lee is referred to as a 'woman' (lines 6–8)
and then as an 'idiot' (lines 15–16). Nick is then similarly described
as a 'woman' in order to insult him. The two terms are used in similar ways – to ridicule, devalue and humiliate. Thus, the equating of
'woman' with 'idiot' means that the negative meaning of the latter term
becomes simultaneously equated with the term 'woman', so that, in this
extract, 'woman = idiot'. This use of the term 'woman' as an insult is not
paralleled in the girls' interactions. They do not use the term 'man' in
a similar way. However, as we have previously seen from some of the
interview data, when girls are perceived as engaging in behaviour that
is culturally and contextually recognisable as 'masculine' (for example,
playing football), this is not evaluated positively, either by boys or girls.

In fact, such behaviour renders the actor's behaviour as 'unintelligible' in terms of gender, or at least in terms of heterosexual gender. Thus, we may conclude that the use of 'woman' as an insult is one linguistic strategy being used by the boys to uphold and reinforce the values of hegemonic masculinity in which there is a need for them to differentiate their own masculine identities from the values and characteristics associated with dominant forms of femininity. When previously analysed from a CDA perspective, I argued that the use of this term is illustrative of a power dimension concerning gender relations – the concept of 'woman' is devalued in terms of power and a gendered hierarchy is therefore (re)constructed through the derogatory use of the term in this extract. In other words, a hierarchy is reinforced between 'man' and 'woman' as they are ascribed differential values within the same context of use.

Although the classroom recordings did not capture any instances of the term 'gay' being used as an insult, data from the interviews suggest that this term was often used in a similarly derogatory way by the boys. This has also been noted and explored in other research (Duncan, 1999; Hunt and Jensen, 2007). In his study of sexual bullying in a UK secondary school, Duncan (1999) found that 'gay' was frequently used as a direct insult to a boy who is not seen to possess the characteristics associated with hegemonic masculinity. Duncan observed a need amongst the boys to shield themselves against accusations of being gay. A key means of achieving this was to call others 'gay' and to produce verbal and visible displays about not being gay. This resulted in the reinforcement of homophobia as a positive masculine trait, as is seen in Extract 5.14 above. Other research has commented on the pervasive use of 'gay' being used to describe an object, experience or process as 'bad'. In both uses of the term, the meanings are always negative. Thus, both homosexuality and femininity are ascribed negative meanings by the boys in the study. This is consistent with Coates's (2003) findings on the study of all-male adult conversations in which male speakers use both strategies in order to discursively construct hegemonic masculinity through their talk. So hegemonic masculinity seems to be at the root of much of the homophobic (and sexist) language which is used, predominantly, by the boys in the study. This has also been noted by DePalma and Jennett (2007), who argue that hegemonic masculinity needs to be challenged and deconstructed in order to begin challenging homophobia and heteronormativity in school contexts. In fact, they go as far as defining 'homophobia' as 'the systematic and purposeful social policing of hegemonic masculinity' (2007: 20). They claim, therefore, that reducing homophobia is more likely to happen through the successful implementation of proactive social change, especially around gender, than simply by reacting to or preventing particular acts of physical or verbal violence. Evidence presented in this chapter further reinforces that view.

Summary and some conclusions

What this chapter has attempted to show is how elements of queer theory overlap with, but also extend the arguments of, CDA and FPDA. In particular, queer theory can extend the interpretations of CDA and FPDA in terms of bringing in a more explicit focus, not just on sexuality, but on the processes which link gender and sexuality. It can also illuminate some of the ways in which genders and sexualities in the classroom context are hierarchised, and the constaints which govern these hierarchies.

What is clear from the analyses presented in this chapter, in conjunction with previous research on sexuality and schooling, is that in order to challenge homophobia and heteronormativity, we have to challenge gender. The two cannot be tackled in isolation. Although the same could be said for gender in relation to a range of different identities (race, ethnicity, age, social class, age and so on), queer theory maintains that there is a special definitional relationship between gender and sexuality. If we are to successfully tackle the evident serious problems of sexism and homophobia in our schools, we need to launch a simultaneous interrogation of both gender and sexuality. Furthermore, what queer theory tells us is that we can no longer simply equate femininity with girls and masculinity with boys – in fact, this is a criticism of aspects of CDA and FPDA (Hultgren, 2008; Swann, 2003). Instead, we have to move towards challenging this unquestioned relationship between sex and gender. What queer theory does, which other approaches are arguably less successful at doing, is offer theoretical frameworks for deconstructing and questioning in a fairly rigorous way this taken-for-granted relationship. Outside linguistics, and drawing on Butler's (1990, 1993, 1998) work on the interrelationship between gender and sexuality, Youdell (2005) has argued that sex, gender and sexuality should be conceptualised as 'constituting constellations' within the school environment. This refers to the idea that the identity categories of gender and sexuality *constitute* subjects in an interrelated way rather than being separate processes. Due to the ideological relationship between sex, gender and sexuality, some constituting constellations are rendered intelligible whilst other possibilities are constituted as unintelligible. If gender were to become truly fluid, and no longer ideologically tied to biological sex, then there would presumably be no grounds for policing it through the use of homophobic language. If homosexuality is no longer a threat to gender, then there is no need for it to have negative associations. Homophobia emerges precisely because homosexuality threatens normative gender. This principle, central to queer theory, is one which informed the work of the *No Outsiders* project. Using action research in UK primary schools, this project explored some of the ways in which gender, sex and sexuality are conflated in the process of constructing normative, or 'appropriate', gendered behaviour for boys and girls in the primary school context. They state that 'sexism, homophobia and transphobia are all deployed in the policing of heteronormativity' (DePalma and Atkinson, 2009: 1). Therefore, all of these forms of social inequality need to be challenged together in a holistic way. In order to successfully effect change in schools, the *No Outsiders* team argue that we need to:

> ...undo homophobia at source, by challenging heteronormativity – the assumption that the world and everything in it is, and should be, based on a heterosexual model – and by challenging heterosexism – the privileging of heterosexual identities and relationships over all others. (*No Outsiders*, 2010: ix)

Challenging heternormativity and heterosexism is essential, therefore, for reducing both sexism and homophobia in schools. The data analysed in this chapter also seem to support this approach. However, what they also reveal, especially the interview data, is that both heteronormativity and heterosexism do not have to be verbally expressed in order for them to permeate the school environment. It is often simply the marked absence of references to non-heterosexual identities which effects a discourse of heteronormativity in school. Thus, we must not only tackle overt forms of heteronormativity and homophobia, but we must also seek to fill the silences around difference and diversity which pervade the school context, and which are reflected in some of the data presented in this chapter.

As a final point, it is worth referring again to some current policy, and especially to the *Equality Act* of 2010, which I discussed briefly in Chapter 1. The *Equality Act* marks out gender and sexuality as areas of inequality which are currently in need of particular attention in UK schools. At the time of writing, it is not yet clear how the *Equality Act* is being implemented, nor how its effectiveness is being assessed.

It is hoped that some of the issues raised and discussed throughout this chapter, and indeed throughout this whole book, are issues which have been considered in the processes of deciding how to implement this new and important piece of legislation. If the Act is really to make a difference to the lives of young people and all those engaged in education, there needs to be recognition that inequalities around gender and sexuality permeate the school system at every level. This includes the level of classroom discourse, as, hopefully, the data and accompanying analysis presented in this and the preceding chapters has shown.

6
Moving Forward? Some Conclusions

What this book has tried to show is that combining different approaches to the analysis of spoken classroom discourse is more fruitful than relying upon a single approach. As discussed earlier, current trends in the wider field of discourse analysis are moving towards using multiple analyses of the same data. No single approach can provide a comprehensive account of what is happening in a particular data-set. And each approach has its own set of limitations and critiques. Through a pragmatic combination, some of these limitations may be effectively addressed. It is hoped that this book-length application of different types of discourse analysis to the same data-set has helped to support, illustrate and contribute to these ongoing developments in both the fields of discourse analysis, and language and gender.

It is hoped that the research presented in this book will provide impetus for other researchers to continue this area of study. As stated in the introductory chapter, gender is still a key issue in all aspects of education, including the interactions that happen on a daily basis inside classrooms. Sexuality is also starting to receive more explicit attention in education, especially in relation to gender. Both are areas imbued with ideological struggle, therefore they are ripe for academic scholarship as well as activist intervention. It is clear that we need to continue to develop our knowledge and understanding of how gender and sexuality operate in education contexts, as understanding is a pre-cursor to change. I would encourage researchers to focus their attention on other aspects of education and schooling in relation to gender and sexuality, in addition to classroom interaction. I would also like to see a continued focus on spoken classroom discourse in relation to gender and sexuality. This book has shown how classroom interaction is a site where gender and sexuality identities are played out on a daily basis. It is a site of ideological struggle for all those involved. Although I have used four approaches to analyse the interactional data, there are, of course, many more discourse-analytic approaches available for use. There is, therefore, much scope for incorporating further analyses in order to enhance our understandings, and also to continue the ongoing methodological debates in the field of discourse analysis.

The research presented in this book has paid particular attention to the ways in which gender intersects with sexuality, although other dimensions have not explicitly been considered. This is mainly because of the scope of the research – within a single project, it is impossible to consider all possible social dimensions in relation to gender, so the research is necessarily selective. It is obviously important to acknowledge other social dimensions which clearly intersect and overlap with gender and sexuality, such as age, ethnicity, social class and so on. And Lazar (2005) urges us to be careful of so-called 'liberal' ideologies which assume that the experiences of all women are similar. She argues that the adoption and prevalence of such ideologies in Western academia has allowed middle-class, white, Western, heterosexual women to represent their partial experiences as universally shared by all women. This is clearly not the case and is, in itself, an enactment and reification of certain kinds of social privilege. Lazar calls instead for a 'serious re-visioning of gender' (2005: 16) which incorporates a critical interrogation of such privileges and encourages a critique of popular post-feminist discourses.

Due to the focus of this research, I would not make any claims about generalising the findings or arguments presented beyond the demographic characteristics of the participants involved in the study. As outlined in Chapter 2, the student participants in the classroom study were predominantly white, aged 11–14, and lived in the same geographical region. The interviews conducted later with the young LGB-identified people involved a greater diversity in terms of ethnicity. And, obviously, all of these participants identified as lesbian, gay or bisexual. Other language-focused studies have examined the ways that gender interacts with other variables in the classroom. For example, Eckert (2000) and Eckert and McConnell-Ginet (1995) examine the ways in which gender intersects with age and class in US high school settings. Norton and Pavlenko (2004) have examined some aspects of the interrelationship between language, gender and ethnicity in second language classrooms. Goodwin (2003) has investigated language in relation to ethnicity, class and gender in children's play talk. Some studies have focused upon gender in relation to other social variables without an explicit focus upon language (for example, Duncan's 1999 study on gender, sexuality, age and ethnicity in school contexts). And in Epstein and Johnson's study (1998: 162), several of their informants explicitly drew attention to 'the ways in that heterosexuality, conventional gender relations and the naturalisation of whiteness are often (re)produced through both the taught and hidden curricula'. Although not all studies can fully explore all possible variables, it is important to acknowledge that the experiences of the people involved in one particular piece of research may not be universal or generalisable to all people.

In addition to making some methodological and analytical contributions, the findings of the research raise a number of important issues concerning gender and young people's academic and social education. The findings potentially have a range of implications for the education of our young people. In terms of academic education, the findings may usefully feed in to ongoing debates around gender, sexuality and education. In addition to contributing to the existing body of research on gender and educational achievement, the findings also draw attention to issues around sexuality and education. Research to date has identified some areas of concern with regard to the academic achievement of LGBT-identified students (Guasp, 2009; Hunt and Jensen, 2007; Pearson, Muller and Wilkinson, 2007; Wilkinson and Pearson, 2009). Through developing our understandings of how gender is enacted and constructed through classroom discourse, we can further our understanding of why there are clear inequities in gender and achievement.

Much of the interactional data shows the girls in the study using language in ways which enable them to complete the tasks they have been set more effectively than the boys. Although there are obviously exceptions to this trend, this emerged from the analyses as being quite a marked pattern. The SFDA in Chapter 3 showed how the girls in their single-sex groups were particularly effective at staying on-task whenever they were required by the class teacher to work on an activity in groups. The mixed-sex and boys' single-sex groups spent more time engaged in off-task talk in these situations. Moreover, the specific discourse structures employed with a higher frequency by the girls in their single-sex groups also may have contributed to their more effective completion of tasks. This perception of girls using group work more effectively than boys was also supported through the student interview data. However, these kinds of arguments do need to be treated with caution as other research has explored the ways in which some of the typical characteristics of the boys' single-sex interaction may actually be effective in terms of learning (see, for example, Head, 1999; Mercer *et al.*, 2004). Because the focus of this research is more on examining classroom interaction in relation to gender as a form of social identity, I would be cautious about making any substantive claims concerning how particular uses of language and interactional patterns resulted in more or less effective learning for the students. Various researchers have warned against making generalisations about both language and gender and gender and education (for example, Swann, 2003). However, the main findings of this research do seem to add both quantitative and qualitative support to Swann's (2003: 631) claim that 'while not identical, the characteristics that have been attributed to feminine "cooperative" styles are consistent with the kind of "collaborative" talk that has been advocated as an aid to learning in educational settings'.

Of course, it is important to remember that effective learning is not simply related to what happens in classrooms at the level of spoken interaction. It also relates to a range of other aspects of schooling such as curriculum design, methods of assessment and learning/teaching methods, to name but a few. However, gender and achievement was an issue in the research simply because the results attained by the students in the study were clearly differentiated by gender. This reflected ongoing national trends in relation to gender and achievement. Therefore, it would appear that the findings of this research suggest that there *is* a relationship between language, gender and achievement, in relation to group classroom interaction. But more research is perhaps needed in order to explore that relationship in more detail and to make more substantive claims. What it does highlight, though, is that educators need to be aware that when they set students tasks to complete in groups this may result in differing interactional patterns across the different types of groups. This may, in turn, result in varying degrees of success between boys and girls.

The implications of the findings also address gender inequities in the social lives of school children more generally, and raise the important question of how local, discursive constructions of gender in the classroom may impact upon young people's experience of school more broadly. As outlined in Chapter 1, there has been much written about the apparent tension between girls' higher attainment than boys in the UK and the inequalities that women and girls are subjected to within and beyond school. Therefore, it is important to consider the social implications of the findings as well as the academic ones. The data analyses presented throughout this book offer some insights into how gender is discursively produced through classroom interaction in ways that perpetuate dominant ideologies of women and girls which potentially disadvantage them within and outside the school. The analyses show how hegemonic masculinity emerges as a particularly powerful gendered discourse through the interactional data, and through some of the interview data as well. Hegemonic masculinity not only creates a hierarchy of masculinities, but it creates a broader gender hierarchy in which girls and women, and the behaviours and characteristics ideologically associated with them, are not valued as highly as boys and men. In a sense, a competition emerges between gendered patterns of academic achievement, in which girls are more successful and therefore attributed a higher value than boys, and gendered discourses in which certain boys (the ones who are the most adept at performing hegemonic masculinity) emerge as the most valued and as having the highest social status. Given the inequalities around gender which exist in life outside the school environment, it would appear that the social discourses around gender which are constructed and sustained through classroom interaction (and other aspects of schooling) emerge as the 'winners', in that they ultimately have more value in the social world beyond the school. This is rather a worrying conclusion as it suggests that no matter how hard girls work in school, and no matter how much higher they attain academically than boys, they are still more likely to be socially disadvantaged in later life. And this will apply more to particular types of girls than others. In this study, for example, lesbian- and bisexual-identifying girls suffered especially badly in school. Although we should not over-generalise such claims, it is clear that the social education of girls and boys is also something that this research has drawn attention to as an area in need of reform. The dominant discourses around gender which pervade classroom interaction need to be challenged more rigorously if any sort of social change concerning gender and education is going to happen. What is revealed through Chapter 5, in particular, is that this kind of radical re-thinking of gender can only happen if heteronormativity and heterosexism are simultaneously challenged. As Epstein (1994) has argued, compulsory heterosexuality is implicit in the dominant gender norms and ideologies which pervade society, including the school environment. This argument has been supported through my own data and findings. Therefore, I would call for all researchers of gender and language to incorporate at least some consideration of sexuality into their work, as excluding sexuality avoids getting to the heart of what gender is really all about. It is clear that focusing only on gender in isolation from sexuality does not tell the whole story of how subjects act in gendered ways, and how gender emerges and acts upon subjects, in the social world.

Finally, it is hoped that the findings and arguments presented throughout this book can provide some contribution to policy developments in education. As discussed in Chapter 1, much educational policy that relates to gender in recent years has been concerned almost exclusively with issues around achievement. Swann (2003: 640) notes that there has been an emphasis on 'the speedy identification of problems such as "underachievement" and the provision of immediate and straightforward solutions'. This has resulted in a rather narrow focus in terms of educational policy around gender and an over-simplification of issues around gender and achievement. The social implications of gender in schools have been largely ignored. And, until recently, sexuality as an integral aspect of gender has also received little attention in terms of either policy or practice. However, sexuality is now emerging as a high educational priority for the current coalition Conservative-Liberal Democrat government. As discussed in the introductory chapter, the Equality Act came into effect in 2010, with its explicit marking out of gender and sexuality as areas in particular need of attention in public institutions, including schools. The current government's *Programme for Government* also highlights sexual orientation as being in need of urgent attention in schools as a means of combating homophobic bullying among young people. Other legislation and government guidance has also highlighted gender and sexuality as key areas of concern in relation to equality and diversity in schools – for example, the *Gender Equality Duty* (2007) and *Transphobic Bullying in Schools* (2008). These are positive signs, but the very fact that gender and sexuality are being singled out so visibly shows that they are still seen as being intensely problematic issues in education (and in other areas of social life).

At the beginning of this book, I stated that my aim, in conducting analyses of classroom interaction in relation to gender and sexuality, was an emancipatory one. As an academic and an activist, I work towards social transformation in relation to gender and sexuality. I hope that the understandings of the complex ways in which gender emerges through classroom interaction, the multiple yet unequal discourses of gender which emerge, and the ways in which gender is inextricably tied to sexuality at the level of spoken interaction, can all contribute to working towards a greater social equality and sense of well-being for all young people and for those involved in their education.

Appendix

A note on the presentation of data extracts and transcription conventions

Using Francis and Hunston's model of SFDA, data is presented in columns. The dialogue is contained in the left column of each extract with the analysis lines presented in the series of columns to the right, starting with the lowest unit of analysis in the system – acts – then moving progressively to the larger units of analysis towards the right. 'E.S' refers to 'element of structure'. In column 3, 'E.S' refers to the specific element of a move that the act constitutes (pre-head, head, or post-head). 'E.S' in column 5 refers to the position of the move (I, R or F) within the exchange. The exchanges have been numbered for ease of reference (exchanges were numbered in each complete transcript so the exchanges presented in each of the extracts do not necessarily start at 1). The speakers have been anonymised but the sex of each speaker is indicated by a letter B if they are a boy and G if they are a girl (this is for brevity purposes only; throughout the rest of the book, when data is presented without the SFDA analysis lines, participants are referred to using a pseudonym).

If other students or teachers are referred to by the speakers throughout the course of the conversation, the names have been altered, as has the name of the school and any other means of identification. The dialogue has been transcribed using no punctuation marks (except when apostrophes are used within words). Punctuation marks are conventions of written language and so are considered inappropriate to the transcription of speech. The following symbols and characters have been used in the transcripts:

( )   Verbal contributions to the dialogue which it has not been possible or necessary to analyse (e.g. inaudible; students reading from text). The information in brackets explains what is happening in stretches of unanalysed discourse which occur in-between stretches of analysed discourse.

⇑   Utterance overlaps with end of preceding utterance.

⇓   Utterance overlaps with beginning of next utterance.

Inaudible part of utterance.

≠   Incomplete utterance.

⌉
          Utterances are produced simultaneously.
⌋

}   Co-constructed utterance (indicated in act analysis column).

?   Utterance spoken with rising intonation (this character is only used when the discourse function of the utterance is ambiguous unless the intonation is indicated).

{aside}   Utterance not intended as a contribution to the conversation.

{laughter} When instances of laughter have been interpreted as serving a function in the discourse (e.g. as an acknowledgement of or response to a preceding utterance), they have been allocated an act in [square brackets] in the act analysis column. If the laughter is interpreted as serving no obvious function within the conversational exchange, it has not been analysed.

[ ]   Square brackets are used in the analysis columns when two (or more) utterances are produced in response to a preceding utterance and, as a result, both responses realise the same move in the exchange. This sometimes happens when there are more than two speakers in the same conversation and when utterances overlap. Square brackets are placed around the act which is not considered to be the main contribution to the exchange. When it is not possible to decide which act is the main contribution to the exchange, the last utterance to be produced is placed in square brackets.

- - - - -   A section of the transcript has been omitted.

Definitions of acts used in SFDA system of analysis (adapted from Francis and Hunston, 1992)

Label	Symbol	Realisation and function
framer	fr	Realised by a closed class of items such as 'OK', 'all right', 'anyway', 'well', 'now', 'good' and their variants. Its function is to mark boundaries in the conversation, where such an interpretation is consistent with considerations of topic.
marker	m	Realised by the same closed class of items as fr. Realises the signalling element of all moves. Its function is to mark the onset of a move.
starter	s	Realised by statement, question, command or mood-less item. Realises the pre-head of an opening, answering, eliciting, informing, directing or behaving move. Its function is to provide information about or direct attention towards the act realising the move head.
meta-statement	ms	Realised by statement, question or command. Realises the head of an opening move in a Structure exchange. Its function is to structure the conversation prospectively in some way, and to obtain a warrant for doing so.
conclusion	con	Realised by a statement or question often with anaphoric reference. Realises the head of an opening move in a Structure exchange.

		Its function is to 'tie up' a particular topic, and to obtain a warrant for doing so.
acquiesce	acq	Realised by 'yes' and other items indicating assent, both verbal and non-verbal.
		Realises the head of an answering move in a Structure exchange.
		Its function is to provide a warrant for a suggestion as to prospective (*ms*) or retrospective (*con*) structuring made by another participant in a conversation.
greeting	gr	Realised by a closed class of items which form the first-pair parts of the adjacency pairs used in the rituals of greeting and leave-taking: 'hello', 'hi', 'good morning', '(good)bye(-bye)', and their variants.
		Realises the head of an opening move in a Greet exchange.
		Its function is self-explanatory.
reply-greeting	re-gr	Realised by a closed class of items which form the second-pair parts of the adjacency pairs used in the rituals of greeting and leave-taking: 'hello', 'hi', 'good morning', '(good)bye(-bye)', 'fine thanks (and you?)', 'yeah see you', and their variants.
		Realises the head of an answering move in a Greet exchange.
		Its function is self-explanatory.
summons	sum	Realised by the calling of somebody's name.
		Realises the head of an opening move in a Summon exchange.

		Its function is to engage another participant in a conversation or to attract his/her attention.
reply-summons	re-sum	Realised by 'yes', 'what?' and other indications of attention (both verbal and non-verbal) given upon hearing one's name called. Realises the head of an answering move in a Summon exchange. Its function is to indicate willingness to participate in a conversation, or that one is giving one's attention.
inquire	inq	Realised by questions which seek information as opposed to a 'yes' or 'no' answer. Realises the head of an eliciting move. Its function is to elicit information.
neutral proposal	n.pr	Realised by questions which seek a 'yes' or 'no' answer. Realises the head of an eliciting move. Its function is to elicit a decision between 'yes' and 'no'.
marked proposal	m.pr	Realised by questions which seek a 'yes' or 'no' answer, where the form of the question indicates the polarity of the expected answer. It is also realised by declaratives said with 'questioning' intonation and declaratives followed by tag questions. Realises the head of an eliciting move. Its function is to elicit agreement.
suggestion	sugg	Realised by questions which seek a 'yes' or 'no' answer but the form of the question does not indicate the polarity of the expected answer.

		Realises the head of an eliciting move at I or R/I in an Elicit exchange. Its function is to elicit agreement.
return	ret	Realised by question, often ellipted. Realises the head of an eliciting move in a Clarify exchange. Its function is to seek clarification of a preceding utterance.
loop	l	Realised by a closed class of items: 'pardon', 'what', 'eh' and their variants, said with rising intonation. Realises the head of an eliciting move in a Repeat exchange. Its function is to elicit the repetition of a preceding utterance which was not clearly heard.
dictate	dict	Realised by a statement, command or mood-less item. Realises the head of an informing move at I or R. Its function is to supply information concerning the construction of a written text.
informative	inf	Realised by statement or by 'yes' and 'no' items and their variants, both verbal. Realises the head of an informing move at I (Inform exchange); or at R/I or R (Elicit exchange) where the head of the eliciting move is realised by either *inq* or *n.pr*. Its function is to supply information or to give a decision between 'yes' and 'no'.
concur	conc	Realised by 'yes' and 'no' items and their variants, both verbal and non-verbal, or by repetition or paraphrase.

		Realises the head or post-head of an informing move at R/I or R (Elicit exchange) where the head of the eliciting move at I or R/I is realised by *m.pr*. Its function is to give agreement.
confirm	conf	Realised by 'yes' and 'no' items and their variants, both verbal and non-verbal, or by repetition or paraphrase. Realises the head of an informing move at R/I or R (Elicit exchange) where the head of the eliciting move at I or R/I is realised by *m.pr*. Its function is to give or assert agreement.
qualify	qu	Realised by 'qualified' statement or by tentative 'yes' and 'no' items and their variants, both verbal and non-verbal. Realises the head of an informing move at R/I or R (Elicit exchanges) where the head of the eliciting move is realised by *n.pr* or *m.pr*. Its function is to qualify a decision or an agreement by indicating that its polarity is not unconditional, or to detail conditions and exceptions.
reject	rej	Realised by statement or by 'yes' and 'no' items and their variants, both verbal and non-verbal. Realises the head of an answering move in a Structure, Greet or Summon exchange or the head of an informing move at R (Elicit exchange). Its function is to refuse to acquiesce to a suggestion as to the structuring of the conversation; or to refuse to give an appropriate answer to a *gr* or a *sum*, or to reject the underlying presuppositions of an *inq*, *n.pr* or *m.pr*, or to indicate unwillingness to comply with a *dir*.

receive	rec	Realised by 'yes' and 'no' items and their variants, both verbal and non-verbal, or by repetition.
		Realises the head or pre-head of an acknowledging move at R and/or F; or the pre-head of an informing move at R (Elicit exchange).
		Its function is to acknowledge a preceding utterance.
react	rea	Realised by 'yes' and 'no' items and their variants, both verbal and non-verbal, or by repetition.
		Realises the head of an acknowledging move at R and/or F.
		Its function is to indicate positive endorsement of a preceding utterance.
reformulate	ref	Realised by statement which paraphrases a preceding utterance.
		Realises the head of an acknowledging move at R and/or F.
		Its function is to acknowledge a preceding utterance or offer a revised version of it.
endorse	end	Realised by statement or mood-less item.
		Realises the head of an acknowledging move at R and/or F.
		Its function is to offer positive endorsement of, or sympathy with, a preceding utterance.
repeat	rep	Realised by a statement or mood-less item.
		Realises the head of an acknowledging move at R or F.
		Its function is to indicate positive endorsement of a preceding *dictate*.

protest	prot	Realised by statement or by 'yes' and 'no' items and their variants.
		Realises the head of an acknowledging move at R and/or F.
		Its function is to raise an objection to a preceding utterance; it acknowledges the utterance while disputing its correctness, relevance, appropriateness, the participant's right to have uttered it, or anything else.
directive	dir	Realised by command.
		Realises the head of a directing move.
		Its function is to request a non-verbal response.
behave	beh	Realised by action.
		Realises the head of a behaving move.
		Its function is to provide a non-verbal response to a preceding *dir*, whether this involves compliance, non-compliance, or defiance.
comment	com	Realised by statement.
		Realises the post-head of all moves except framing.
		Its function is to exemplify, expand, explain, justify, provide additional information, or evaluate one's own utterance.
engage	eng	Realised by 'mm', 'yeah' etc.
		Does not realise any element of move structure.
		Its function is to provide minimal feedback while not interrupting the flow of the other participants' utterances.

Notes

1 Introduction: Language, Gender, Sexuality and Schooling

1. Statistics available from http://www.statistics.gov.uk.
2. See, for example, http://www.bbc.co.uk/news/uk-11875321.

2 Data and Methods

1. Examinations in various subjects, taken by almost all 16-year-olds. The starred A to C grades represent the range of passes considered acceptable/good to excellent and a school is often judged by the number of A* to C grades achieved. Achieving these grades can also determine which children go on to study for higher (A-level) examinations. For a full breakdown of 2010 GCSE results by gender, see http://guardian.co.uk/news/datablog/2010/aug/24/gcse-results-2010-exam-breakdown#data.
2. For more information about the Design and Technology and English subject sections of the National Curriculum, see http://www.qca.org.uk/curriculum.

3 From Form to Function: Structural-Functional Discourse Analysis

1. Other exchange types are identified in the system of analysis (Greet, Summon, Clarify, Repeat and Re-initiation) but, because they only occur in the data very rarely, it does not seem necessary to define or discuss them here.
2. The total number of exchanges (and moves and acts) is higher for the boys' interaction than it is for the girls' and mixed-sex groups' interaction because there was more data collected from the boys than from the other two groups. This was because there were more boys than girls in the classes involved in the study.

5 Beyond Identity: Queer Theory

1. The homophile movement was an international movement active during the 1950s and 1960s, whose main agenda was to work towards political reform surrounding sexuality.
2. These statistics are discussed in a BBC News article ('Hate crime figures published for the first time', *BBC News*, 30 November 2010) and an *Independent* article ('Hate crime figures paint a grim portrait of life in Britain', *The Independent*, 1 December 2010).
3. Details of these and other relevant studies are provided on the *Schools Out* website – http://www.schools-out.org.uk/research/contents.htm.

Bibliography

Airton, L. (2009) From sexuality (gender) to gender (sexuality): the aims of anti-homophobia education. *Sex Education* 9 (2): 129–39.

Althusser, L. (1971) Ideology and ideological state apparatuses. In *Lenin and Philosophy*. London: New Left Books.

Arnot, M. and Mac an Ghaill, M. (eds.) (2006) *The Routledge Falmer Reader in Gender and Education*. London: Routledge.

Arnot, M. and Weiner, G. (eds.) (1987) *Gender and the Politics of Schooling*. London: Unwin Hyman.

Atkinson, E., DePalma, R., Reiss, M., Givens, N. and Nixon, D. (2009) *No Outsiders: Researching Approaches to Sexualities Equality in Primary Schools*. ESRC-funded project 2006–2009 (RES 062230095).

Austin, J.L. (1962) *How to Do Things with Words*. Oxford: Oxford University Press.

Baker, P. (2005) *Public Discourses of Gay Men*. London: Routledge.

Baker, P. (2008) 'Eligible' bachelors and 'frustrated' spinsters: corpus linguistics, gender and language. In K. Harrington *et al.* (eds.), pp. 73–84.

Bakhtin, M. (1981) *The Dialogic Imagination: Four Essays*. Texas: University of Texas Press.

Barnes, D. (1976) *From Communication to Curriculum*. Harmondsworth: Penguin.

Barthes, R. (1977) *Image-Music-Text*. New York: Hill and Yang.

Baxter, J. (2002a) Competing discourses in the classroom: a poststructuralist analysis of pupils' speech in public contexts. *Discourse and Society* 19 (6): 827–42.

Baxter, J. (2002b) A juggling act: a feminist post-structuralist analysis of girls' and boys' talk in the secondary classroom. *Gender and Education* 14 (1): 5–19.

Baxter, J. (2003) *Positioning Gender in Discourse: A Feminist Methodology*. Basingstoke: Palgrave Macmillan.

Baxter, J. (2008) Feminist post-structuralist discourse analysis: a new theoretical and methodological approach? In K. Harrington *et al.* (eds.), pp. 243–55.

Bellack, A., Kliebard, H., Hyman, R. and Smith, F. (1966) *The Language of the Classroom*. New York: Teachers College Press.

Bergvall, V. (1996) Constructing and enacting gender through discourse: negotiating multiple roles among female engineering students. In V. Bergvall, J. Bing and A. Freed (eds.) *Rethinking Language and Gender Research: Theory and Practice*. London: Longman, pp. 173–201.

Bing, J. and Bergvall, V. (1998) The question of questions: beyond binary thinking. In J. Coates (ed.) *Language and Gender: A Reader*. Oxford: Blackwell, pp. 495–510.

Bourdieu, P. (2006) Masculine domination: permanence and change. In M. Arnot and M. Mac an Ghaill (eds.), pp. 91–100.

Brown, P. and Levinson, S. (1987) *Politeness: Some Universals in Language Use*. Cambridge: Cambridge University Press.

Bucholtz, M. and Hall, K. (2004) Theorising identity in language and sexuality research. *Language in Society* 33: 469–515.

Butler, J. (1990) *Gender Trouble: Feminism and the Subversion of Identity*. New York: Routledge.

Butler, J. (1993) *Bodies that Matter: On the Discursive Limits of 'Sex'*. New York: Routledge.

Butler, J. (1997) *Excitable Speech*. New York: Routledge.

Butler, J. (1998) Afterword. In S. Munt (ed.) *Butch/femme: Inside Lesbian Gender*. London: Cassell, pp. 225–30.

Butler, J. (2004) *Undoing Gender*. New York: Routledge.

Butler, J. (2006) Performative acts and gender constitution: an essay in phenomenology and feminist theory. In M. Arnot and M. Mac an Ghaill (eds.), pp. 61–71.

Caldas-Coulthard, C. (1996) Women who pay for sex and enjoy it: transgression versus morality in women's magazines. In C. Caldas-Coulthard and M. Coulthard (eds.) *Texts and Practices: Readings in Critical Discourse Analysis*. London: Routledge, pp. 250–70.

Cameron, D. (1992) *Feminism and Linguistic Theory* (2nd edition). London: Macmillan.

Cameron, D. (1997) Performing gender identity: young men's talk and the construction of heterosexual masculinity. In S. Johnson and U. Meinhof (eds.), pp. 47–64.

Cameron, D. (2001) *Working with Spoken Discourse*. London: Sage.

Cameron, D. and Kulick, D. (2003) *Language and Sexuality*. Cambridge: Cambridge University Press.

Campbell-Kibler, K., Podesva, R., Roberts, S. and Wong, A. (eds.) (2002) *Language and Sexuality: Contesting Meaning in Theory and Practice*. Stanford, CA: CSLI.

Clarricoates, K. (1983) Classroom interaction. In J. Whyld (ed.) *Sexism in the Secondary Curriculum*. New York: Harper and Row.

Coates, J. (1996) *Women Talk: Conversation between Women Friends*. Oxford: Blackwell.

Coates, J. (2003) *Men Talk: Stories in the Making of Masculinities*. Oxford: Blackwell.

Coates, J. (2007) 'Everyone was convinced that we were closet fags': the role of heterosexuality in the construction of hegemonic masculinity. In H. Sauntson and S. Kyratzis (eds.) *Language, Sexualities and Desires: Cross Cultural Perspectives*. Basingstoke: Palgrave Macmillan, pp. 41–67.

Cole, M. (ed.) (2000) *Education, Equality and Human Rights: Issues of Gender, 'Race', Sexuality, Special Needs and Social Class*. London: Routledge Falmer.

Connell, R.W. (1987) *Gender and Power*. Oxford: Polity Press.

Connell, R.W. (1995) *Masculinities*. Cambridge: Polity Press.

Connell, R.W. (2006) The big picture: masculinities in recent world history. In M. Arnot and M. Mac an Ghaill (eds.), pp. 101–14.

Corson, D. (1997) Gender, discourse and senior education: ligatures for girls, options for boys. In R. Wodak (ed.), pp. 140–64.

Coulthard, R.M. (ed.) (1992) *Advances in Spoken Discourse Analysis*. London: Routledge.

Coulthard, R.M. and Montgomery, M. (eds.) (1981) *Studies in Discourse Analysis*. London: Routledge and Kegan Paul.

Creese, A. (2010) Linguistic ethnography. In L. Litosseliti (ed.) *Research Methods in Linguistics*. London: Continuum, pp. 138–54.

Cullen, R. (2002) Supportive teacher talk: the importance of the F-move. *ELT Journal* 56 (2): 117–27.

Davies, B. (2006) Identity, abjection and otherness: creating the self, creating difference. In M. Arnot and M. Mac an Ghaill (eds.), pp. 72–90.

Davies, J. (2003) Expressions of gender: an analysis of pupils' gendered discourse styles in small group discussions. *Discourse and Society* 14 (2): 115–32.

Davies, J. (2005) 'We know what we're talking about, don't we?' An examination of girls' classroom-based learning allegiances. *Linguistics and Education* 15: 199–216.

Delamont, S. (1990) *Sex Roles and the School.* London: Methuen.

DePalma, R. and Atkinson, E. (eds.) (2009) *Interrogating Heteronormativity in Primary Schools: The Work of the* No Outsiders *Project.* Stoke-on-Trent: Trentham Books.

DePalma, R. and Jennett, M. (2007) Deconstructing heteronormativity in primary schools in England: Cultural approaches to a cultural phenomenon. In L. Van Dijk and B. van Driel (eds.) *Challenging Homophobia: Teaching about Sexual Diversity.* Stoke-on-Trent: Trentham Books, pp. 19–32.

Duncan, N. (1999) *Sexual Bullying: Gender Conflict and Pupil Culture in Secondary Schools.* London: Routledge.

Duncan, N. (2006) Homophobia, misogyny and school bullying. Paper presented at the *British Educational Research Association* conference, University of Warwick, September 2006.

Eckert, P. (1989) *Jocks and Burnouts: Social Categories and Identity in the High School.* New York: Teachers College Press.

Eckert, P. (1996) Vowels and nail polish: the emergence of linguistic style in the preadolescent heterosexual marketplace. In N. Warner, J. Ahlers, L. Bilmes, M. Oliver, S. Wertheim and M. Chen (eds.) *Gender and Belief Systems.* Berkeley: Berkeley Women and Language Group, pp. 183–90.

Eckert, P. (2000) *Linguistic Variation as Social Practice.* Oxford: Blackwell.

Eckert, P. and McConnell-Ginet, S. (1995) Constructing meaning, constructing selves: snapshots of language, gender and class from Belten High. In K. Hall and M. Bucholtz (eds.) *Gender Articulated: Language and the Socially Constructed Self.* London: Routledge, pp. 469–507.

Edwards, A.D. and Westgate, D. (1994) *Investigating Classroom Talk* (2nd edition). London: Methuen.

Ellis, V. and Forrest, S. (2000) One of them or one of us? Sexuality, identity and equality. In M. Cole (ed.), pp. 78–98.

Elwood, J. (2005) Gender and achievement: what have exams got to do with it? *Oxford Review of Education* 31 (3): 373–93.

Epstein, D. (ed.) (1994) *Challenging Lesbian and Gay Inequalities in Education.* Buckingham: Open University Press.

Epstein, D. (1998) Real boys don't work: 'underachievement', masculinity and the harassment of 'sissies'. In D. Epstein *et al.* (eds.), pp. 96–108.

Epstein, D., Elwood, J., Hey, V. and Maw, J. (eds.) (1998) *Failing Boys? Issues in Gender and Achievement.* Buckingham: Open University Press.

Epstein, D. and Johnson, R. (1998) *Schooling Sexualities.* Buckingham: Open University Press.

Erickson, F. (2004) *Talk and Social Theory.* Oxford: Polity Press.

Fairclough, N. (1992) *Discourse and Social Change.* Cambridge: Polity Press.

Fairclough, N. (1995) *Critical Discourse Analysis*. London: Longman.

Fairclough, N. (2001) *Language and Power* (2nd edition). London: Longman.

Fairclough, N. (2003) *Analysing Discourse: Textual Analysis for Social Research*. London: Longman.

Forrest, S. (2000) Difficult loves: learning about sexuality and homophobia in schools. In M. Cole (ed.), pp. 99–117.

Foucault, M. (1972) *The Archaeology of Knowledge*. London: Tavistock.

Foucault, M. (1984) What is enlightenment? In P. Rabinow (ed.) *The Foucault Reader*. London: Penguin, pp. 32–50.

Foucault, M. (1990) *The History of Sexuality* (trans. R. Hurley). London: Penguin.

Francis, B. (1998) *Power Plays*. Stoke-on-Trent: Trentham.

Francis, B. (2000) *Boys, Girls and Achievement: Addressing the Classroom Issues*. London: Routledge.

Francis, B. and Skelton, C. (2001) Men teachers and the construction of heterosexual masculinity in the classroom. *Sex Education* 1 (1): 9–21.

Francis, B. and Skelton, C. (2005) *Reassessing Gender and Achievement*. London: Routledge.

Francis, B., Skelton, C. and Read, B. (2010) The simultaneous production of educational achievement and popularity: how do some pupils accomplish it? *British Educational Research Journal* 36 (2): 317–40.

Francis, G. and Hunston, S. (1992) Analysing everyday conversation. In R.M. Coulthard (ed.), pp. 123–61.

Fuss, D. (ed.) (1991) *Inside/Out: Lesbian Theories, Gay Theories*. New York: Routledge.

Gilligan, C. (1982) *In a Different Voice*. Cambridge, MA: Harvard University Press.

Gipps, C. and Murphy, P. (1994) *A Fair Test? Assessment, Achievement and Equity*. Buckingham: Open University Press.

Goodwin, M. H. (1990) *He-Said-She-Said: Talk as Social Organization among Black Children*. Bloomington, IA: Indiana University Press.

Goodwin, M. H. (1998) Co-operation and competition across girls' play activities. In J. Coates (ed.) *Language and Gender: A Reader*. Oxford: Blackwell, pp. 121–46.

Goodwin, M. H. (2003) The relevance of ethnicity, class, and gender in children's peer negotiations. In J. Holmes and M. Meyerhoff (eds.), pp. 229–51.

Graddol, D. and Swann, J. (1989) *Gender Voices*. Oxford: Blackwell.

Guasp, A. (2009) *The Teachers' Report: Homophobic Bullying in Britain's Schools*. London: Stonewall.

Gumperz, J. (1982) *Discourse Strategies*. Cambridge: Cambridge University Press.

Halberstam, J. (1998) *Female Masculinity*. Durham, NC: Duke University Press.

Hall, D. (2003) *Queer Theories*. Basingstoke: Palgrave Macmillan.

Halliday, M.A.K. (1985) *Spoken and Written Language*. Victoria: Deakin University Press.

Hammersley, M. (1992) *What's Wrong with Ethnography?* London: Routledge.

Hammersley, M. (2003) Conversation analysis and discourse analysis: methods or paradigms? *Discourse and Society* 14 (6): 751–81.

Hammersley, M. (2006) Ethnography: problems and prospects. *Ethnography and Education* 1: 3–14.

Harrington, K., Litosseliti, L., Sauntson, H. and Sunderland, J. (eds.) (2008) *Gender and Language Research Methodologies*. Basingstoke: Palgrave Macmillan.

Head, J. (1999) *Understanding the Boys: Issues of Behaviour and Achievement.* London: Falmer.

Hennessy, R. (1993) *Materialism Feminism and the Politics of Discourse.* New York: Routledge.

Hewitt, R. (1997) 'Boxing out' and 'taxing'. In S. Johnson and U. Meinhof (eds.), pp. 27–46.

Hey, V. (1997) *The Company She Keeps: An Ethnography of Girls' Friendship.* Buckingham: Open University Press.

Hey, V., Leonard, D., Daniels, H. and Smith, M. (1998) Boys' underachievement, special needs practices and questions of equity. In D. Epstein *et al.* (eds.), pp. 128–44.

Hildebrand, G. (1996) Redefining achievement. In P. Murphy and C. Gipps (eds.), pp. 149–72.

Hoey, M. (ed.) (1993) *Data, Description, Discourse: Papers on the English Language in Honour of John McH Sinclair.* London: HarperCollins.

Holden, C. (1993) Giving girls a chance: patterns of talk in co-operative group work. *Gender and Education* 5 (2): 179–89.

Holmes, J. (1992) Women's talk in public contexts. *Discourse and Society* 3 (2): 131–50.

Holmes, J. (1995) *Women, Men and Politeness.* London: Longman.

Holmes, J. (1996) Women's role in language change: a place for quantification. In N. Warner, J. Ahlers, L. Bilmes, M. Oliver, S. Wertheim and M. Chen (eds.) *Gender and Belief Systems.* Berkeley, CA: Berkeley Women and Language Group, pp. 313–30.

Holmes, J. and Meyerhoff, M. (eds.) (2003) *The Handbook of Language and Gender.* Oxford: Blackwell.

Holmes, J. and Stubbe, M. (2003) 'Feminine' workplaces: stereotype and reality. In J. Holmes and M. Meyerhoff (eds.), pp. 573–99.

Holmes, J., Stubbe, M. and Vine, B. (1999) Constructing professional identity: 'doing power' in policy units. In S. Sarangi and C. Roberts (eds.) *Talk, Work and Institutional Order: Discourse in Medical, Mediation and Management Settings.* Berlin: Mouton de Gruyter, pp. 351–85.

Howe, C. (1997) *Gender and Classroom Interaction: A Research Review.* Edinburgh: Scottish Council for Research in Education.

Hultgren, A. K. (2008) Reconstructing the sex dichotomy in language and gender research: some advantages of using correlational linguistics. In K. Harrington *et al.* (eds.), pp. 29–42.

Hunt, R. and Jensen, J. (2007) *The School Report: The Experiences of Young Gay People in Britain's Schools.* London: Stonewall.

Hymes, D. (1977) *Foundations in Sociolinguistics.* London: Tavistock.

Jackson, D. (1998) Breaking out of the binary trap: boys' underachievement, schooling and gender relations. In D. Epstein *et al.* (eds.), pp. 77–95.

Jagose, A. (1996) *Queer Theory: An Introduction.* New York: New York University Press.

Jaworski, A. and Coupland, N. (eds.) (1999) *The Discourse Reader.* London: Routledge.

Johnson, S. and Meinhof, U. (eds.) (1997) *Language and Masculinity.* Oxford: Blackwell.

Kehily, M. and Nayak, A. (2006) 'Lads and laughter': humour and the production of heterosexual hierarchies. In M. Arnot and M. Mac an Ghaill (eds.), pp. 131–46.

Kelly, A. (1987) The construction of masculine science. In M. Arnot and G. Weiner (eds.), pp. 127–39.

Kendall, S. (2003) Creating gendered discourses of authority at work and at home. In J. Holmes and M. Meyerhoff (eds.), pp. 600–23.

Kenway, J. and Epstein, D. (1996) The marketisation of school education: feminist studies and perspectives. *Discourse* 17 (3): 301–14.

Kessler, S., Ashenden, D., Connell, R. and Dowsett, G. (1987) Gender relations in secondary schooling. In M. Arnot and G. Weiner (eds.), pp. 223–36.

Kiesling, S. (2002) Playing the straight man: displaying and maintaining male heterosexuality in discourse. In K. Campbell-Kibler *et al.* (eds.), pp. 249–66.

Kimmel, M. (2009) Hostile high school hallways. In W. Martino, M. Kehler and M. Weaver-Hightower (eds.) *The Problem with Boys' Education.* New York: Routledge, pp. 169–97.

Krolokke, C. and Sorensen, A. (2006) *Gender Communication: Theories and Analyses.* London: Sage.

Landry, D. and MacLean, G. (eds.) (1996) *The Spivak Reader.* London: Routledge.

Langton, R. (1993) Speech acts and unspeakable acts. *Philosophy and Public Affairs* 22: 293–330.

Lazar, M. (ed.) (2005) *Feminist Critical Discourse Analysis: Gender, Power and Ideology in Discourse.* Basingstoke: Palgrave Macmillan.

Leap, W. (1996) *Word's Out: Gay Men's English.* Minneapolis: University of Minnessota Press.

Leap, W. (2008) Queering gay men's English. In K. Harrington *et al.* (eds.), pp. 283–96.

Lemke, J. (1985) *Using Language in the Classroom.* Victoria: Deakin University Press.

Lingard, B., Martino, W. and Mills, M. (2009) *Boys and Schooling: Beyond Structural Reform.* Basingstoke: Palgrave Macmillan.

Litosseliti, L. and Sunderland, J. (eds.) (2002) *Gender Identity and Discourse Analysis.* Amsterdam: John Benjamins.

Livia, A. (2002) The future of queer linguistics. In K. Campbell-Kibler *et al.* (eds.), pp. 87–97.

Livia, A. and Hall, K. (eds.) (1997) *Queerly Phrased: Language, Gender, and Sexuality.* Oxford: Oxford University Press.

Mac an Ghaill, M. (1994) *The Making of Men: Masculinities, Sexualities and Schooling.* Milton Keynes: Open University Press.

Mackinnon, A., Elgqvist-Saltzman, I. and Prentice, A. (eds.) (1998) *Education into the 21st Century: Dangerous Terrain for Women?* London: Falmer Press.

Maybin, J. (2003) Language, relationships and identities. In M. Kehily and J. Swann (eds.) *Childrens' Cultural Worlds.* Chichester: John Wiley, pp. 89–132.

Maybin, J. (2006) *Children's Voices: Talk, Knowledge and Identity.* Basingstoke: Palgrave Macmillan.

McElhinny, B. (2003) Theorising gender in sociolinguistics and linguistic anthropology. In J. Holmes and M. Meyerhoff (eds.), pp. 21–42.

Mendick, H. (2006) *Masculinities in Mathematics*. Maidenhead: Open University Press.

Mercer, N. (1995) *The Guided Construction of Knowledge: Talk amongst Teachers and Learners*. Clevedon: Multilingual Matters.

Mercer, N., Dawes, L., Wegerif, R. and Sams, C. (2004) Reasoning as a scientist: ways of helping children to use language to learn science. *British Educational Research Journal* 30 (3): 359–77.

Meyerhoff, M. (2004) Doing and saying: some words on women's silence. In M. Bucholtz (ed.) *Robin Tolmach Lakoff's 'Language and Woman's Place': Text and Commentaries*. Oxford: Oxford University Press, pp. 209–15.

Morrish, E. and Sauntson, H. (2007) *New Perspectives on Language and Sexual Identity*. Basingstoke: Palgrave Macmillan.

Morrish, E. and Sauntson, H. (2010) Performing sexual identity through spoken discourse. In B. Scherer (ed.) *Queering Paradigms*. Oxford: Peter Lang Press, pp. 27–47.

Murphy, P. and Gipps, C. (eds.) (1996) *Equity in the Classroom: Towards Effective Pedagogy for Girls and Boys*. London: Falmer Press.

No Outsiders Project Team. 2010. *Undoing Homophobia in Primary Schools*. Stoke-on-Trent: Trentham Books.

Norton, B. and Pavlenko, A. (2004) Addressing gender in the ESL/EFL classroom. *TESOL Quarterly* 38 (3): 504–14.

OFSTED (1993) *Boys and English: A Report by Her Majesty's Chief Inspector of Schools*. London: HMSO.

OFSTED (1996) *The Gender Divide: Performance Differences between Boys and Girls at School*. London: HMSO.

O'Higgins-Norman, J. (2009) Still catching up: schools, sexual orientation and homophobia in Ireland. *Sexuality and Culture* 13 (1): 1–16.

Pearson, J., Muller, C. and Wilkinson, L. (2007) Adolescent same-sex attraction and academic outcomes: the role of school attachment and engagement. *Social Problems* 54 (4): 523–42.

Rampton, B., Roberts, C., Leung, C. and Harris, R. (2002) Methodology in the analysis of classroom discourse. *Applied Linguistics* 23 (3): 373–92.

Rampton, B., Tusting, K., Maybin, J., Barwell, R., Creese, A. and Lytra, V. (2004) UK linguistic ethnography: a discussion paper. www.ling-ethnog.org.uk (Accessed 1 September 2010).

Reay, D. (1991) Intersections of gender, race and class in the primary school. *British Journal of Sociology of Education* 12: 93–110.

Reay, D. (2006) 'Spice girls', 'nice girls', 'girlies' and 'tomboys': gender discourses, girls' cultures and femininities in the primary classroom. In M. Arnot and M. Mac an Ghaill (eds.), pp. 117–30.

Renold, E. (2007) Primary school 'studs': (de)constructing young boys' heterosexual masculinities. *Men and Masculinities* 9 (3): 275–98.

Renold, E. (2009) Tomboys and 'female masculinity': (dis)embodying hegemonic masculinity, queering gender identities and relations. In W. Martino, M. Kehler and M. Weaver-Hightower (eds.) *The Problem with Boys' Education: Beyond the Backlash*. London: Sage, pp. 224–41.

Rich, A. (1993) Compulsory heterosexuality and lesbian existence. In H. Abelove, M. Barale and D. Halperin (eds.) *The Lesbian and Gay Studies Reader*. London: Routledge, pp. 227–54.

Richards, K. (2006) 'Being the teacher': identity and classroom conversation. *Applied Linguistics* 27 (1): 51–77.

Rubin, G. (1984) Thinking sex: notes for a radical theory of the politics of sexuality. In C. Vance (ed.) *Pleasure and Danger: Exploring Female Sexuality*. New York: Routledge, pp. 267–319.

Sauntson, H. (2007) Girls' and boys' use of acknowledging moves in pupil group classroom discussions. *Language and Education* 21 (4): 304–27.

Sauntson, H. (2008) The contributions of queer theory to gender and language research. In K. Harrington *et al.* (eds.), pp. 271–82.

Sauntson, H. and Simpson, K. (2011) Investigating sexuality discourses in the UK secondary English curriculum. *Journal of Homosexuality* 58 (6–7).

SEAC (1991) *APU Technology Surveys*. London: HMSO.

Sedgwick, E. (1990) *The Epistemology of the Closet*. Berkeley, CA: University of California Press.

Seedhouse, P. (2004) *The Interactional Architecture of the Language Classroom: A Conversation Analysis Perspective*. Oxford: Blackwell.

Silverstein, M. (2003) Indexical order and the dialectics of sociolinguistic life. *Language and Communication* 23: 193–229.

Sinclair, J. and Brazil, D. (1982) *Teacher Talk*. Oxford: Oxford University Press.

Sinclair, J. and Coulthard, R. M. (1975) *Towards an Analysis of Discourse: The English Used by Teachers and Pupils*. Oxford: Oxford University Press.

Sinclair, J. and Coulthard, R. M. (1992) Towards an analysis of discourse. In R. M. Coulthard (ed.), pp. 1–34.

Skelton, C. (1997) Primary boys and hegemonic masculinities. *British Journal of Sociology of Education* 18: 349–69.

Skelton, C. (2001) *Schooling the Boys: Masculinity and Primary Education*. Buckingham: Open University Press.

Skelton, C. and Francis, B. (2009) *Feminism and 'The Schooling Scandal'*. London: Routledge.

Skelton, C, Francis, B. and Smulyan, L. (eds.) (2006) *The Sage Handbook of Gender and Education*. London: Sage.

Skidmore, D. (2000) From pedagogical dialogue to dialogical pedagogy. *Language and Education* 14 (4): 283–96.

Spender, D. (1982) *Invisible Women: The Schooling Scandal*. London: The Women's Press.

Stanworth, M. (1981) *Gender and Schooling: A Study of Sexual Divisions in the Classroom*. London: Hutchinson and Co.

Stokoe, E. (1998) Talking about gender: the conversational construction of gender categories in academic discourse. *Discourse and Society* 9 (2): 217–40.

Stokoe, E. and Smithson, J. (2001) Making gender relevant: conversation analysis and gender categories in interaction. *Discourse and Society* 12 (2): 217–44.

Stubbe, M., Lane, C., Hilder, J., Vine, E., Vine, B., Marra, M., Holmes, J. and Weatherall, A. (2003) Multiple discourse analyses of a workplace interaction. *Discourse Studies* 5 (3): 351–88.

Stubbs, M. (1976) *Language, Schools and Classrooms*. London: Methuen.

Stubbs, M. (1983) *Discourse Analysis: The Sociolinguistic Analysis of Natural Language*. Oxford: Blackwell.

Sunderland, J. (2002) From representation towards discursive practices: gender in the foreign language classroom revisited. In L. Litosseliti and J. Sunderland (eds.), pp. 223–55.

Sunderland, J. (2004) *Gendered Discourses*. Basingstoke: Palgrave Macmillan.

Sunderland, J. and Litositeli, L. (2002) Gender identity and discourse analysis: theoretical and empirical considerations. In L. Litosseliti and J. Sunderland (eds.), pp. 3–42.

Sunderland, J. and Litosseliti, L. (2008) Current research methodologies in gender and language study: key issues. In K. Harrington *et al.* (eds.), pp. 1–18.

Swann, J. (1992) *Girls, Boys and Language*. Oxford: Blackwell.

Swann, J. (1998) Language and gender: who, if anyone, is disadvantaged by what? In D. Epstein *et al.* (eds.), pp. 147–61.

Swann, J. (2002) Yes, but is it gender? In L. Litosseliti and J. Sunderland (eds.), pp. 43–68.

Swann, J. (2003) Schooled language: language and gender in educational settings. In J. Holmes and M. Meyerhoff (eds.), pp. 624–44.

Swann, J. and Graddol, D. (1995) Feminising classroom talk? In S. Mills (ed.) *Language and Gender: Interdisciplinary Perspectives*. London: Longman, pp.135–48.

Swann, J. and Maybin, J. (2008) Sociolinguistic and ethnographic approaches to language and gender. In K. Harrington *et al.* (eds.), pp. 21–8.

Talbot, M. (2010) *Language and Gender* (2nd edition). Cambridge: Polity Press.

Tannen, D. (ed.) (1993) *Gender and Conversational Interaction*. Oxford: Oxford University Press.

Thorne, B. (1993) *Gender Play: Girls and Boys in School*. Milton Keynes: Open University Press.

Tolmie, A. and Howe, C. (1993) Gender and dialogue in secondary school physics. *Gender and Education* 5 (2): 191–209.

Tusting, K. and Maybin, J. (2007) Linguistic ethnography and interdisciplinarity: opening the discussion. *Journal of Sociolinguistics* 11 (5): 575–83.

Walkerdine, V. (1990) *Schoolgirl Fictions*. London: Verso.

Walters, S. (1996) From here to queer: radical feminism, postmodernism and the lesbian menace (Or why can't a woman be more like a fag?) *Signs* 21 (4): 830–69.

Weaver-Hightower, M. (2003) The 'boy turn' in research on gender and education. *Review of Educational Research* 73 (4): 471–98.

Wells, G. (1986) *The Meaning Makers: Children Learning Language and Using Language to Learn*. London: Hodder and Stoughton.

Wells, G. (1999) *Dialogic Inquiry: Toward a Sociocultural Practice and Theory of Education*. Cambridge: Cambridge University Press.

Wetherall, M. (1998) Positioning and interpretative repertoires: conversation analysis and post-structuralism in dialogue. *Discourse and Society* 9 (3): 387–412.

Wilkinson, L. and Pearson, J. (2009) School culture and the well-being of same-sex attracted youth. *Gender and Society* 23 (4): 542–68.

Willis, J. (1992) Inner and outer – spoken discourse in the language classroom. In R.M. Coulthard (ed.), pp. 162–82.

Willis, P. (1977) *Learning to Labour: How Working Class Kids Get Working Class Jobs*. London: Hutchinson and Co.

Wittig, M. (1993) One is not born a woman. In H. Abelove, M. Barale and D. Halperin (eds.) *The Lesbian and Gay Studies Reader.* London: Routledge, pp. 103–9.

Wodak, R. (2001) What CDA is about: a summary of its history, important concepts and its developments. In R. Wodak and M. Meyer (eds.), pp. 9–21.

Wodak, R. (2008) Controversial issues in feminist critical discourse analysis. In K. Harrington *et al.*(eds.), pp. 193–210.

Wodak, R. and Meyer, M. (eds.) (2001) *Methods of Critical Discourse Analysis.* London: Sage.

Yates, L. (1997) Gender, equity and the boys debate: what sort of challenge is it? *British Journal of Sociology of Education* 18: 337–47.

Youdell, D. (2005) Sex-gender-sexuality: how sex, gender and sexuality constellations are constituted in secondary schools. *Gender and Education* 17 (3): 249–70.

Zuengler, J. and Mori, J. (2002) Microanalyses of classroom discourse: a critical consideration of method. *Applied Linguistics* 23 (3): 283–8.

Internet references

A Fairer Future: The Single Equality Bill (2009) – http://www.equalities.gov.uk/equality_bill.aspx (accessed 1 August 2010).

Every Child Matters – http://www.dcsf.gov.uk/everychildmatters (accessed 1 August 2010).

Equality Act (2006) – http://www.legislation.gov.uk/ukpga/2006/3/contents (accessed 1 August 2010).

Equality Act (2010) – http://www.equalities.gov.uk/equality_act_2010.aspx (accessed 1 August 2010).

The Gender Equality Duty (2007) – http://www.teachernet.gov.uk/wholeschool/equality/genderequalityduty/ (accessed 1 August 2010).

Hate crime figures paint a grim picture of life in Britain. *The Independent*, 1 December 2010 – http://www.independent.co.uk/news/uk/crime/hate-crime-figures-paint-a-grim-portrait/ (accessed 2 December 2010).

Hate crime figures published for the first time. *BBC News*, 30 November 2010 – http://www.bbc.co.uk/news/uk-11875321 (accessed 2 December 2010).

National Curriculum for England and Wales – http://www.qca.org.uk/curriculum (accessed 1 August 2010).

Primary National Strategy (SEAL strand) – http://nationalstrategies.standards/dcsf.gov.uk/primary/publications/banda/seal (accessed 15 September 2010).

Programme for Government – http://www.cabinetoffice.gov.uk/media/409088/pfg_coalition.pdf (accessed 3 July 2010).

Schools Out – http://www.schools-out.org.uk/research/contents/htm (accessed 16 November 2010).

Transphobic Bullying in Schools (2008) – http://www.gires.org.uk/transbullying.php (accessed 17 November 2010).

Index